THE JUSTICE PROJECT

EDITED BY

BRIAN McLAREN,

ELISA PADILLA,

AND ASHLEY BUNTING SEEBER

BakerBooks

a division of Baker Publishing Group
Grand Rapids, Michigan

Published by Baker Books
a division of Baker Publishing Group
P.O. Box 6287, Grand Rapids, MI 49516-6287
www.bakerbooks.com

Printed in the United States of America

Library of Congress Cataloging-in-Publication Data
The justice project / edited by Brian D. McLaren, Elisa Padilla, and Ashley Bunting Seeber.
    p. cm.
  Includes bibliographical references and index.
  ISBN 978-0-8010-1328-7 (cloth : alk. paper)
  1. Christianity and justice. 2. Postmodernism—Religious aspects—Christianity.
3. Emerging church movement. I. McLaren, Brian D., 1956– II. Padilla, Elisa. III. Seeber,
Ashley Bunting.
BR115.J8J877 2009
261.8—dc22   2009016214

In keeping with biblical principles of
creation stewardship, Baker Publishing Group advocates the responsible
use of our natural resources. As a
member of the Green Press Initiative,
our company uses recycled paper
when possible. The text paper of
this book is comprised of 30% post-
consumer waste.

ēmersion is a partnership between Baker Books and Emergent Village, a growing, generative friendship among missional Christians seeking to love our world in the Spirit of Jesus Christ. The ēmersion line is intended for professional and lay leaders like you who are meeting the challenges of a changing culture with vision and hope for the future. These books will encourage you and your community to live into God's kingdom here and now.

The Justice Project is the second community call in the ēmersion line. The first was *An Emergent Manifest of Hope*. These books are written not with a single voice but in concert with many voices. Some topics simply require the contribution of many, and this book is intended to be just that—a collective expression of the need for and possibility of justice.

But more importantly it is an invitation—an invitation for you and your community to join the project with your own ideas and gifts. This book comes from a community of activists, thinkers, practioners, and dreamers. And, as the ēmersion line has always done, it is meant to encourage, instruct, and, more importantly, invite individuals and communities to join in the hopes, dreams, and aspirations God has for our world.

Emergent Village resources for communities of faith

 **ēmersion**

Emergent Village resources for communities of faith

www.emersionbooks.com

CONTENTS

Section Two: The Book of Justice

Section Three: Justice in the U.S.A.

Conclusions

FOREWORD

In ominous red and black, an April 2009 cover of *Newsweek* carried the headline "The Decline and Fall of Christian America." The magazine's cover story by editor Jon Meacham provoked a wide array of reactions from across the spectrum, from dismay to jubilation. This is not the first time the demise of Christianity and religion in general has been predicted. In 1966, a *Time* magazine cover asked "Is God Dead?" and the writers for that issue certainly did not foresee the developments in American public life over the past forty years.

This volume, and the authors it brings together, point not to a "decline and fall" of Christianity in America but a shift that is reshaping and renewing both the church and its role in the public square. These "new kind of Christians" are not as easily identified, quantified, or labeled as Christians have been in the past. But their commitment to the mission of the Gospel and the vision of Christ in this world is transforming everything from coffee shops to churches, neighborhoods, and cities. The conversation the authors of this book engage in get to the root of the two greatest hungers in our country and our world today: the hunger for spiritual fulfillment and the hunger for social justice.

We are in the midst of a profound religious shift in this country, the reverberations of which are being felt throughout our society. This shift is a religious shift, a cultural and racial shift, a genera-

tional shift, and a political shift. The leadership and perspective of
new and different voices—African-American, Latino, and Asian
Christians—along with a new generation of the faithful in white
America are participating in a new conversation. The breadth, depth
and effectiveness of this shift have been so pervasive and effective
that even those who had avoided its reality and some of the difficult
questions it raises are now feeling the pull of its vision.

As I read through the pages of this book, what inspires me and
gives me great hope is to recognize all of the leaders, voices, and communities that are wrestling with the question that has animated the
Church since the first days of Pentecost: "How do we as the people
of God live out God's mission for the world?" After two thousand
years we are still challenged and humbled by Jesus's first sermon, his
"Nazareth Manifesto," in which he proclaimed, "The Spirit of the
Lord is on me, because he has anointed me to preach good news to
the poor. He has sent me to proclaim freedom for the prisoners and
recovery of sight for the blind, to release the oppressed, to proclaim
the year of the Lord's favor" (Luke 4:18–19 NIV).

History has taught us that when the Church takes seriously its
mission in this world, when it truly believes and lives out the Gospel
as not just good news for another world but good news here and
now to a broken and hurting planet, "great awakenings" and revivals
begin to burn and grow. I see it across the country in people young
and old who have turned away from churches but are overwhelm-
ingly attracted to communities of Christ's followers that care deeply
about issues of justice.

What Christianity in America looks like will continue to shift. The
church's role in public life will go on changing. But as long as the
people of God have the leadership, sincerity, and depth of thought
as represented in this book, "renewal and growth," not "decline and
fall," is imminent.

Jim Wallis
President, Sojourners
www.sojo.net
May 2009

ACKNOWLEDGMENTS

First, thanks to Tony Jones, Doug Pagitt, and Chad Allen for their patience and persistence in challenging me (Brian) to take on this project. They were right: *An Emergent Manifesto of Hope* needed to be complemented by cries for justice. Thanks also to Elisa Padilla for bringing important Latin American voices to the table, for translating their work into English, and for living out the message of this book so passionately. And special thanks—from me and from all our contributors—to Ashley Bunting Seeber, who proved herself a first-rate project manager, an excellent editor, and an absolute pleasure to work with at every turn.

Of course, most of all, the contributors to this work deserve enthusiastic appreciation. For many of the authors, to contribute a chapter to this book meant late nights and early mornings, extra pressures on hearts that already bear so much on behalf of people in need. Some of them repeatedly told me how much they "hate writing": their main work is doing justice, not writing about it. But I think you'll agree: these are exactly the kinds of people the rest of us should hear from. I hope readers will echo to our contributors my sincere gratitude thousands of times over.

Finally, on a personal note, I wish to thank my mentors and friends who helped nudge me out of the comfortable, privatized, complacent, hyper-personalized, escapist, consumerist, colonial, justice-evading, and utterly convenient understanding of the Christian gospel that I once enjoyed and considered orthodox. You know who you are. You knew me when I was exactly where many future readers of this book now are: sincere, earnest, open, and terribly uninformed about the biblical message of justice. You patiently but firmly challenged me to see the faith in larger dimensions, and for doing so, sometimes I thought you were heretics, disturbers of the peace, "liberal," and otherwise a pain in the neck. But in the end, you got through, and my greatest hope is that this book will do for others what you have done for me.

No, that's my second greatest hope. My greatest hope is that we will find ourselves swept up in a Spirit-inspired movement that brings transformation not only to our lives and our faith communities but to our world . . . our world that cannot survive unless God's justice rolls like mighty waters and flows like a never-ending stream.

You can participate in bringing that movement from dream to reality—by reading these chapters with an open heart and mind; by forming a reading group or class and inviting others into conversation about this book; by putting the wisdom of this book into practice in your life day by day; by following and joining the work of these and others like them who are speaking up and acting up for justice; by praying for, volunteering with, and financially supporting people and groups for whom God's justice is their life's project.

INTRODUCTION
A Conversation about Justice
BRIAN D. MCLAREN

A few days ago, my wife and I stood in a crowd of about two million joyful people in my hometown of Washington, D.C. Grace and I wanted to be part of what we believed was a historic moment: not just the inauguration of the first African American U.S. president, which was wonderful enough, but also the turning of a page in history. We hoped, and continue to hope, that Barack Hussein Obama's election signaled a repudiation of both the partisan, culture-war politics of recent decades and the polarizing, paralyzing theology that legitimized those politics.

The President's Inaugural Address, although lacking some of the spark and sparkle of his best campaign speeches, exceeded them in depth and intensity. Recalling Paul's words in 1 Corinthians 13, he said it was time to put childish things behind us, time to grow up and out of the facile thinking that had brought our nation and world to a moment of unparalleled global crises. It's too early to tell how successful he and all of us will be in turning our hope for change into a reality; since the inauguration, we've gotten a greater sense of the economic meltdown into which we have been plunged, and nobody knows what the future holds. But the book you are now reading represents a passionate and intelligent call towards hope and creative action, whatever the circumstances of the moment, because the work of justice is not simply the work of presidents and governments, nor is it the exclusive domain of activists and humanitarians: it is a vital project to which we are all summoned. To paraphrase the prophet Micah, if you want to know what God requires of all humanity, start with doing justice.

I was a freshman in college when John Stott, Billy Graham, René Padilla, and others convened a group of Christian leaders from around the world to (among other things) compose and affirm a document known as the Lausanne Covenant. I remember feeling a certain thrill that there was a section of the document called "Christian Social Responsibility," excerpts of which you will encounter in chapter 4.

Now, twenty-five years later, it's depressing to see how little effect that document has had on the sectors of the Christian community to which it was addressed. But perhaps its intention has been slowly advancing in secret, and perhaps now is the moment for the Covenant's promise to be fulfilled. Perhaps now our diverse Christian communities in the U.S. and around the world—especially their younger generations—are ready to engage more deeply with God's justice project. Perhaps momentum for change has been quietly building all these years, and now the time has come for a global, Christ-centered, cross-confessional, justice-oriented spiritual/social movement to be born.

My path to this moment came through getting involved with what is now referred to in the U.S. as "the emergent conversation." When the conversation began in the 1990s, it was primarily a group of younger evangelical leaders gathered under the auspices of Leadership Network (leadnet.org).[1] We didn't know it at the time, but similar conversations were well underway in the UK and Europe; in Africa and Latin America; and in Canada, Australia, and New Zealand. In many ways we in the U.S. were latecomers to an emerging global phenomenon. We were a little band of lonely misfits on the fringes of the American evangelical world, glad to know that we weren't completely alone. At that point, we had little to say about matters of justice.

Mostly we were preoccupied with the priorities of the "church growth movement" of the 1990s. Mega-church pastors brought together through Leadership Network did many things well, one of which was counting attendees. As good counters, many of them noticed an alarming trend: there were disproportionately few people in their churches between the ages of eighteen and thirty-five.[2]

This realization launched a flurry of conferences and books to see what the problem was with "Generation X." Soon, when some bona fide Generation X people were invited to the table to speak for themselves, they said, "No, this isn't just about generational fads; we're dealing with a deep cultural shift here, a transition from the familiar modern world to an uncharted postmodern world." This was a conclusion I had reached as well; even though I was a middle-aged boomer in body, I felt I had found my soul-tribe when I got to know these brilliant and passionate younger leaders.

In the mid and late 1990s, this conversation focused not on "doing justice" but on "doing church"—doing evangelism, doing worship, doing leadership, doing preaching, and so on. But it was unavoidably clear to many of us that our doing couldn't be separated from our knowing, and so we also became deeply interested in philosophy and theology. While many of our friends were saying that theology and praxis could be separated into distinct bins so that we could "change the methods" without "changing the message," we were realizing— with Marshall McLuhan—that media/methods and message are not mechanically related like a bottle and Coke or a computer and a program.[3] Instead, they are more organically related, like skeleton and muscles, or brain and thought. You can't simply change one without also changing the other. To quote Jesus, you can't put new wine into old skins. (You can, however, put old wine into new skins . . . a rather pointless exercise in which many of us have wasted a lot of time.)

Scholars and writers like Sally Morgenthaler, Leonard Sweet, Alan Roxburgh, Nancey Murphy, Stanley Grenz, John Franke, Dallas Willard, Robert Webber, Todd Hunter, Joe Myers, and many others were invaluable to us at this time. They gave us permission to think in ways we normally weren't allowed to think. They helped us create "safe space" for questions and conversations about Christian faith in a postmodern world . . . questions that wouldn't be allowed in many of our churches, denominations, and seminaries. Like skittish animals in a forest full of creatures with sharp teeth and long claws, more and more of us began stepping into a remote clearing and finding safety with one another—safety to question, to rethink, to wonder, to imagine. That process continues today.

I remember the first time I nervously went public with an idea that had been brewing in me for some time. Many of us had been accused of "pandering" to postmodernity, of engaging in syncretism with postmodernism, of watering down the gospel to make it appealing to postmoderns, and so on—often by people who had only a vague or distorted idea of what the slippery, vaporous terms in question actually might mean. I was on a panel discussion at a conference and said something like this: *I'm not really interested in figuring out how the gospel can be adapted to fit into the postmodern mind; I'm more concerned with figuring out how the gospel we communicate has already been trimmed and flattened and shrunk to fit into the modern mind. Some of our critics are worried about us sliding down a slippery slope into accommodation with postmodernity, but they're assuming they're at the top of the mountain with a pure understanding of the gospel, looking down-slope at the rest of us. My hunch is that everyone is already halfway down the mountain because our understanding of the gospel became a subset of the modern, Western mindset centuries ago. I think we've already accommodated more than we realize, which is why a lot of us are reopening the question of what the gospel really is.*

That kind of talk struck a chord with some people, but it frightened or even angered others. Some participants coalesced around the familiar and less-unsettling conviction that "we can change the methods but we've already got the pure message," while the rest of us continued in our explorations that were opening up questions of both praxis and theology.

So many people and groups played important roles in this process. From the beginning, Rudy Carrasco (harambee.org) had been a key person in the emergent network, and he brought us into contact with the Christian Community Development Association (urbanministry .org/ccda), which included people like John Perkins, Mary Nelson, Tony and Peggy Campolo, Bart Campolo, and Shane Claiborne. Jim Wallis and the Sojourners community (sojo.net) became our friends and conversation partners as well, and we developed relationships with groups like the One campaign (one.org) and Bread for the

World (bread.org). We also got to know Native American Christian leaders like Randy Woodley, Richard Twiss, Terry LeBlanc, and Ray Aldred; African American Christian leaders like Anthony Smith, Efrem Smith, Adam Taylor, and Melvin Bray; Latinos like David Ramos, Gabriel Salguero, Alexie Torres Fleming and Belinda Passafaro (see latinoleadershipcircle.typepad.com); and Asian American leaders like D. J. Chuang, Soong-Chan Rah, and Eugene Cho. Each of these friendships cemented social justice as a matter of deepening concern for the emergent conversation.

As we pursued this path, we found more and more mainline Protestants eager to be involved. Their companionship helped us in at least two ways. First, our thinking was further challenged by scholars such as Walter Brueggemann, Walter Wink, Diana Butler Bass, Jürgen Moltmann, and Stanley Hauerwas, who brought fresh intellectual and theological resources to our conversation. Second, with more mainline Protestants involved, we welcomed even more women and people of color into our conversation as well, since nonwhite and non-male speakers and leaders had simply been hard to find in the conservative circles from which most of us had come. We continued to discover and learn from Roman Catholic and Eastern Orthodox conversation partners too. With expanding theological and demographic diversity came more and more theological foment—leading us deeper and deeper into matters of social justice.

Another key factor: several of us—notably Doug Pagitt, Tony Jones, and I—were filling up our passports with international travel. People from around the world were asking us to share what we were learning. I think we'd all agree that we "Americans abroad" felt we were learning far more from our hosts in our travels than we were teaching. Along the way, we discovered the work of René Padilla and lareddelcamino.org in Latin America, the work of Mabiala Kenzo and Claude Nikondeha (amahoro-africa.org) in Africa, and many others. The more we ventured outside the echo chamber of the U.S., the more we were being radicalized—and the process was aided and abetted back home, no doubt, by the increasingly shrill, constricting rhetoric of the religious right and a painful and polarizing presidency.

Through all of this foment, it was the Bible to which we always returned, and the Bible, we were discovering, had more to say about justice than we had ever realized. The theme had been simmering there all along, but we had been trained to see other things, and to ignore or marginalize social justice.[4] Looking back, my personal pilgrimage is, I think, typical of what thousands have experienced or are right now experiencing:

1. I became disillusioned with a way of "doing church" that was not working, especially for younger and more educated people.
2. I first focused on pragmatics, but then began asking theological questions as well.[5]
3. Those questions eventually led me to ask, "What is the gospel anyway?"[6]
4. That gospel-centered question led me back to the Scriptures, and especially the Gospels.[7]
5. There, I was confronted with a message into which justice was inextricably woven.[8]

This conversation is not finished.[9] Far from it. But this book represents an important turn in the conversation: many of us are coming together to say, *The Christian faith isn't all about getting to heaven. It isn't all about the church. It isn't all about the individual spiritual life or "personal relationship with God." It is about all of these things, but they aren't the whole point, or even the main point. The main point is God's saving love for creation, God's faithfulness to all of creation, God's ongoing mission of healing a world torn by human injustice so that it can fulfill God's original dream. It is about God's kingdom coming to earth, and it is about God's will being done on earth as it is in heaven.*[10]

Like any good conversation, then, this one has been unfolding, moving from topic to topic, circling back again to previous topics, but then venturing out into new territory again. Doing church, understanding the gospel, and seeking justice . . . these strands are integral for us now: they have been joined by God and cannot be put asunder.

What follows in these pages are snippets of a conversation among many voices—some well known, many not-yet-well-known; some evangelical, some mainline, some Catholic, one Jewish, and some all-and/or-none-of-the-above; many from the U.S., but many important voices from other parts of the world too.[11] You'll notice that we have tried to avoid bleaching these voices into a white-bread sameness; although we have translated them into English and edited in terms of spelling and grammar, we have also tried to let the full flavor of each unique multi-grain accent come through; the "otherness" of "the other" is part of the message of justice that we all need to hear. You will discern among these diverse voices differing emphases and at some points, differences of opinion, reflecting their different backgrounds, experiences, and convictions. You shouldn't assume each author will agree with all the others on every detail. Again, in the pursuit of justice, we must learn to respectfully acknowledge difference and joyfully sing in harmony without requiring homogeneity. Beyond all differences, be assured that all our contributors share a profound desire to seek first the kingdom and justice of God—which, we believe, can be paraphrased as God's will being done on earth as in heaven.

But in spite of this attention to otherness and difference, this book is being published in the U.S., and that fact points to a peculiar and complex problem. We in the U.S. need to realize that we only make up about 5 percent of the world's population, but we are generally acknowledged as the world's most self-centered, consumptive, arrogant, and inconsiderate minority. On average, we consume thirty-two times the resources of a person living in the global South and produce thirty-two times the waste. Because of our military and economic dominance, we have the capacity to cause more injustice than any other nation, and with that capacity goes a corresponding responsibility. In addition, because the Christian religion in its various forms is highly dominant in U.S. culture, as go the churches, so goes the nation. In other words, if our churches are preaching, praying, studying, working, singing, and worshiping in the spirit of justice, then our members will work, organize, and vote for justice and have the chance to steer our nation toward more just paths. The opposite would be true as well.

So, we in the U.S. need simultaneously to be knocked down from our pedestal of self-importance, and to recognize how important we are. Much has been given to us, and much, our Lord said, is expected.

For this reason, although we have been careful to include voices from many countries, we have slanted the focus of this book toward the United States. Thankfully, grassroots conversations and friendships centered around justice are springing up around the world. In the future, we are confident they will become increasingly networked so that the church of Jesus Christ, in all its forms, will become an increasingly integrated global force for justice. This force, as we envision it, does not force itself or exert itself with "earthly" or "fleshly" weapons like swords or guns, chariots or tanks, shields or bombs, spears or artillery, insult or propaganda. Rather, this incoming force infiltrates and expands through harmless and unarmed faith, hope, and love—the greatest of these being love.

This book has been written to contribute in some small way to this exciting process. May this book, and all the writers who have contributed to it, stimulate needed conversation about justice in light of the gospel of Jesus Christ, so that we, as people walking humbly with God and walking kindly with the earth and all who share it, will seek and do justice until it rolls down like mighty waters and flows like a never-failing stream.[12]

WHAT IS JUSTICE?

BRIAN D. MCLAREN

The subject of our book is notoriously hard to define. If you look in a dictionary, you will find a lot of circular reasoning: justice means equity, which means fairness, which means . . . justice.

You get a feel for the simultaneous importance and opaqueness of the word in reflections on justice by postmodern philosopher and "father of deconstruction" Jacques Derrida. For him, justice was the one un-deconstructable reality that guided all deconstruction. Yet all definitions of justice could be and should be deconstructed to protect the untamed and untamable reality of justice from being obscured by the words used to define it.

Will and Lisa Samson define justice as "acting right in our relationships,"[1] and that's as good a definition as any. Gary Haugen also builds on the word *right*, and brings in the important dimension of power: justice is the right use of power, and injustice is the abuse of power. Both definitions, of course, leave us wondering how we define *right*.

At this point, we as Christians refer to God. *Right*, *fair*, and *just*, ultimately, are determined by and reflective of God. "So justice occurs on earth," Gary Haugen says, "when power and authority between people is exercised in conformity with God's standards of moral excellence."[2] By resorting to God at this point, we need to be careful and humble because, as Scripture says, God's ways are above our ways and God's thoughts are above our thoughts. We must acknowledge from the outset that we, like the Pharisees in the Gospels, can never underestimate our power to be wrong about God and God's view of things. We human beings are famous for our adventures in missing the point, for straining at legal gnats and swallowing camels of injustice, for cleaning the outside of the cup with detergent while leaving the inside full of salmonella.

In referring to the Pharisees and alluding to Jesus, we are acknowledging that we best know justice not simply through definitions and synonyms, but through stories and biographies. For example, when Jesus stoops and writes in the ground in front of a group of religious leaders who want to stone an adulterous woman, we know he is just and they are misguided. When Jesus hangs on a cross—the punishment, in Rome's eyes, for perpetrators of gross injustice—we know Jesus exposes their injustice instead. In more recent history, we know that justice was at work in the fight against slavery, in the work of Dr. King or Desmond Tutu and Nelson Mandela. We see it today in the struggles of today's heroes who work for the poor, the oppressed, the excluded, and the forgotten.

So in the pages that follow, we will be thinking about justice as *the right use of power in our relationships with others*. And we will seek to be rooted and resourced at every point by the stories of Scripture and their echoes through history. And most of all, we will focus again and again on Jesus, our leader, liberator, and Lord.

GOD'S CALL TO DO JUSTICE
C. RENÉ PADILLA

The practice of justice is at the center of God's purpose for human life. It is so closely related to the worship of the living God as the only true God that no act of worship is acceptable to him unless it is accompanied by concrete acts of justice on the human level. Micah 6:8, which may be regarded as a synthesis of Old Testament ethics, points in this direction: "He has told you, O mortal, what is good; and what does the LORD require of you but to do justice, and to love kindness, and to walk humbly before your God."

The Basis for Justice

For the biblical writers justice is a central concern—it is not incidental that the main words for *justice* in Hebrew (*mishpat* and *sadiqah*)

C. RENÉ PADILLA was born in Quito, Ecuador, and reared in Bogota, Colombia. He received a BA in Philosophy from Wheaton College, an MA in Theology from Wheaton College Graduate School, and a PhD in New Testament from the University of Manchester, England. In 1992 he was given a DD by Wheaton College. He is a founding member of the Latin American Theological Fellowship and of the Kairos Foundation in Buenos Aires, Argentina. He is President of the Micah Network and Executive Director of Ediciones Kairos. He is married to Catharine Feser and has four daughters, one son, and twenty grandchildren.

and Greek (*dikaiosune* and *krisis*) occur over a thousand times in the Bible. They almost take it for granted that God is a God of justice—justice is intrinsic to his being and to his action. In order to understand this concept, however, it is essential to overcome the common misconception of justice as an abstract ethical principle. Abraham J. Heschel is quite correct in maintaining that very few ideas are so deeply rooted in the mind of the biblical writers as the idea that justice and righteousness are inherent to God's character. "This is not an inference," he says, "but an *a priori* of biblical faith, self-evident; not an attribute added to His essence, but belonging to the idea of God. It is inherent to His essence and is identified with His ways."[1]

Because God is a God of justice, *in any situation in which power is misused and the powerful take advantage of the weak, God takes the side of the weak.* In concrete terms, that means God is *for* the oppressed and *against* the oppressor, *for* the exploited and *against* the exploiter, *for* the victim and *against* the victimizer. Because God loves justice, he is "a stronghold for the oppressed" and "the needy shall not always be forgotten, nor the hope of the poor perish forever" (Ps. 9:9, 18); "the LORD works vindication and justice for all who are oppressed" (Ps. 103:6). Because God loves justice, on the other hand, "his soul hates the lover of violence" and "on the wicked he will rain coals of fire and sulfur; a scorching wind shall be the portion of their cup" (Ps. 11:5–6). In summary, *God's justice is a corrective, remedial, restorative justice.*

God's justice is the basis for the practice of justice on a human level. God calls us, in conformity with his restorative justice, to practice justice and correct inequity in all forms of power relationships. That is the sense of the expression "God's preferential option for the poor," coined in Roman Catholic circles in Latin America.

Many people react against this way of speaking about God. Their objection is that because God is just, God does not take sides but deals with everyone on an equal basis. In response to this objection, I offer the following comments. First, because God loves justice, God requires that justice be done not only by the rich but also by the poor, and not only to the poor but also to the rich. Judges in the courtroom are obliged to be strictly impartial. Any form of injustice on their part, whether it favors the rich or the poor, is unpleasing to

God. In this regard, the injunction in Leviticus 19:15 is clear: "You shall not render an unjust judgment; you shall not be partial to the poor or defer to the great: with justice you shall judge your neighbor." God's *retributive justice* is impartial. Therefore, it excludes any form of favoritism—there is no person above the law, no place for impunity on the basis of social or economic position (cf. Deut. 1:16–17). Accordingly, judges are exhorted against the danger of being co-opted with bribes, "for a bribe blinds the eyes of the wise and subverts the cause of those who are in the right" (Deut. 16:19; cf. Mic. 7:3–4).

Second, precisely because God is impartial, God intends to correct any kind of imbalance of power created by sinful—and therefore biased—human beings. The partiality present in any situation of injustice is not God's but ours, as is clearly seen in Deuteronomy 10:17–19, one of many biblical passages that could be quoted:

> The LORD your God is God of gods and Lord of lords, the great God, mighty and awesome, who is *not partial* and takes no bribe, who *executes justice for the orphan and the widow, and who loves the strangers, providing them food and clothing.* You shall also love the stranger, for you were strangers in the land of Egypt (emphasis mine).

Aside from pointing to the relationship between God's impartiality and God's action on behalf of the orphan, the widow, and the stranger—the poor and oppressed—this passage throws into relief what God expects of Israel in terms of its practice of justice to the poor. The provision of food and clothing is God's provision, given through God's people to satisfy basic needs of the poor. God's justice to the poor is executed through God's covenant people.

God's justice applies to every form of abuse of power, unjust economic distribution, or violation of human rights present in society. It is not restricted to the retributive justice of the courtroom. God's justice embraces every human relationship and seeks to abolish every manifestation of injustice. It is corrective, rectifying, restorative justice, and in this sense *partial*.

God's preferential option for the poor was demonstrated in the person and work of Jesus Christ, who claimed to be anointed by

25

the Spirit to bring good news to the poor, to proclaim release to the captives and recovery of sight to the blind, to let the oppressed go free, to proclaim the year of the Lord's favor (Luke 4:18–19). While there is good reason for a warning against a socio-political reduction of his ministry, no proper understanding of the teaching of the New Testament is possible unless one sees Jesus' mission as the fulfillment of God's purpose to establish his kingdom of justice and peace. In anticipation of the end, the kingdom of God has come into history, the new era has started, and the basis has been laid to proclaim good news to the poor.

God's Call to Do Justice in a Globalized World

One of the most urgent needs in today's globalized world is for the practice of justice, not only on personal, regional, and national levels but also on an international level. As President Jimmy Carter, winner of the 2002 Nobel Peace Prize, has rightly stated, "The greatest challenge we face [at the beginning of the twenty-first century] is the growing chasm between the rich and the poor people on earth. . . . More than half the world's poor people live on less than $2.00 a day, and 1.2 billion people have to survive on half that amount."[2]

No attempt at a full discussion of the causes of poverty can be made in this introduction. Poverty is a very complex problem, and one must be careful to not appeal to simplistic explanations of its causes. An undeniable fact, however, is that one of the greatest causes—if not *the* greatest—for "the growing chasm between the rich and the poor on earth," as well as for the destruction of the environment, is the global economic system, which Michael S. Northcott has rightly described as *tyrannical*. In his own words, "Its growing power over the planet involves systematic erosion of local sources of power and freedom as the well-being of human communities and ecosystems are sacrificed to sustain 'freedoms' of global corporations and wealthy consumers to accumulate regardless of the costs to others and the earth system."[3]

Despite the negative results of the globalization of the neo-liberal capitalist system, its advocates insist that the only hope for humankind to eliminate poverty and to establish justice lies in giving free reign to the free market all over the world. Free-market fundamentalism, closely related to the ideology of consumerism, ignores the catastrophic consequences of the unilateral emphasis on economic growth and obstinately perseveres in following a course of action that leads to both ecological and human destruction.

From the perspective of the neo-liberal transnational class that controls the global economic system, the state is conceived as the political institution responsible for promoting investments for the sake of economic growth, protecting the right to private property, encouraging production, and making sure that the free market functions in an efficient and transparent way. Thus conceived, the national governments have no jurisdiction over economic relationships in society, which depend on the market. It is taken for granted that "the invisible hand" of the market will regulate those relationships for the benefit of all. What generally happens in practice, however, is that the free market widens the gap between rich and poor. In E. F. Schumacher's words, "Nothing succeeds like success and nothing stagnates like stagnation. The successful province drains the life of the unsuccessful, and without protection against the strong, the weak have no chance; either they remain weak or they must migrate and join the strong; they cannot effectively help themselves."[4] Indeed, the agenda of neo-liberal economics does not include the common good, nor is it designed to function according to ethical principles on questions of human relationships or the ecosystem.

In contrast with the *laissez-faire* view of the state promoted by today's global economic system, Scripture indicates that the state is responsible for ensuring that socio-political and economic justice is highly honored in society. Throughout the Old Testament it is assumed that the primary responsibility of the power-holders is to mediate God's justice—to make sure that the weak are protected from the strong, that no one is a victim of oppression, and that all have access to the goods of the land needed to sustain life. Justice is regarded as so important that, in addressing the kings of Judah in the midst of the national crisis produced by King Nebuchadnezzar's Babylonian invasion, the prophet Jeremiah makes the call to practice justice the main thrust of his message. He says to King Zedekiah:

> Execute justice in the morning, and deliver from the hand of the oppressor anyone who has been robbed, or else my wrath will go

27

forth like fire, and burn, with no one to quench it, because of your evil doings. (Jer. 21:12)

He exhorts King Shallum:

Woe to him who builds his house by unrighteousness, and his upper rooms by injustice; who makes his neighbors work for nothing, and does not give them their wages; who says, "I will build myself a spacious house with large upper rooms," and who cuts out windows for it, paneling it with cedar, and painting it with vermillion. Are you a king because you compete with cedar? Did not your father [Josiah] eat and drink and do justice and righteousness? He judged the cause of the poor and needy; then it was well with him. Is this not to know me? says the LORD. But your eyes and heart are only on your dishonest gain, for shedding innocent blood, and for practicing oppression and violence. (Jer. 22:13–17)

Among the many that could be quoted from Scripture, these passages from Jeremiah should be sufficient to lead us to the following conclusions:

First, God demands that the power-holders practice justice in their personal lives as well as in their exercise of government. In no way is power given to them for their own benefit.

Second, the practice of justice is closely related to God's special concern for the poor, represented in the Jeremiah passages, as in many other Old Testament passages, by the alien, the orphan, and the widow—in one word, the powerless.

Third, the knowledge of God is so closely related to the practice of justice that the following question can be legitimately raised: could practicing justice be equivalent to knowing God?

Christians living under the aegis of a global capitalist system, which takes for granted the benefits of "the invisible hand" of the market, need to take seriously, in both their reflection and in their action, God's call to the power-holders to do justice. In faithfulness to the teaching of Scripture, their mission includes a prophetic stance against every form of institutionalized injustice and a lifestyle that illustrates in concrete ways the meaning of the beatitude, "Blessed are those who hunger and thirst for righteousness, for they will be filled" (Matt. 5:6).

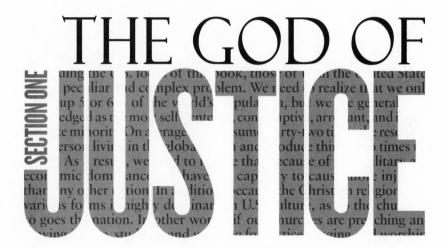

THE GOD OF JUSTICE

SECTION ONE

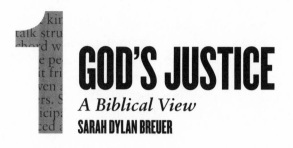

GOD'S JUSTICE
A Biblical View
SARAH DYLAN BREUER

I was learning to surf. Or, at least, that's what I was trying to do; mostly, I was learning how "unfun" it is to not catch waves, or to have them crash on top of you. And then an older, wiser surfer pulled me aside with some advice: "You're missing the waves because you're acting like it's your paddling that will move you forward," he said. He explained to me that a wave is really a kind of slippery hill, and it's gravity, not frenetic paddling, that moves you forward on it. The trick in surfing is to line yourself up with the wave in such a way that the place where you want to go is downhill. In other words, surfing is really strategically planned falling: if you start where the wave is forming and, as the wave curls, point yourself toward where the wave is still forming, gravity takes care of the rest, and you're in for an exhilarating ride.

Justice and reconciliation are like that. If they were a matter of us deciding individually where the world needs to be and paddling frenetically toward it, we wouldn't see much of them, and the effort would leave us exhausted and disappointed. But what if justice and reconciliation are what God is doing in the world? "Justice is like a

SARAH DYLAN BREUER is a writer, preacher, and retreat leader with particular passions for Scripture, faith, and justice. She has an MPhil in biblical studies from the University of St. Andrews (Scotland) and is a PhD candidate in early church history at the University of California at Los Angeles. In her spare time, she loves cooking, playing guitar, and teaching self-defense.

mighty stream," Abraham Heschel writes, referring to Amos 5:24, "and to defy it is to block God's almighty surge."[1] In other words, for those who worship the God we find in the Hebrew bible and in Christian scripture, engaging God's mission of justice and reconciliation in this world isn't an optional add-on; justice is to disciples what waves are to surfers. Align yourself with God's justice, and you're in for an exhilarating ride; watch it roll in from a distance, and you're not living as a disciple, not following what God is doing.

That's what I believe as a student of Scripture. I believe that God set that wave of justice rolling from the moment humanity was created:

> Then God said, "Let us make humankind in our image, according to our likeness." . . . So God created humankind in his image, in the image of God he created them, male and female he created them. . . . God blessed them, and God said to them, "Be fruitful and multiply" (Gen. 1:26–31).[2]

God made the earth fruitful, and gave the benefit and stewardship of that fruitfulness to the *adam*—that is, to humanity. The plurality of that gift and that charge is clear from the writer's reference to God's creating "them, male and female." God's first command to human beings is to be fruitful.

But how on earth can a human being be fruitful without clean water, without good food, without health and safety, without a chance to live to adulthood? God made the earth abundantly fruitful, with more than enough resources to give every child a chance— that is, if humanity exercises stewardship of God's gifts, as does the God who "makes his sun rise on the evil and on the good, and sends rain on the righteous and on the unrighteous" (Matt. 5:45). That abundance is God's intent for creation and for all people. When human systems distribute God-given resources in a way that places a small fraction of humanity in luxury while a billion people live—or die—on less than a dollar a day, can that be anything other than sin? And when our action and inaction perpetuate those systems that have created unprecedented wealth among the richest nations and left billions of others to starve, can that be anything other than sin?

We live in a sinful world, then. Some might suggest that the dream of every life being fruitful is just for Eden. But that's not the character of the God we see in Scripture. We worship a God who "rose up to establish judgment, to save all the oppressed of the earth" (Ps. 76:9).

Consider the story of the great flood. The version in Genesis shares a great deal with other ancient stories, such as the Greek myth of Deucalion or the Mesopotamian Epic of Gilgamesh, one of humanity's earliest known works of literature. But compare the character and concerns of the gods of Gilgamesh with those of the God of Genesis. The gods of Gilgamesh decide to exterminate humanity because the growing population brings noise that disturbs the gods' sleep. The God of Genesis, however, is concerned specifically with the behavior of human beings toward one another. The "wickedness" and "evil" raised in Genesis 6:5 are clarified very specifically in verse 11: "the earth was filled with violence." And after the flood subsides, God's blessing comes with a charge: "for the blood of another, I will require a reckoning for human life," followed by a restatement of the command to humanity to be fruitful on the earth (9:5–7). Considering the bloodshed on earth in our lifetime, what reckoning will God require?

Or consider the great story to which many point as the formation of God's people: the exodus from Egypt and the giving of the Torah in the desert. Our God forms God's people by liberating them from slavery. For all the fuss and hubbub around posting the Ten Commandments in public places, few remember that they begin with a reminder: "I am the LORD your God, who brought you out of the land of Egypt"; we are commanded to have no gods other than this liberator of slaves (Exod. 20:2).

God chooses the oppressed, those counted least by the most powerful, and commands, "You shall not deprive a resident alien or an orphan of justice; you shall not take a widow's garment in pledge." This is followed by one of many injunctions to "remember that you were a slave in Egypt and the LORD your God redeemed you from there; therefore I command you to do this" (Deut. 24:17–18). This is a theme central throughout the Torah: God is concerned particularly for the poor, the oppressed, the widow, and the orphan. God's justice is defined around these emphases, and God's people are called to order their lives around them so that, as emphasized by Paul (2 Cor. 8:12–15) as well as Exodus (16:18), no one has too much or too little.

I once had the privilege of listening to Rabbi Alexander Schindler speak; he pointed out that the Hebrew name for Egypt, *Mitzrayim*, means "the narrow places." God is still raising up prophets, he said, to lead us out of all these "narrow places." God's prophets cry out— how will we respond to the call, to those whose spirits are crushed by poverty, trauma, and abuse; whose intellect and imagination could lift whole families and villages out of poverty but for the lack of an education; whose bodies are wounded or killed by hunger, disease, and violence? Prophets throughout Scripture challenge us to raise these questions and to address them with all the resources we have— with our money and our goods, certainly, but also with our intellects, our voices, and our power. Public outcry against "sodomites" often, if not always, ignores what Isaiah told the "rulers of Sodom" and the "people of Gomorrah" was "the evil of [their] doings": failure to "seek justice, rescue the oppressed, defend the orphan, plead for the widow" (1:10, 16–17). "The LORD rises to argue his case," Isaiah says, "he stands to judge the peoples. . . . It is you who have devoured the vineyard; the spoil of the poor is in your houses" (3:13–14). The writings of all scriptural prophets carry such indictments. How many of us are missing the wave of God's justice?

For many people, to speak of God's justice evokes only doom and gloom. But Walter Brueggemann distinguishes two kinds of justice. First, there is *retributive justice*: being sure those who harm others and do evil get what they deserve. Then there's *distributive justice*: God making the world a more just place by bringing justice for the oppressed. Both kinds of justice are important.

For example, there are instances—lots of them—in which God's people complain to God about a lack of retributive justice: the wicked prosper while the righteous suffer, and punishment is too long in coming or too easily dropped in God's mercy. Jonah is my favorite example, but he is hardly alone in Scripture. The Psalms are just some of the pastoral treasures in Scripture for anyone who has ever wondered why bad things happen to good people, and why people who would call themselves good commit public and private atrocities and yet seem to prosper.

Deprived of justice, God's people weep and even yell at God, demanding both retributive and distributive justice, expressing both the agony of their suffering and the intensity of their innate longing for a more just world. I have felt this agony and intensity again and again when I come close to the sufferings of others. My heart has been broken, and it breaks still when I hear the stories of women struggling to get out of abusive relationships that threaten their very lives; when I see shantytowns without clean water; when I listen to people who have nothing to sell and therefore no way to survive other than to sell their bodies and make choices between almost equally horrifying risks and damage. Somehow in this grieving, mourning, and thirsting for justice, I have known that God suffers with us, that our tears and rage at injustice are in harmony with the heartbreak of God.

Think about it—if God's character is really constant, then the suffering of our Christ, who was nailed to a cross by an imperial power and bureaucracy, says something truly surprising. It says that the living God of justice has true solidarity with all who suffer, any time, anywhere.

God's heart breaks. But God knows where history is headed. God knows that the universe God made arcs toward justice. God's justice and mercy are not so much in tension as some proclaim, I think; God looks at us as our Creator, our Redeemer, and our Sustainer, and God's justice is as perfectly consonant with God's mercy as God's love is with God's anger. God in grace created a world of abundance and created humanity for distributive justice, through which the world's abundance sustains joyful, abundant life available to all people.

I've spent most of my adult life studying the Scriptures full-time. I've learned to read six languages or so, trying to understand the Scriptures and what other thoughtful people have to say about them. What has kept me going all those years isn't the hope of some particular job at the end of it, but the way those Scriptures sustain me when I'm face-to-face with real, heartbreaking suffering. What keeps me going in my studies—and in my work with abused women, in praying and working for an end to extreme poverty, in confronting injustice and experiencing abundant life in doing so—is the vision I see in Scripture of the character and mission of God.

I see that we—all of humanity—are made in the image of God. We all are called by our very nature as created beings to be visible icons of what God is doing in the world.[3] If we believe that God frees from oppression, feeds the hungry, and cares for all that God has created—and if we believe Genesis's contention that we are created in the image of this very God—then we live into our identity as God's children and the adventure of God's redemption as we engage God's mission of distributive justice.

Sometimes it seems overwhelming. The systems that keep human beings in "narrow places," cycles of poverty and violence that crush and kill, are bigger than the sum of their parts. It's not for nothing that Ephesians tells us that our struggle is "against the rulers, against the authorities, against the cosmic powers of this present darkness" (6:12). Our increasingly global societies have fallen far short of God's justice and have dramatically increased the gap between the richest and poorest; I want to cry with Paul, "Who will rescue me from this body of death?" (Rom. 7:24). Who can overcome such powerfully and deeply entrenched systems of injustice?

Paul provides the answer to which I cling. God justifies—that is, brings justice. Christ intercedes for us, and no power on earth can overcome the love of God in Christ (Rom. 8:31–39). The power of God's love in Christ will bring God's mission to fulfillment. Jesus saves—and is saving, and will save.

And we are Christ's body in the world. As enfleshed icons of God's image, as Christ's body present on earth, we are called to participate in God's mission, God's victory over every oppressive power. That's not a pipe dream. It's God's dream for the world that God made. That's one powerful wave.

We all are surfers. If you picked up this book, you're clearly interested in who God is, what God is doing in the world, and how we might respond. Every wave I miss (and I miss a great deal) reminds me of how much I need to listen to those around me. We huddle amidst the swells. But just imagine the excitement we'll share when the wave comes in. A surfer's call is waiting, and watching, and lining up with what's going on. I can hardly wait.

JUST SON

What Does Jesus' Message of the Kingdom Have to Do with Justice?
ADAM TAYLOR

Prior to the 2006 midterm election, I was honored to serve as one of the youngest voices within a speakers bureau launched by Sojourners called the Red Letter Christians, which was aimed at reclaiming all of what Jesus said, including justice and the good news. During the 2004 election the "values voter" became a new political category synonymous with the narrow agendas of abortion, gay marriage, and family values promulgated by the religious right. Somehow in the minds of many Christians and non-Christians alike, Jesus had become pro-rich, pro-war, and only pro-American. Sojourners felt as though Jesus had become the victim of identity theft and that it was time to rescue the words of Jesus, often written in red ink in many Bibles. This was an attempt not to dismiss or undermine the rest of the Bible, but to shine a necessary spotlight on what Jesus actually stood for and proclaimed. Somehow themes of justice had

ADAM RUSSELL TAYLOR currently serves as the senior political director at Sojourners, a thirty-four-year-old Christian organization that integrates spiritual renewal with social justice. He cofounded Global Justice, and also worked as an associate at the Harvard University Carr Center for Human Rights. He earned a Master's degree in public policy from the J.F.K. School of Government at Harvard University (2001) and a BA from Emory University (1998) in international studies. Taylor currently serves on the board of Micah Challenge USA and as an Associate Minister at Shiloh Baptist Church in Washington, D.C.

been hidden or ignored, as though Jesus came only for our salvation, redemption, and personal piety, and not to inaugurate an entirely new kingdom built upon justice and peace.

In the film adaptation of C. S. Lewis's famous book *The Lion, the Witch and the Wardrobe*, when Lucy asks Mr. Tumnus whether Aslan is a tame lion, Mr. Tumnus replies, "Oh no, he's not tame . . . but he is good." Too often the church has sanitized and domesticated Jesus into a tame savior. We easily associate Jesus with God's goodness and love made flesh. But what about Jesus also being the personification of God's justice? Jesus was both pastoral and prophetic, demonstrating unconditional love as well as real righteous anger against the abuse and misuse of power. The same Jesus who heals lepers and multiplies loaves and fishes to feed thousands also overturns the tables of the moneychangers for defiling the temple and exploiting God's people.

In a sermon entitled "The Transformed Nonconformist," Dr. Martin Luther King Jr. preached, "The saving of our world from pending doom will come, not through the complacent adjustment of the conforming majority, but through the creative maladjustment of a nonconforming minority." Dr. King called Jesus the world's most dedicated nonconformist, whose ethical nonconformity still challenges the conscience of humankind. Seeing Jesus as a "dedicated nonconformist" and as an agent of justice requires placing Jesus within his proper historical context.

Placing Jesus in His Proper Context

We must learn to reread the Gospels through the lens of oppression, removing many of the presuppositions that blind us to the full meaning behind Jesus' words and actions. In the seminal book *Jesus and the Disinherited*, Howard Thurman emphasizes that Jesus was a poor Jew born during Herod's slaughter of innocent children. After his birth, Jesus became a refugee, fleeing to Egypt until Herod's death. Jesus' words were directed to the House of Israel, a minority within the Greco-Roman world and an occupied nation smarting under the loss of status, freedom, and former greatness. Severing Jesus from the political, social, and economic context of Roman oppression is like removing Moses from the context of Jewish slavery under Pharaoh's rule. Or using more contemporary examples, it is like separating the words of Gandhi from the context of the British colonial occupation of India, or of Dr. King's words from the context of the evils of Jim Crow segregation.

Within his context, Jesus served as an agent of justice through his ministry and teaching, resisting and defying the powers of the religious leaders and the Roman authorities. In *The Great Awakening*, Jim Wallis points out that Jesus faced a number of political and religious choices in his time. He could have chosen the way of the Pharisees and become a religious leader who enforced the strict piety code of Hebrew law. Instead, Jesus criticized their hypocrisy because they "tithe mint, dill, and cumin, and have neglected the weightier matters of the law: justice and mercy and faith" (Matt. 23:23). Jesus could have taken up arms with the Zealots and led a violent political revolution to secure the kind of worldly kingship hoped for by the Jewish people suffering under the yoke of Rome. Instead, while being arrested for treason, Jesus told Peter to drop his sword and said, "Those who use the sword will die by the sword" (Matt. 26:52 NLT). Jesus could have joined the monastic order of the Essenes and modeled an alternative, ascetic life withdrawn from society. Instead, Jesus chose to intervene in the brokenness of peoples' lives, performing miracles and challenging the powers and principalities of his time.[1] Jesus' message called for change in individual hearts, but it also demanded sweeping and comprehensive change in the political, social, and economic structures in his setting of occupied Israel.

However, Jesus did not lay out a detailed political manifesto. His words can be selectively proof-texted and taken out of context to defend almost any position. While we can't naively leap from Jesus' parables, teachings, and words to specific policies and programs, we can glean a series of values and principles that must undergird our understanding of justice. Echoing the biblical prophets, Christ showed a particular concern for the poor, the weak, and the marginalized. While Christ's love, grace, and mercy are equally available to everyone, Christ is continually seen siding with the least, the last, and the lost. In Matthew 25 Christ conditions salvation and God's judgment around our treatment of the "least of these among us." James Forbes cleverly summarizes Matthew 25 by suggesting that "no one will get to heaven without a letter of reference from the poor."[2] During Jesus' first sermon at Nazareth, he quotes Isaiah 61, saying, "The spirit of the Lord is upon me, because he has anointed me to bring good news to the poor" (Luke 4:18). Jesus aligns himself with the prophetic tradition, becoming the new Moses who fulfills scriptural prophecy. Throughout the Gospels we find an overriding theme of justice connected to Jesus' proclamation of the kingdom of God.

Jesus and the Kingdom of God

One of the dominant themes in the preaching and teachings of Jesus is the coming of the kingdom. This term or closely related ideas occur some seventy times in the synoptic Gospels and have both present and future associations. For instance, Jesus says in Matthew 6:33, "Seek first his kingdom and his righteousness, and all these things will be given to you as well" (NIV). The Bible's definition of righteousness is broad and more akin to our understanding of justice, or the way things ought to be. Therefore, the kingdom is inextricably linked to our pursuit of justice. The kingdom already "has come near" (Mark 1:15), Jesus says, but its full realization is yet to come. In the meantime, Christians are called to embody this "kingdom come" and to bear in our lives and work the fruits of the kingdom. Thus the Christian believer is caught up in the tension between the "now" and the "not yet." In *The Politics of Jesus*, Dr. Obery Hendricks underscores this point by putting the Lord's Prayer in the political context of Caesar's empire in order to shed new light on its seditious and subversive nature. During the time of Christ, publicly saying that Jesus is Lord instead of Caesar constituted treason under Roman law, the very crime for which Jesus was executed.[3] Similarly, declaring "thy kingdom come, thy will be done" was to pledge allegiance first and foremost to God's kingdom instead of to Caesar's rule.

Jesus sets out the values and characteristics of the kingdom in his Sermon on the Mount. The sermon outlines new principles, or Beatitudes, that reverse the logic, patterns, and political options of his time as well as ours. The Beatitudes contrast kingdom values with worldly values. Living according to these Beatitudes is like taking a sojourn, a spiritual journey of being in, but not of, this world. We are called to embody these counter-cultural values in ways that give others a foretaste of the coming kingdom. However, our politics and culture often exhibit an exact opposite set of values. Instead of blessing the poor in spirit, we bless the proud and self-serving. "Blessed are the meek" is replaced by blessing the arrogant and powerful. "Blessed are the peacemakers" gets overshadowed by those who pursue war as a first option rather than as a last resort. Although Jesus says that those who are persecuted for justice's sake are blessed, our culture says that those who freely pursue self-interest are blessed.

Barriers to Justice

Christians have been impeded from embracing Jesus' call to justice and the kingdom due to three misnomers that I call the *privatized Jesus*, the *prosperity Jesus*, and the *apolitical Jesus*. Too often we privatize Jesus, reducing the gospel to only personal salvation. God does want a personal relationship with each of us, but that relationship isn't simply fire insurance from hell; it instead enlists us in God's kingdom project. Many churches in the global South understand this connection, embracing a commitment to "integral mission" in which "justice and justification by faith, worship and political action, the spiritual and the material, personal change and structural change belong together."[4] A "prosperity Jesus" makes Jesus into a heavenly ATM machine, doling out comfort and material blessings to faithful believers. According to this view, the crown we wear precedes the cross we bear. Jesus does promise an abundant life but never an ostentatious life. Following Christ also involves denying ourselves and picking up our cross to serve others. Lastly, an apolitical faith often blocks justice ministry. Many Christians feel burned out and bruised by the political example of the religious right, which sought to take over one political party to achieve an often-narrow agenda. Yet as Dr. King often said, "The church must be reminded that it is not the master or the servant of the state, but rather the conscience of the state."[5] Yet the moment Christians abdicate their civic and prophetic role we give greater power to the forces of injustice. Thus, according to the Confer-

41

ence of Catholic Bishops, we must be engaged but never used, and political but never ideological.[6]

A Contemporary Application

The crisis of AIDS provides a contemporary example of how to apply Jesus' concern for justice. In many respects, AIDS has become the leprosy of the twenty-first century. The disease is often shrouded in a cloud of stigma, shame, inequality, and injustice. Just as the virus attacks the weakest part of the human body, the disease often attacks the most marginalized members of society. The disease is devastating communities across the world, particularly on the continent of Africa, where a generation of orphans is being left in its wake. Fortunately the church is moving from a posture of stigma and judgment to one of compassion, mercy, and love. Modern medicine has created a Lazarus effect, transforming AIDS from a brutal death sentence to a manageable disease. However, the cost of these drugs is still prohibitively high and out of reach for the majority of people living with HIV. Christians agree that Jesus would respond to the AIDS pandemic with acts of miraculous healing and practical love. At the same time, I picture Jesus overturning the tables of the pharmaceutical industry for blocking access to generic drugs. I imagine him calling on wealthy creditors like the World Bank and International Monetary Fund to remember the Jubilee Year and cancel the debts of many impoverished nations that still spend more money each year on interest payments than health care for their people. Jesus would confront root causes and seek to redress systemic injustices that so often fuel the epidemic.

Conclusion

Jesus loved speaking in parables; it was a critical medium through which he explained the world and offered timeless wisdom. In my favorite parable in Luke 18, Jesus offers wisdom on what it will take to be an agent of justice. In the parable there's a judge "who neither feared God nor had respect for people" (v. 2). A widow comes to the judge seeking justice regarding a dispute from an enemy. The judge ignores her first few entreaties, but finally relents as a result of her persistent and unremitting pressure. If God can use a widow—who during the time of Jesus represented one of the most marginalized and powerless members of society—to seek and achieve justice, then God can use each and every one of us. Pursuing justice and realizing the kingdom will require the same kind of dogged determination and tireless commitment.

There's a popular adage in the church that too many Christians are "so heavenly minded that we have become no earthly good." Yet it is because Christians are so heavenly minded that the earth as we know it should never look or feel the same as we engage in the work of justice. By addressing the most pressing justice issues of our time, such as ending the scandal of extreme poverty, preventing the genocide in Darfur, and stopping global climate change, we will yank bits and pieces of heaven closer to this earth. We will provide a foretaste of what is already promised and made possible by Christ's victory over death, sin, and injustice. We are called to follow Jesus into the highways and byways of this world, seeking to embody the kingdom's values and creating kingdom space here on earth.

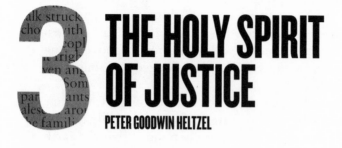

3 THE HOLY SPIRIT OF JUSTICE

PETER GOODWIN HELTZEL

Because of the Pentecostal explosion in the twentieth century, you could say that the doctrine of the Holy Spirit is on fire.[1] While evangelical theology has focused its pneumatological energy on personal sanctity and liberal theology on liberation, emerging theologies seek to integrate both in a vision of justice. Jesus inaugurates God's realm of justice on and for the earth. His entire life, death, and resurrection unveil for all people in all times a true portrait of God's justice. Justice empowers the wronged by making wrongs right. Jesus' teaching and ministry show us what justice looks like in every dimension of human life—individual, social, and cosmic.

When Jesus ascended into heaven, he sent the Holy Spirit of justice to empower the missional church. It is through the sanctifying energies of the Holy Spirit that the church actualizes its mission of neighbor love and creation care. Emerging holistic pneumatol-

PETER GOODWIN HELTZEL is assistant professor of theology at New York Theological Seminary. An ordained minister in the Christian Church (Disciples of Christ), he holds theological degrees from Wheaton College (BA), Gordon-Conwell Theological Seminary (MDiv), and Boston University (PhD). He is a co-founder of New York Faith and Justice and the Envision Conference. He has edited *The Chalice Introduction to Disciples Theology* and coedited *Evangelicals and Empire* and *Theology in Global Context*. Forthcoming publications include *Jesus and Justice: Evangelicals, Race, and American Politics*. He lives in New York City with his wife, Sarah, who is an opera singer.

ogy understands the Holy Spirit as the Spirit of justice-making that energizes Christian missional movements to actively proclaim and embody Christ's peaceable kingdom.

Justice becomes a lens through which we can see an emerging biblical theology of the peaceable kingdom. In pneumatological terms, we are challenged to ask the question, "What would it look like to imagine the Holy Spirit throughout the scriptural narrative as the divine person and powerful presence who is tenaciously committed to the concrete materialization of justice on earth as it is in heaven?" Throughout Scripture we witness the Holy Spirit of justice seeking to weave together a broken creation. *Ruach*, the Hebrew word for Spirit, is a feminine term that can also be translated "wind" or "breath." In the creation accounts of Genesis, this wise wind brooded over the face of the deep, bringing form to the formless. The Spirit played an active role in knitting together the natural elements—water, air, earth, and fire—to create a "good creation." This wise wind blows throughout Scripture, forming creation and weaving the community together in the earthly struggle for justice.

Within the Garden of Eden, Adam and Eve lived in a state of *shalom*—the presence of justice in all aspects of human life.[2] This order of well-being, peaceful and just, provides the theological basis for right relations with others and the good creation. *Shalom* provides the conditions for human flourishing in the midst of God's good creation.

According to the Genesis 3 narrative, God's *shalom* in the community of creation was dramatically broken. The radical disruption was a break in creation on multiple relational levels: relationships between God and humanity, humanity and creation, and man and woman. God's reign of *shalom*, love, and justice was replaced by worldly powers of sin, evil, and injustice. This episode in Eden was a cataclysmic break in the peaceable creation, a fracture that went all the way down into the very depths of human-being and earth-being.

After the break in creation, *shalom* was no longer the normative state of creation, but rather the *telos* of the people of God, their ultimate destination. *Shalom* was the collective goal to be attained by the twelve tribes of Israel as they sojourned together through the wilderness and into the Promised Land in search of God's realm of

45

peace, healing, and justice. In Jewish teaching, this struggle to restore God's *shalom* in the world is often referred to as *tikkun olam*, the healing of the world. Across the arc of redemptive history, we see God's Spirit empowering people in this earthly struggle for healing and justice, gathering and repairing the fragments of a broken world. Restoring *shalom* through seeking God's justice is a leitmotif of the drama of redemption.[3]

God's justice is a social form of God's holiness.[4] The revelation of God's holiness is a revelation of an ancient "unsaid" name (1 Sam. 2:2; Isa. 6:3).[5] Holiness is so close to the mystery of divinity that it must be meditated on in silence, a tradition kept in Judaism through the unspoken *tetragrammaton*.[6] Holiness designates God's moral excellence in excess (Deut. 1:16–17; Exod. 18:21–23). God's *holiness* broadly reaches out to the *whole* earth (Gen. 18:25): it embraces and exceeds creation in the horizon of a Messianic future. God's holiness is inclusive and integral, embracing the integrity of human person-hood and humanity's integration into the community of creation. Because of the presence of sin, death, and evil in the world, Israel's pursuit of being a holy people was an ongoing struggle to be in right relationship with God, humanity, and creation.

The prophetic literature offers vignettes of the social dimension of holiness. The Hebrew prophets deploy a dyad—justice and righteousness, *mishpat* and *sadiqah*—to call Israel to restore creation's *shalom* as a concrete way of worshiping their Creator (Gen. 18:19; Amos 5:21–24; Mic. 6:6–8). Justice-making is an essential component of being the holy people of God.

The prophets offer Israel a clarion call to embody salvation in the earthly struggle to end injustice and live together in *shalom*.[7] The people of God are called to end injustice because God hates injustice and longs for justice within *shalom*. While injustice results from broken people's evil actions, justice empowers the wronged through making their wrongs right and restoring broken relationships. Thus, the people of Israel express their holiness through their struggle for justice. Justice as social sanctity includes the just treatment of all God's children, especially the marginalized ones. Central to the Jewish law was the call to diligently care for those located on the margins of the tribes of Israel—the widows, orphans, strangers, and poor (Zech. 7:9–10).

46

When those on the margins were mistreated, God raised up and anointed prophets to blow the ram's horns of jubilee justice, awakening God's people from their deep slumber (Lev. 25:8–12; Deut. 15:1–7). The Jubilee Year sought to embody a stouthearted weaving together of broken people, communities, and creation. During this seventh year, the land lays fallow, debts are forgiven, slaves are freed, and the poor are fed. Thus, in Hebrew Scripture the Spirit fell on prophets who called the people of Israel to practice God's justice, while they also predicted the coming of a Messiah who would usher in the age of love, justice, and peace.

In the Luke-Acts narrative, the Holy Spirit is poured out upon human flesh, first entering the Jewish flesh of Mary's womb (Luke 1–2), and then being poured out on all flesh, both Jewish and Gentile, at Pentecost (Acts 1–2).[8] In Luke's Gospel, the Holy Spirit is present at many of the most important moments in Jesus' life.[9] It was through the power of the Holy Spirit that the very justice of God is woven in the flesh in Mary's Jewish womb (Luke 1:35). The early Christian theologian Proclus of Constantinople conceived of Mary's womb as a loom, where the pure and sinless cloak of Christ's flesh was woven.[10] The human, Jewish flesh of Jesus Christ is the crimson thread that ties together God and creation. The thread of Christ's flesh holds together the rent garment of creation as the mischievous Holy Spirit mysteriously binds and bonds creation's disparate parts. Through the incarnation of the just Son, the Triune God enters fully into creation, creating the conditions for a new realization of God's new creation, a space where God's justice is fully present within *shalom*.[11] Mary responds to the Spirit's call with a passionate prophecy, calling the people of God to honor the holiness of God's name through social justice directed toward those on the margins (Luke 1:43–55; cf. Ps. 111:9).

The Holy Spirit anoints Jesus as he preaches his first sermon reclaiming Isaiah's vision of jubilee justice, proclaiming good news for the poor, freedom for prisoners, sight for the blind, and liberation for the oppressed (Luke 4:16–19). Jesus both inaugurates and *is* the peaceable kingdom.[12] Throughout his ministry, anointed by the Holy Spirit, Jesus proclaimed and performed the loving justice of God in his compassion for the "least of these" (Matt. 25:31–46). Jesus shows humanity that the way of holiness is treating other people's needs as holy.[13] Jesus models justice-making through his "life for the other," culminating his crucifixion on a Roman cross and being raised to life by the Spirit, as the source and inspiration of our own journey into Spirit-filled, cruciform discipleship.

After his resurrection, Jesus stayed with his disciples for forty days teaching them about the kingdom, asking them to wait for the Father's promised Holy Spirit (Acts 1:1–5; 2:33; cf. Luke 24:49). As the Spirit had fallen on his own Jewish flesh in the incarnation it would now fall universally on the early Christians, empowering them to be witnesses from Jerusalem "to the ends of the earth" (Acts 1:8). With the whirring of a rushing wind, Pentecost came suddenly. The sky was filled with the brightness of tongues of fire as the multitude was filled with the Spirit and spoke all the languages of the world (2:1–6). Pentecost provides a template for the Christian movement as a Spirit-empowered, transnational, multilinguistic, intercultural movement for justice.

The outpouring of the Holy Spirit at Pentecost empowers the early Christians to justice-making in individual, social, economic, and ecological dimensions. Individuals are called by the apostle Peter to repent and be baptized (2:37–38). Social hierarchies between men and women, young and old, slave and free are turned "upside down" as the early church becomes a radically egalitarian counter-imperial prophetic community in the heart of the Roman Empire (Acts 2:17–18; 17:6; cf. Joel 2:28–32). Instead of an economy of exchange, they practiced a gift economy through living in intentional community (Acts 2:42–46; 4:32–37). The healings, signs, and wonders they performed were seen as acts of creation care, honoring their "Sovereign Lord, who made the heaven and the earth, the sea, and everything in them" (4:24). Thus, Pentecost provides a portrait of God's justice being materialized in the Spirit-filled prophetic community of the early Christian movement.

America's Pentecost, the Azusa Street revival of 1906, began as a prophetic, black Christian movement and quickly grew into a global missionary movement.[14] Under the leadership of William J. Seymour, an African American Holiness preacher, the Azusa Street Mission gathered people together for Spirit-filled worship of God in Christ across the boundaries of race, gender, class, and language. Yet Charles F. Parham, one of Seymour's white Bible teachers, soon

joined by other white leaders, tried to wrestle leadership of the movement from Seymour, demonstrating the racial tension within the
church in Jim Crow America.[15] The Holy Spirit of justice that had
flowed like a river through slave religion in the antebellum South and
empowered the struggle to abolish slavery now flowed once again in
the attempt to achieve an interracial community of love and justice
on Azusa Street in Southern California. But the forces of colonization, social conservatism, and white racism had deep roots and stood
undaunted. Christ's peaceable kingdom will only materialize in the
Americas as emerging Christian communities disrupt the logics of
racism, nationalism, materialism, and militarism and form counter-
imperial communities of justice and hope.

With roots in the third wave Charismatic movement, the emerging
church movement is, at its best, a global "Pentecostal" movement for
justice. Yet since the emerging conversation began primarily among
white elite in the United States and the United Kingdom, who are
beneficiaries of the world's largest militaries and global economy,
emerging theologies must account for the dark colonial legacies of
injustice. In the North American context this means articulating
how the Holy Spirit of justice has empowered the justice struggles
of black and brown peoples against the racism and colonialism of a
white, largely evangelical modernity.[16] This will include narrating a
counter-genealogy of Christianity in the Americas that foregrounds
the genocide of Native Americans and the enslavement of African
Americans. It also calls for a mutual transformation between Anglo-
American emerging communities and emerging communities of
color worldwide. Vital to this post-colonial, intercultural theological
task is dislocating the emerging conversation from a white colonial
modernity and relocating in the freedom struggles of black and
brown Christians.

Pentecost prefigured a new history and body politic inaugurated
by Christ's incarnation, while the Azusa Street Revivals were a more
recent parable of Christ's peaceable kingdom. Yet these pneumatological moments are fleeting unless the whole of creation pulls
together to seek God's love and justice. God's cosmic call for love
within justice is presented poetically by Paul in Romans 8.[17] In contrast to the way of the Law and sin, Paul shows that we can actually
experience life in the Spirit because of the righteousness (*dikaios* =

justice), peace, and joy of Jesus Christ (Rom. 8:10). We have often thought that these are individual experiences, but Paul means that peaceable kingdom conceived as a new creation is the Holy Spirit creating in and through and among us justice, peace, and joy in multiple, concrete ways.

After the incarnation and Pentecost, Paul proclaims that the life of holiness is not only a possibility but also an earthly and experiential reality now and into the future. We receive the sanctifying energies of God through the gift of the eschatological Spirit, allowing our inner person to participate in the Triune life of God. Thinking (Rom. 8:6), praying (vv. 15–17, 26, 27), and acting holy (vv. 12–14) are present choices we can make through the power of the Spirit. Amidst our efforts to do justice, we still groan with the whole creation at the very depth of our struggle with sin, death, evil, and suffering, amidst the magnitude of our current global moral crises (vv. 22–27).[18] These groans are eschatological cries for Christ's coming kingdom. Through the Spirit we are gathered into intimate communion with the Holy Trinity, opening ourselves up to be an "iconic space" through which God can speak through us and to us through the intercessory prayers of the Spirit and the Son (vv. 26, 34).[19] As the Holy Spirit of justice flows through us as bearers of Christ's image, together we can herald and hasten Christ's rapidly emerging new creation.

The Holy Spirit of justice produces bold prophets, who call God's people to live in *shalom*, who sing of an upside-down kingdom, who proclaim the year of the Lord's favor, and who speak of God's universal love and justice in every tongue. Living as truly human in the *imago Christi* is only possible through the Holy Spirit of justice being resident in the life of Christ's followers. When emerging communities live fully in the Spirit, we will witness God restoring the *shalom* of the world through a radical out-breaking of new creation into the brokenness of the old—liturgies of healing, acts of justice, arts of transformation, miracles of reconciliation, and multifarious forms of life out of death. The Holy Spirit of justice is moving us forward toward the new creation when Christ's peaceable and just reign will be fully present to the whole creation.

A TRADITION OF JUSTICE

Snapshots of the Church Pursuing Justice
Across the Major Periods of Church History

JENELL WILLIAMS PARIS

My friend Tricia Elisara lives in Julian, California, a small mountain settlement in San Diego County. Julian has no shopping mall and no movie theatre, but it does have a park—just one public space for baseball and skateboarding, play dates, and spontaneous conversation with neighbors. Well, it had one park until the people voted against a property tax assessment necessary for park upkeep. The park was fenced shut and closed down. Tricia was inspired to take action, and was instrumental in a local campaign that worked to influence the first vote, request a revote, and campaign hard to influence the results of the revote. Tricia, a Christian, partnered with others through the local political process to work for the common good.

Preserving a small park in a small town may seem like a small story, and it is. Justice is a grand abstraction that gets worked out in concrete ways by individuals and groups doing right in their spheres of influence. Social justice involves acts of charity: by our actions we show how the poor, excluded, forgotten, or oppressed should be treated in light of God's justice and love. But it must

JENELL WILLIAMS PARIS is professor of sociology and anthropology at Messiah College in Grantham, Pennsylvania. She blogs at The Paris Project, www.jenellparis.blogspot.com.

also go beyond acts of charity to addressing the systemic inequities that make people vulnerable and put them in need. In this chapter I will argue that justice has been a central concern of Christians throughout the ages, not merely a special interest of an occasional few. We'll take an aerial view of the issue, covering lots of ground as we look across the Christian tradition. By necessity this telling won't be comprehensive, or even representative, of all the ways Christians have worked for justice in the world; if time and space allowed, we could consider William Wilberforce's work against slavery in England, Pandita Ramabai's campaign for justice for women in India, Martin Luther King Jr.'s work for racial justice in the United States, and many others.[1] Nevertheless, even in this brief treatment we will see that justice has been important to the church throughout its history.

Emergent worship and devotional practices often appropriate the ancient into the new. This way of doing church and personal spirituality carries wonderful potential for doing justice. In our rapidly changing context, we can be inspired, empowered, and sometimes warned through knowledge of Christian activism throughout church history. Additionally, drawing from the emergent emphasis on generative friendships, we can create unprecedented conversations about justice across doctrinal and denominational boundaries, and we can form unexpected new partnerships in the practice of justice, opening unexplored new potential.

Early Church

One key question for believers in the first centuries of the Christian movement involved the nature of their relationship to society. If Christians had eternal security through faith in Christ, they could have de-emphasized their concern about real-life conditions in this world, this society, this town. Fortunately, the faith of the early Christians led them in the opposite direction. Because Christians felt sure about their true citizenship in God's kingdom, they were emboldened to take risks and work for the good of the societies in which they lived on earth. Just as Hebrews were to invest in their communities of exile, the early Christians were to live as "resident aliens," recalling the words of Jeremiah 29:7: "Seek the welfare of the city." They did so by supporting widows and the poor, saving babies from infanticide, and nursing the sick.[2] Indeed, an early church document describes Christians this way:

> For Christians cannot be distinguished from the rest of the human race by country or language or customs. They do not live in cities of their own; they do not use a peculiar form of speech; they do not follow an eccentric manner of life. . . . Yet, although they live in Greek and barbarian cities alike, as each man's lot has been cast, and follow the customs of the country in clothing and food and other matters of daily living, at the same time they give proof of the remarkable and admittedly extraordinary constitution of their own commonwealth. They live in their own countries, but only as aliens.[3]

Middle Ages

The history of justice and the church is far from seamless; individually and collectively through the institutional church, Christians have at various times abused the weak while amassing power for themselves. Many of the most winsome stories of Christians doing justice occurred in the context of church renewal, during which believers tried to redirect and restore the larger church that had become complacent, self-aggrandizing, or otherwise unjust. One such story of the Middle Ages is that of St. Francis, a young man in Assisi, Italy, in the thirteenth century. Born into privilege, Francis turned to a life of religious zeal. He quickly gained a following, and together he and his followers committed to a life of poverty. Francis and his followers worked in the fields in solidarity with peasants, rebuilt dilapidated churches, and made particular effort to sit with lepers, helping them with their daily bodily needs. A like-minded local woman, Clare, joined the Franciscan vision; and eventually several Catholic orders were formed, the two main ones being the Franciscans and the Second Order of St. Francis, or the Poor Clares. Today, Franciscans still commit to lives of poverty, chastity, and obedience; and concern for the poor remains central to their religious practice.[4]

Reformation

While they broke with the Roman Catholic Church in many ways, the Protestant reformers carried on the church's historic tradition of caring for the poor. John Calvin, for example, carried forward the General Hospital of Geneva, an institution that housed orphans and foundlings, the elderly, sick, and incapacitated adults. The hospital also gave food to the hungry and hospitality to travelers. In France, churches negotiated apprenticeships for poor boys, and gave dowries to poor young women so they could marry. Churches worked to help people find employment, marriage, and families, all of which contributed to broader social harmony and stability.[5]

Modern

Christians in the modern era have worked for social justice in many ways, sometimes taking the lead and at other times cooperating with people of other worldviews toward a common good. My tradition, evangelicalism, was derailed for much of the twentieth century in this regard by using social justice as a pawn in the struggle for self-definition. Liberals, in this (mis)characterization, cared about social justice but not Scripture, whereas evangelicals emphasized the Bible, Jesus, and evangelism, which pushed social justice far down the list of religious priorities. Even though twentieth-century evangelicals often minimized social justice as an element of mission, their behavior often surpassed their rhetoric, and the 1974 Lausanne Covenant reaffirmed a more healthy integration of social justice in evangelical identity.

Article 5 of the Lausanne Covenant, titled "Christian Social Responsibility," summarizes this perspective:

> We affirm that God is both the Creator and the Judge of all men. We therefore should share his concern for justice and reconciliation throughout human society and for the liberation of men and women from every kind of oppression. Because men and women are made in the image of God, every person, regardless of race, religion, colour, culture, class, sex or age, has an intrinsic dignity because of which he or she should be respected and served, not exploited. Here too we

express penitence both for our neglect and for having sometimes regarded evangelism and social concern as mutually exclusive. Although
reconciliation with other people is not reconciliation with God, nor
is social action evangelism, nor is political liberation salvation, nevertheless we affirm that evangelism and socio-political involvement are
both part of our Christian duty. For both are necessary expressions
of our doctrines of God and man, our love for our neighbour and
our obedience to Jesus Christ. The message of salvation implies also
a message of judgment upon every form of alienation, oppression
and discrimination, and we should not be afraid to denounce evil and
injustice wherever they exist. When people receive Christ they are born
again into his kingdom and must seek not only to exhibit but also to
spread its righteousness in the midst of an unrighteous world. The
salvation we claim should be transforming us in the totality of our
personal and social responsibilities. Faith without works is dead.[6]

There are too many interesting social justice initiatives in the modern
era to even attempt an overview, but the one that most impacted
my life was the late–twentieth-century urban ministry movement.
I volunteered in youth ministry for two summers in Philadelphia
for KingdomWorks (now reconfigured as Mission Year), an organization founded by Bart Campolo.[7] I networked more broadly with
the Christian Community Development Association, a collection
of like-minded urban ministries appreciative of John Perkins's philosophy of "relocation, redistribution, and reconciliation."[8] This
movement of Christians toward economic, racial, and interpersonal
right relationships changed my life. I eventually earned a doctorate
in urban anthropology, studying how ghettos form and how ghetto
residents take action on their own behalf, and spent thirteen years
living in needy areas of Philadelphia, Washington, D.C., Buffalo,
and Minneapolis.

Christians in the modern era, evangelicals as well as others, have
also failed, and these lapses are important to acknowledge along with
the success stories. In the modern era Christians have at times failed
to recognize the gospel's message about just treatment of women, and
have refused to address racism and slavery more preemptively and
effectively. We not only have failed to work against colonialism but
have often actively benefited from it. We have even ignored injustice

and scandal within the church itself, including pedophilia, moral failings of church leaders, and the prosperity gospel scam.

Postmodern

We must hear the call to social justice if we are serious about addressing the problems in nearly every sector of our world: environmental degradation, human slavery and abuse, the effects of patriarchy on both women and men, political injustice, and poverty, just to name a few. Postmodern approaches to social justice—which are being created as we speak—include creative uses of technology, cyber-activism, and new collaborations between people who might have seen themselves as antagonists in the modern era. One innovative project is the relational tithe, which uses Internet technology to connect resources with needs across geographic boundaries.[9] Another interesting form of activism is blogosphere leadership. Numerous times I've seen one blogger launch a fund-raiser on a blog or Facebook page on behalf of another blogger in personal crisis, and PayPal accounts fill up along with comment sections and email inboxes. A group of women bloggers once supported a dying woman by giving her money, words of encouragement in blog comments, emails, and, when possible, face-to-face visits and physical support. Christians are already involved in creating these kinds of possibilities, and in dialoguing about the interface between cyber-activism and real-world acts of justice.

Conclusion

Like Christians in each of these eras, Tricia made use of existing technologies, political structures, and communication venues as she worked for justice in her locality. She worked with all willing partners to make phone calls, write letters, and pursue conversations that would influence voters. I heard about her story because she shared her story with far-flung friends and family who prayed and encouraged her efforts. Justice is supposed to be big, describing the fullness of relationships made right, but it's also wonderfully small—in this story, a park remains open in a California mountain settlement for the enjoyment of its people.

I was rasied in the twentieth-century polarities of social justice versus evangelism and evangelicalism versus liberalism. There is much in my heritage I cherish, but I must choose how to make the most of it in my life and my generation. The emergent conversation offers hope for assessing and appropriating reigning, recent, and ancient paradigms and practices in wise ways, creating fresh ways to nourish ourselves and our world. In deconstructing reigning paradigms and pursuing new contextualizations of faith and life, we will by necessity learn from and appropriate practices from Christian brothers and sisters of all times and places. There's nothing new about Christian concern for justice, but it's a new day in which we may carry forward the cause.

(DE)CONSTRUCTING JUSTICE

What Does the Postmodern Turn Contribute to the Christian Passion for Justice?
TONY JONES

In the spring of 2007, Emergent Village hosted an intriguing event. It was our annual "Theological Conversation," but that year we took a different tack and hosted a "~~Theological~~ Philosophical Conversation." For three days we conversed with John Caputo and Richard Kearney, the premier representatives of the second and third generation of postmodern philosophers.

As you might guess in a gathering with two prominent postmodern philosophers, our conversation included lots of talk about "truth," "justice," "love," and "the gift." But here's something you might not expect: these two postmodernists did not deny the reality of any of these things. Instead, they argued vehemently that Truth, Justice, Love, and The Gift do indeed exist. They are real things. They are, you might say, absolutes. In the lingo of Caputo and Kearney, they are "undeconstructible."[1]

TONY JONES is the author of *The New Christians: Dispatches from the Emergent Frontier* and is theologian-in-residence at Solomon's Porch in Minneapolis. A doctoral fellow in practical theology at Princeton Theological Seminary, he is the author of many books on Christian ministry and spirituality, and a sought-after speaker and consultant in the areas of the emerging church, postmodernism, and Christian spirituality. Tony has three children and lives in Edina, Minnesota.

They went on to say that our human articulations of these absolutes, on the other hand, are fully and entirely deconstructible. Take laws, for instance. We Americans live in the most litigious society in the history of humankind. The IRS tax law alone covers seventeen thousand pages, and the "pocket edition" of the federal criminal code is fourteen hundred pages long. Everyone in the U.S. is covered by a multitude of federal statutes, state laws, and local ordinances. They range from kidnapping across a state line to how long you're allowed to grow the grass in your yard.

But not one of those laws is perfectly just. Each one is, instead, an attempt at justice—a reaching, grabbing, hoping for justice. Keeping people from driving over the speed limit or being sure they don't walk down Main Street naked are the ways that we, as a society, attempt to enforce a sense of justice. Taken all together, the hundreds of thousands of pages of law in every jurisdiction is our culture's attempt at an all-comprehensive system of justice.

But every year, we add some new ones and we drop some old ones. That undeconstructible justice that hovers just out of reach still compels us to keep trying, keep reaching, keep hoping. And so we keep amending, voting, and debating about the laws most resonant with justice.

The passion for justice among Christ-followers, of course, is more than some ethereal "sense." Instead, it's based on a text and a history that give us some very compelling examples of what justice is. In fact, it seems that justice was very much on God's mind when dealing with the Israelites. For instance, in Moses' final exhortations to God's people before they crossed the Jordan into the Promised Land, he made it abundantly clear that how those people treated "the stranger" was very important to God. In fact, it seems it was right near the top of God's agenda.

That was the big picture. But even in the minutiae, in the jots and tittles of the Levitical law, justice was the compelling motivation. When the Israelites were commanded by the Law to let each of their fields lie fallow every seventh year, there was one caveat: although the field could not be cultivated, wayfarers and wild animals were allowed to eat whatever they could glean from what the field naturally produced. Thus even in the Sabbath laws, which were so important to Israel, justice for those on the margins of society was accounted for.

Years later, when Jesus stepped onto the scene, he pointed to these very Sabbath laws, particularly their application and enforcement, as a place where his theological opponents had missed the point. "The Sabbath was made for humans," he said, "not humans for the Sabbath." In other words, the law had a purpose, and that purpose was to invoke a sense of rhythm in human life. But when that law was interpreted legalistically, it was not serving that purpose any longer. Then Paul cranked it up a notch when he convinced the rest of the apostles that, thanks to Jesus, God's family was now open to non-Jews as well. This truly scandalous notion took a while to sink in, but Peter and company finally got the message that Gentiles were no longer "the Other."

Of course, we live in very different times today. Years ago, Max Weber saw the brilliance of the synergy between Calvinism and capitalism. The former curbed the immoral greed of the latter, and the latter spurred entrepreneurialism in the former. But as the religious tendencies of Westerners have shifted, the "Protestant work ethic" can no longer be relied upon to keep capitalism in check. While some Christians have always been skeptical of capitalism, it seems that many of us today are more acutely aware of capitalism's weaknesses. Indeed, former U.S. Secretary of Labor Robert Reich argues that we live in an era of "supercapitalism," in which market forces and the sheer amount of money and futures being exchanged every day have overwhelmed the democracy on which the United States (and many other countries) are based. In *Supercapitalism: The Transformation of Business, Democracy, and Everyday Life*, Reich argues compellingly that Americans need to push back against the corporate takeover of America . . . before it's too late. The problem, he writes, is that we want to pay Wal-Mart prices.[2]

But we can't have it all. So we have to make some choices about how we, as citizens of a twenty-first-century, globalized world work toward justice in an era very unlike Jesus' day. And, believe it or not, those aforementioned postmodernists can help. Here's how:

Firstly, the postmodern turn has reminded us of our own limitations. Postmodern theorists like Hans-Georg Gadamer and Paul Riceour have written much on the idea of hermeneutics—that is, different theories of interpretation. What they've taught us is that we must move forward in this globalized world with *humility*. The first step is to recognize the all-encompassing nature of hermeneutics, to acknowledge that all our conversations about reality involve layers of limited perception and human interpretation, and are therefore open to question and correction. Although some will argue this claim, there is no one, clear, plain-and-simple answer to, "What is truth?" or "How shall we interpret that verse?" or "What is the most just thing to do in this situation?" If we lived in more homogenous groups, the reality of interpretation would be unnecessary. Imagine if you lived in an area where everyone had the same skin color, spoke the same language, and practiced the same religion, for example. Chances are that you and your neighbors would pretty much agree on what laws would be most just.

But the advent of massive global travel and telecommunications has brought us, like no other time in history, into proximity with those who perceive and interpret the world differently from us. In Great Britain, for instance, there has been a great influx of Africans and Arabs, many of them Muslim. That led Rowan Williams, the archbishop of Canterbury, to suggest in 2007 that Britons might need to find a way for British law to coexist with Shari'ah law. A firestorm of criticism of the archbishop ensued, but even Williams' utterance of such a suggestion indicates that we've entered a new time.

Thus, when faced with multiple interpretations of Truth, Justice, and Love, even within the borders of a single nation-state, Christians must think carefully about our hermeneutical posture. Is ours the one, true interpretation? How do we deal with the diversities within our own Christian tradition? Contrary to popular opinion, the postmodernists do not tell us to avoid these questions. Instead, they argue that absolutist answers lead to fascism. But humble, circumspect answers lead to peace. This is also, arguably, the most Christlike posture as well.

Secondly, postmodern theorists have taught us about our inevitable *embeddedness in community*. Stanley Fish, for instance, has written much about the "authority of interpretive communities."[3] How we interpret a Bible verse, or answer the question, "What is the most just thing to do in this situation?" is ineluctably and inescapably influenced by the communities that shape and have shaped us. Where and by whom I was reared; the institutions in which I was educated; my friends, coworkers, and family members all affect my answers.

While this is another area of frequent criticism against postmodernists like Fish because it seems to promote relativism at the cost of moral absolutes, it should not intimidate those of us who follow the way of Christ; for ours is a way completely circumscribed by the story of a community. The Bible tells of justice not in some objective, non-embodied way, but instead in the story of a people who have followed after God for five millennia. We who are committed to Christ decide every day to submit ourselves to a community of faith that extends through these millennia and across the planet. This community—both its history and its present—then implicate us in every decision we make, and in how we answer questions of justice.

And thirdly, the postmodernists have opened us to the *power of stories*. In surely the most often quoted characteristic of the postmodern condition, Jean-François Lyotard wrote that we live amidst an "incredulity toward meta-narratives."[4] In other words, we're less likely to believe someone (like Hitler) who tells us that he has the answer to who we are as a human race.

Instead, we're more likely today to listen to micro-narratives.[5] In fact, it seems that the only way to cut through the massive amount of information available to us today (an amount, we are told, that doubles every eighteen months!) is to listen to each other's stories. It's stories that give meaning to the reams of data in our lives, and it's ultimately stories that provoke us to action. And what is the Bible and the Christian tradition other than an ever-increasing compendium of stories? Heroes and villains, sinners and saints, noblemen and peasants—our stories are written into this collection as we work out our own faiths with fear and trembling.

Some bemoan the merits of postmodern theory; they think it might produce a generation of nihilistic slackers. But just the opposite is true. The younger generation of Christians around the world today are more passionate about justice than anyone would have guessed they'd be. They are causing the powers-that-be in evangelicalism to broaden their political agenda, and they're provoking the leadership in the mainline to think less about political posturing and more about missional action.

With a hermeneutic of humility, Christians are less apt to spend their time writing books on apologetics and more likely to link arms with those with whom they disagree (even those from other religions) and fight for justice. With an awareness of our embeddedness in community, Christians are less likely to think of the faith as a distant and ancient set of directives and are more likely to roll up their sleeves and get involved in transforming their own neighborhoods.

And with an appreciation for the power of stories, Christians are less likely to demonize our neighbors (down the street and across the world), and more likely to listen to one another. And listening, really listening, to one another may actually be the first and most important step in expediting real, biblical justice in our lifetimes.

One final word: none of these characteristics of the postmodern turn mitigates our distinctives as Christians. This is not a course of watering down the faith. It is, instead, a meditation on *how* we hold and live out our beliefs. It may seem counterintuitive, but the postmodern turn actually cultivates the Christian passion for justice, and thanks be to God for that!

THE BOOK OF

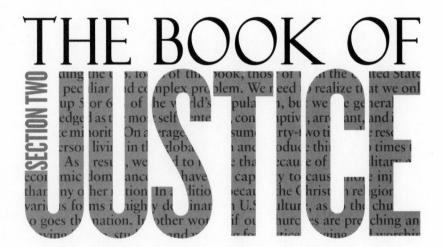

6 READING THE BIBLE UNJUSTLY

How Has the American Church Read the Bible Unjustly?

RICHARD TWISS

When Jerry Yellowhawk prayed over me in a Lakota naming ceremony where I was given the name *Taoyate Obnajin* ("He Stands With His People"), and Vincent Yellow Old Woman gifted me with his eagle feather war bonnet to confirm the name and Creator's gifting in my life, it was a defining moment in my journey as a Lakota follower of Jesus.

My father is Oglala Lakota Sioux from the Pine Ridge Reservation, and my mother is Sicangu from the Rosebud Lakota Sioux Tribe, both in South Dakota. I was born among my mother's people but grew up away from the reservation.

In 1972, along with six hundred others, I participated in the American Indian Movement's (AIM) forced takeover and occupation of the Bureau of Indian Affairs office building in Washington,

RICHARD TWISS and his wife Katherine live in Vancouver, Washington. They are cofounders of Wiconi International and are committed to seeing Native people emerge as a dynamic voice for justice, reconciliation, and healing. Their vision is "removing barriers and building bridges for better communities for generations to come." He is a DMiss candidate at Asbury Theological Seminary and serves as co-chair of the North American Institute of Indigenous Theological Studies. You can contact Richard at www.wiconi.com.

D.C., protesting the U.S. government's breaking of more than seven hundred Congressionally ratified treaties that it made with tribes in the United States.

I became a follower of Jesus in 1974. I learned to forgive my enemies, love my neighbor, and follow Christ with a humble heart. I also learned that "biblical Christians" were conservative Republicans, raised their children on James Dobson, abstained from almost everything, judged different churches because they were wrong, and thought everybody spoke in tongues and were expected to embrace strange Anglo cultural behavior in the name of "sound doctrine."

For many years I had resisted the pressure to accept interpretations of the Bible that suggested that I must leave the context of my Native cultural ways, music, dance, drumming, and ceremony, in order to follow Christ. In reference to my Native culture, I was informed the Bible said, "Touch not the unclean thing," or "Come out from among them and be separate," or "What fellowship does light have with darkness?" This meant I needed to leave my Indian ways behind me because I had a new identity in Christ—and it wasn't Indian! The Bible was used to demonize just about everything important to our culture's sense of being one with God and creation.

In this chapter I invite you to join me in examining how the Bible was used in the colonizing of "Turtle Island"—the Native term for North America. For America to gain its freedom to become a "Christian nation," "founded on the Word of God," it cost our First Nations people the loss of our lands, the decimation of our populations, and colonization of our nations, all in the name of the glory of God.

The founders and leaders of the U.S. credited America's growth with God's favor or blessing. Its origins were understood to be "inspired" by biblical notions, recharged through the Reformation, of the predestined, redemptive role of God's chosen people in the Promised Land.

The world as God's "manifestation" and history as predetermined "destiny" had been ideological staples of the strongly providentialist period in England between 1620 and 1660, during which, of course, the initial migration to New England took place. Any genealogy, in short, must begin with the religious sources.[1]

The term "manifest destiny" is often credited to journalist John L. O'Sullivan, who coined it in 1845 to signify the mission of the United States: "to overspread the continent allotted by Providence for the free development of our yearly multiplying millions."[2] I remember feeling so conflicted when reading about manifest destiny in grade school. I was the Native guy in the illustration of that story being crushed under the lady angel's foot as she blessed wagonloads of pioneers flooding from St. Louis to settle the "Wild West" and kill Indians, the bad guys. Manifest destiny, as a pseudo-biblical ideology, carried the weight of providence and privilege. It became thoroughly institutionally embedded, politically and religiously, and part of America's self-identification as a "Christian nation." This self-conception was supported by the notion of being founded by Christian leaders under the guidance of the Spirit of God, biblical truth, and sense of divine calling to establish the kingdom of God.

The Christian colonizers of the Americas—including the Spanish and the Portuguese—understood their endeavors as sacred enterprises. As Anders Stephanson points out, "The Puritan reenactment of the Exodus narrative revolved around a powerful theology of chosenness that was to be decisive for the course of colonialization as well as for the later American self-concept." He summarizes this with four fundamental biblical themes: (1) election and covenant; (2) choice and apostasy; (3) prophecy, revelation, and the end of history; (4) territory, mission, and community.[3]

Biblical narratives were formally used to justify the civilization of the new world beginning in 1629 with the striking of the Great Seal of the Massachusetts Bay Colony as Puritans prepared to depart England for America. The seal's central figure was an Indian man holding a bow in one hand and an arrow in the other, naked except for some appropriately placed leaves. From his mouth flowed a ribbon with the words "come over here and help us,"[4] a reference to the apostle Paul's "Macedonian call." This invoked a sense of God's leading the Puritans to evangelize the inhabitants of the new world.

Around this time in England there were also speculations that Indians were part of the lost tribes of Israel.[5]

The discussion in the 1640s and 1650s depended on the belief that conversion of Jews would precede universal Christianity. Thus if Indians were gentiles, their conversion to Christianity could not signal the initiation of end-time events but was rather a taste of the massed conversions to come. If, however, Indians were members of the lost tribes of Israel, their conversion to Christianity could indicate Christ's imminent return.[6]

Puritan writers used biblical typologies to identify Indian converts. In Ezekiel's vision of dry bones coming back to life, for example, they found a parallel to Christian Indians—people who, they asserted, had been "dead" in their sin before hearing the Word.[7]

> Truly the work [of evangelism] is honorable . . . it tending so much to be of good for the souls of these poor wild creatures, multitudes of them being under the power of Satan, and going up and downe with the chains of darkness rattling at their heels. Other missionaries wrote of the Native communities as "miserable captives—slaves to the devil from birth—poor soules captive to Satan."[8]

The first Christians in America used the Old Testament exodus narrative to explain the viral epidemics that decimated Native coastal communities. John Winthrop claimed in 1639 that "God hath consumed the natives with a great plague in those parts," and thus Puritan settlers had a "warrant" to settle in New England. In Pequot War descriptions, Puritan victors exulted in the terrible deaths of their foes: "But God was above them, who laughed at his Enemies and the Enemies of his People to Scorn, making them as a fiery Oven. . . . Thus did the Lord judge among the Heathen, filling the Place with dead Bodies."[9] The many who died from disease, they believed, had been willing occupants of the devil's territories and therefore merited death.[10]

Reinforcing America's national identity as a "Christian nation," Thomas Jefferson in his second inaugural address appealed to the biblical theme of chosenness, evoking the providential hand that had led "our fathers, as Israel of old, from their native land and planted them in a country flowing with all the necessaries and comforts of life."[11] Our American one-dollar bill reflects this view in the image of the Great Seal of the U.S. with the Latin phrase *Annuit Coeptis*, which translates roughly, "Providence has favored our beginnings," or "Providence has favored our undertakings."[12]

Biblical themes also served to inform government policy decisions about how best to handle the "Indian problem." Beginning in 1869, "Indian agencies were assigned to religious societies,"[13] which served as "duly subordinate and responsible"[14] agents to the United States Department of the Interior. The Federal Government, along with denominational and missionary groups, believed this plan might improve the ability of government policies to stimulate "the slow growth of the savage beasts" leading to the "moral and religious advancement of the Indians."[15]

In 1882, then Commissioner of Indian Affairs, Hiram Price, reported on the positive effects of this ongoing partnership. He stated,

> One very important auxiliary in transforming men from savage to civilized life is the influence brought to bear upon them through the labors of Christian men and women as educators and missionaries. Civilization is a plant of exceeding slow growth, unless supplemented by Christian teaching and influence. I am decidedly of the opinion that a liberal encouragement by the government to all religious denominations to extend their educational missionary operations among the Indians would be of immense benefit.[16]

Hiram Price referred to the Bible in support of the combined efforts of federal policy and Christian missions to serve, as Steven Newcomb describes it, "some huge Christian European reclamation project metaphorically conceiving American Indians as needing to be 'reclaimed' or 'recalled from wrong or improper conduct.'"[17]

Viewing Native people through the lens of Scripture, European people saw idolaters who were spiritually deceived, lost in rebellion, and hell-bound. While it is true that all peoples and cultures are stained by sin and the rejection of the Creator's path of beauty, and desperately need reconciliation to God, it is also true that European enlightenment thinking so colored their understanding of Scripture that manifest destiny and biblical mission became indistinguishable; one appeared the same as the other. Furthermore, it led to the conclusion that "Christian European missionaries and educators needed to lead the Indians to a moral way of life, which, from a

Christian European perspective, was considered to be a 'civilized' and 'Christian' way of life."[18]

Early missionary John Sergeant, while pastoring a Christian native community, emphasized to his converts "their cultural inadequacy and their personal responsibility for overcoming that inadequacy. . . . Only through a complete sense of their own inadequacy can Natives be properly Christianized."[19] He felt they could not fulfill this mandate, and began a school to assist them toward Christianity with the goal of the "total eradication of all that marks them as native . . . to root out their vicious habits, and to change their whole way of living."[20]

I receive many letters and emails reflecting these same ethnocentric biblical interpretations. A friend sent me an email from some evangelical ministry leaders and seminary graduates in which they expressed concerns about Native culture. "For the sake of the gospel," they questioned the legitimacy of my friend's desire to leverage a huge interest in Native culture, by writing:

> We don't know what His plans are, but as we consider Native American culture, we see core values that are not just questionable, but values that are an abomination to God; its pagan religion has roots in witchcraft. Specifically, because Native American culture is based in pagan religion—which is ultimately demonic—and their culture can't be separated from their religious practices . . . we don't believe God wants any efforts associated with the Gospel mingled with false religion which is under Satan's dominion.

Though I have written specifically of how the Bible has been read unjustly with respect to our First Nations people, the same negative attitudes are also found in the marginalization of women, the horrific injustice of African slavery, the demonizing and sanctifying of political parties or ideologies, and the pillaging of our environment. If our reading of the Bible isolates us from other believers, rationalizes sectarianism, marginalizes minorities, and creates adversarial camps among believers with differing theological views, then are we not reading the Bible unjustly?

When I go back to 1972 and reflect on my AIM experience, I believe at a fundamental level our protest was a theological one.

We were actually protesting the colonizers' unjust interpretation of Scripture to justify their theft of what was not rightfully theirs, but rather belonged to our First Nations people. When I look at the church today, and when I consider the church of the future, I wonder whether the descendents of the colonizers have honestly faced those old unjust ways of using Scripture, and whether there has been much in the way of real repentance.

Of course, over the past thirty-four years I too have, at times, been guilty of reading the Bible unjustly. Reading the Bible unjustly is not solely the problem of "white people" or those of European origins; it is at its core a temptation all human beings face. That's why I hope you will join me in relearning to read the Bible with a heart for justice, reconciliation, and the restoration of all things . . . so we can, in the language of my ancestors, return to the "Beauty Way" in Jesus, who is our Waymaker.

JUST TORAH

No Justice, No Peace—The Heresy of the World Ignored

J. SHAWN LANDRES

Dedicated to the memory of my father, Dr. Peter Landres, whose life as a healer was committed to ensuring just treatment for the mentally ill and bringing peace to those whose minds tormented them.

One of the greatest heresies of Jewish faith, caution my friends and teachers Rabbi Shai Held and Rabbi Sharon Brous, is the belief that the world is as it must be. This heresy contradicts the core principle of Judaism that we are covenanted with God to be partners in creation, instruments of revelation, catalysts of redemption. If the world were as it must be, Abraham would not have argued with God to save the people of Sodom and Gomorrah. If the world were as it must be, Jacob would not have wrestled with the angel of the Lord. If the world were as it must be, then Moses would not have defended the Hebrew slave or marveled at the incongruity of the burning bush. If the world were as it must be—okay, you get the idea.

J. SHAWN LANDRES is CEO and Research Director of Jewish Jumpstart (www.jewishjumpstart.org), which develops, strengthens, and learns from community-building organizations at the nexus of spirituality, learning, social activism, and culture. As the architect of Synagogue 3000's Jewish Emergent Initiative, Shawn worked with Tony Jones to organize the groundbreaking January 2006 meeting of Christian and Jewish Emergent leaders. Shawn and Ryan Bolger have published a number of essays on emergent Christianity and Judaism.

So the world isn't the way it's supposed to be. If that's the case, then three questions follow: (1) Why isn't the world living up to its potential, as it were? (2) What is our vision for the world? (3) How do we get there from here?

Major religions have risen (and some have fallen) on that first question, so I'm going to focus here on the second and third. Since we Jews have a habit of answering a question with another question, or better, a comment about the question, I'll begin with one of my favorites. Sometime around the turn of the second century, the great sage Rabbi Tarfon observed, "The day is short, the work is vast, the workers are lazy, and the Master is impatient."[1] In other words, it's not just that the world needs a rather spectacular amount of fixing, but also that we don't have a lot of time to get it done, we human beings are taking our own sweet time, and God—well, God is getting a bit fed up waiting for us to do the job.

For those who consider themselves followers of Jesus, this theological dilemma may sound familiar: God has high expectations of us which we can't possibly fulfill on our own. Historically, however, that's not really a specifically *Christian* problem. In fact, this dilemma occupied the Jewish people throughout Rabbi Tarfon's lifetime, from the catastrophic destruction of the Temple through the expulsion from Jerusalem. Without the Temple for performance of the required sacrifices, and without anywhere to obey the many laws specific to the land of Israel, how could we possibly do the job we thought we were called—commanded—to do? How could we ever finish the work? How could we transform the world that is into the world that must be?

Nearly two thousand years since the destruction of the Temple, contemporary, living, rabbinic Judaism bears little practical resemblance to its Israelite forebear. In reflecting on my assignment here—to reflect on the lessons of the Torah for an emergent understanding of justice—I began to think about all the connotations of the word *Torah*, the name for the five books of Moses, in the strictest sense to the magisterium of the entire Jewish tradition in the broadest sense. Realizing that one of our remaining links to the Judaism of Rabbi

Tarfon's day is the language of our worship, I started to consider the way we as Jews pray: what, through the liturgy, we ask of God and what we ask of ourselves. If justice is the vehicle through which we do our part to create a perfected world, then prayer is the language through which we express our deepest yearnings and aspirations for that world.

I discovered that for a people whose history is in so many ways (though never enough) identified with epic struggles for justice, our liturgy contains remarkably little to do with "justice."[2] On Friday nights as we greet the Sabbath, for example, we recite Psalm 92, which promises that the *tzadik*[3] will flourish like the date-palm tree. But we don't especially bless God as an instrument of justice, nor during the week (when we recite petitionary prayers) do we ask God to bring us justice. The daily litany in most liturgies asks God to bring us "peace, goodness and blessing, grace, loving-kindness, and compassion."[4] The two weekday petitionary prayers most directly concerned with justice use the word *tz'dakah*, or "righteousness," a term that has a more individual than collective connotation. The first prayer calls for the restoration of our judges, as in days of old, and blesses God "who loves righteousness [*tz'dakah*] and civil order [*mishpat*]." This is to say liturgically that God is concerned both with personal comportment and with the conduct of society as a whole. The second prayer calls on God to show compassion to righteous people (*tzadikim*) and blesses God as their "support and trust."

In short, there's not a lot of talk about *tzedek* or *tz'dakah* in Jewish liturgy. A little righteousness sprinkled here and there, and some civil order, but not so much justice. So what is there? *Shalom*, and lots of it.

Because we often reflexively translate the word *shalom* as "peace," we tend to forget that the root *slm* connotes wholeness, completion, and the enduring stability of perfection. It suggests the kind of wholeness that imagines a return to the safety of the womb, the Garden of Eden, ultimate reassurance that everything is and always will be okay. Not only does *shalom* appear throughout Jewish liturgy, but it appears as something only God can bring.

Shalom is so important to our relationship with God that we dare to ask for it even on the Sabbath, when virtually all petitionary prayer ceases (for God rested on the seventh day). *Shalom* is the ultimate promise of the *Birkat Kohanim*, the threefold priestly blessing recited at the climax of numerous communal liturgies. In the full *Kaddish* prayer, which is repeated in various forms as a kind of liturgical punctuation to mark transitions and conclusions, *shalom* is so important that we ask for it twice—once in Aramaic, once in Hebrew. In every case, *shalom* originates in heaven and it is God who brings it to earth. If it is God who "loves *tz'dakah*" found on earth, then we are the ones who love the great *shalom* of heaven.

Shalom is an essential element of Jewish prayer because it is that which God, in covenant with humanity, promises not as our reward but as the complement to our achievement of justice, *tzedek*, through lives of righteousness, *t'zdakah*. We fulfill the commandment to pursue justice by acting righteously. God's heavenly answer to humanity's earthly *tzedek* is *shalom*. As we are partners in creation and partners in revelation, so too are we partners in redemption.

My assignment here was to reflect on the lessons of the Torah for an "emergent" understanding of justice. Yet the entire Torah, the entire body of the radical revelation at Sinai, is itself emergent, revolutionary, paradigm-shifting. It is the extraordinary notion that, together with God, we can perfect heaven and earth through a covenantal partnership that unites *tzedek* and *shalom*, justice and peace.

Our covenant with God, then, is this: we pursue justice, and God redeems us with peace. The instrument of our covenant is Torah, the commandments, stories, exhortations, and interpretations through the centuries that provide the roadmap for connecting God and humanity. The great charge to humankind recited in the *Aleinu* prayer at the end of every service—*l'taken olam b'malchut Shaddai*, "to heal the world in the kingdom of God"—is our holy errand to achieve perfection and wholeness through the reconciliation of earthly justice and heavenly peace.

The world is not as it must be. So we must act, with all of our heart, with all of our soul, with all of our might. We must pursue justice, for its own sake, not only for our generation but also for generations to come, and for the sake of our covenant with God. Our Jewish tradition, grounded in the radical, revolutionary words of the

Torah, teaches that only humans can bring justice to the world. And if we do so, if we choose life and creation, if we are instruments of God's revelation, then we shall be catalysts of the redemption and the peace that only God can bring. In the climactic words of the *Kaddish* prayer, may the one who brings peace to the high heavens bring peace to us, to all God's people Israel, and indeed to all the inhabitants of the world; and let us say, Amen.

PROPHETS OF JUSTICE

How Can We Read the Prophetic Books in Their Socio-Political Context?

JEREMY DEL RIO

For the Hebrew prophets, justice is more than a theologian's hermeneutical exercise. Their conception of justice exists beyond the pale of partisan bickering, penetrates pop culture sloganeering, and transcends the speculations of the academy. More than a theoretical construct or philosophical pursuit, for the Hebrew prophets justice was a central point, if not *the point*, of the story.

> What does the LORD require of you? To act justly and to love mercy and to walk humbly with your God. (Mic. 6:8 NIV)

Justice and its sisters Mercy and Grace are what a loving God offered fallen humanity. In justice, mercy, and grace, God forgave sin, provided redemption, and promised the Messiah. They fueled the exodus from slavery and comforted a dejected mountaintop cleric in a still, small voice. They empowered the stutterer-turned-spokesman,

JEREMY DEL RIO consults churches and community groups on youth development, social justice, and cultural engagement. He is a cofounder and lead strategist for 20/20 Vision for Schools, a campaign to transform public education within a single generation of students. He directs Community Solutions, Inc., which provides after-school programs and summer camps through Generation Xcel and hosts service learning trips nationally through Chain Reaction. Jeremy is the founding youth pastor at Abounding Grace Ministries, and has also worked as a corporate attorney in New York (www.jeremydelrio.com).

the prostitute-turned-great-grandmother to a king, and the shepherd boy-turned-giant slayer.

Follow justice and justice alone, so that you may live. (Deut. 16:20)

Justice restores fractured relationships. It's both the pathway and the destination of the law of God codified on Sinai and fulfilled by Jesus. It foreshadowed the incarnate Christ whose mission became good news for the poor, freedom for prisoners, healing for the sick, and release for the oppressed.

For I the LORD love justice. (Isa. 61:8)

The contributors to this book understand this, which is why we repeatedly cite the prophets throughout its chapters. Read in context, the prophets challenge us to see God—and our world—in a new way. Rick Warren's public confession at a Pew Forum in 2005 serves as a model for so many of us:

> I had to say, "God, I repent, because I can't think of the last time I thought of widows and orphans." . . . And so I went back and I began to read Scripture, and it was like blinders came off. . . . I've got three advanced degrees. I've had four years in Greek and Hebrew and I've got doctorates. . . . I went to two different seminaries and a Bible school; how did I miss the 2,000 verses on the poor?

Many of those two thousand verses can be found in the writings of what Christians term the Old Testament prophets. They define how to love God and others well even in a broken world characterized by pain and degradation. Consider the following Old Testament case study about a teenager who internalized a prophet's plea for justice.

―

"'For I know the plans I have for you,' declares the LORD, 'plans to prosper you and not to harm you, plans to give you hope and a future'" (Jer. 29:11 NIV). Ironically, the prophet Jeremiah wrote these words to political exiles, slaves who had been conquered by a

Babylonian dictator; stripped of their power, possessions, and positions; and forced to march hundreds of miles across the desert from Jerusalem to what is now Baghdad.

No one ever told me that growing up. As a preacher's kid practically born with a Bible in my hand, as some of my youth group kids facetiously liked to say, and raised on a steady evangelical diet of Sunday school, VBS, youth group, youth camps, and Christian schools, I had heard dozens of sermons preached from this passage in Jeremiah. The inspirational messages usually came around springtime to mark graduations or weddings. Promises of prosperity and safety resonated, especially while enjoying life's milestones and awaiting further blessing.

But no one ever put the promise in context for me. They wouldn't have had to dig very far to find the backstory. (Nor would I, for that matter, but as a teenager I deferred to the preachers.) The first four verses of the chapter spell it out for us. Verse one reads: "This is the text of the letter that the prophet Jeremiah sent from Jerusalem to . . . [all those] Nebuchadnezzar had carried into exile from Jerusalem to Babylon."

Second Kings 24 and Daniel 1 further elaborate, describing waves of conquest and exile over a three-year period that ultimately included ten thousand of Jerusalem's elite, seven thousand soldiers, and one thousand artisans and craftsmen. "Only the poorest of the land were left" (2 Kings 24:14 NIV) to inhabit a burned-out shell of a city.

One of the letter's recipients may have experienced a different side of the conquest. As a child of nobility, Daniel would not have been affected by the same hunger, corruption, and street-level violence others would have faced. The buffer of privilege would have protected the upper crust from much political unrest.

But the siege made hunger real. The invading army had already looted nearby farms and peasants. The blockade cut off trade routes, and the soldiers dammed fresh waterways. The city's storehouses rapidly depleted. Outright starvation replaced hunger pangs, and malnutrition made an already-demoralized citizenry further susceptible to disease. Waterborne maladies spread, and the body count escalated. The cries from the street began to echo in the places of privilege where Daniel would have been at home. No longer immune to the pain and frustrations of commoners, he must have begun, perhaps for the first time, to confront the injustices they lived with every day.

Months later, the attack ended with Jerusalem's fall. A paranoid king blamed everyone else for the invasion. Suspecting treachery and fearing a coup, he cut a deal, surrendering as slaves many of his best and brightest, including young Daniel—trophies from a war they didn't start and would have preferred to avoid.

Compelled to march shackled through the Arabian Desert, Daniel and his three friends didn't know where they were headed. Iraq—then known as Babylonia—was a faraway nation shrouded in mystery. They certainly did not expect the double humiliation of being hand-picked from among the exiles to work in the personal service of the conquering king. Possessing aptitude for learning, good looks, and royal pedigree, Daniel and his friends Hananiah, Mishael, and Aza-riah qualified to serve in the king's court. Stripped of their Hebrew names and forced to assimilate into palace culture, like the house slaves of America's own sordid past, the boys were coerced into the king's *intelligentsia*.

It is to Daniel, his friends, and other exiles whom Jeremiah writes his letter. He told them to ignore the false prophets promising easy fixes and a quick return to Jerusalem. Settle down, he exhorted them; establish families and homes and businesses. Plan for the future stability of your children and grandchildren. Not exactly the kind of news political prisoners hoped to hear.

Yet Jeremiah raised the standard even higher than this. He encour-aged them to not isolate themselves from the conquerors, harbor bitterness, or plot revenge. Instead, "Seek the peace and prosperity of the city to which I have carried you into exile. Pray to the LORD for it, because if it prospers, you too will prosper" (Jer. 29:7 NIV).

God revealed through the prophet that the exiles' pursuit of justice for themselves would begin when righting other people's wrongs in Babylonia mattered more than avenging their blight in Jerusalem. After pursuing mercy—indeed, "prosperity"—for the enemies who caused them untold horrors, God promised to right the wrongs that beset them and return them to Jerusalem—*seventy years* hence.

It's against this backdrop that verse 11 speaks. God's plans to prosper and not to harm take on a decidedly different meaning for conquered Israelite slaves seeking the *shalom* of ancient Baghdad than twenty-first-century Christians chasing health, wealth, and safety in the West. The promised future hope comes as we pursue peace for and with others in the present, despite a painful personal past.

Jeremiah continues: "Then you will call upon me and come and pray to me, and I will listen to you. You will seek me and find me when you seek me with all your heart. I will be found by you . . . and will bring you back from captivity" (vv. 12–14 NIV). Jeremiah makes clear that the promise of answered prayer is conditional. The promise of finding a relationship with God is conditional. And the promise of experiencing liberation is conditional. The condition: pursuing justice and peace, even in the midst of captivity.

For Daniel and his friends, seeking the peace of Babylon meant first dining at the king's table. Traumatized by conquest and degraded by slavery, they nevertheless confronted the temptations that came with access to power and resolved to not defile themselves. But not eating the king's food—a religious defilement because it had previously been sacrificed to Babylonian idols—meant defying a royal edict, a crime punishable by death.

The men recognized that access to influence brought both the temptation to be corrupted and the opportunity to change things. To seize the opportunities required courage and great risk. With nothing but their lives left to lose, Daniel and his friends lobbied the overseer to change an unjust law. They understood that not every public policy is a just policy, and they were positioned to bring reform. They could have protested without a plan, but instead they proposed a test. Change the law, they said, but first hold us accountable for measurable results. They suggested milestones, specifically a ten-day pilot after which their performance could be compared to the status quo.

That was the first of many tests, including the peril of a fiery furnace and a den of hungry lions. But Daniel and his friends, rooted in faith convictions that allowed them to rise above their circumstances, consistently outperformed their peers. They overcame their own expectations of captivity and those of their captors. For activists and justice crusaders this means offering more than band-aid solutions to entrenched pathologies; digging deep to overcome core issues; proposing structural changes where needed; under-promising and over-delivering; and being accountable for performance. At the end of their training, the king found none equal to the four exiles from Jerusalem. When was the last time the same could be said of us, much less by an oppressive boss, abusive bureaucrat, or conquering king?

How did God honor Daniel's pursuit of justice in the midst of captivity? What "prosperity" came his way? For starters, this "slave boy-turned-advisor-to-kings" survived three empirical conquests (Babylon was subsequently overcome by the Medes and Persians), and enjoyed a political career that outlasted seventy years of captivity. He was still advising kings when Cyrus of Persia fulfilled Jeremiah's promised return of the exiles to Jerusalem—sending them home with a blank Medo-Persian check to rebuild what Nebuchadnezzar had earlier destroyed. Further, Daniel's pursuit of the peace of Baghdad included introducing personal justice with God to his original captor Nebuchadnezzar, King Darius, and others. And ultimately God entrusted to Daniel prophetic insights foretelling the coming King of kings, whose "everlasting kingdom" (Dan. 7:27) would right wrongs and restore justice for us all.

Too many Bible readers have been trained, as I was, to approach the biblical text through the priestly lens, not the prophetic one. That is, they look at the priestly theme of personal justification and ignore the prophetic theme of social justice. They're concerned about pleasing God with personal piety rather than public policy. They are more interested in being blessed than in being a blessing, quicker to bomb their enemies than to love and serve them, more preoccupied with evading justice than with seeking it first. They've been taught to cherry-pick certain comforting verses (such as, "Come now, let us reason together. . . . Though your sins are like scarlet, they shall be as white as snow" [Isa. 1:18 NIV]), while ignoring the challenging verses that come immediately before ("Seek justice, rescue the oppressed, defend the orphan, plead for the widow" [v. 17]) and after ("How the faithful city has become a whore! . . . Zion shall be redeemed by justice" [vv. 21, 27]).

Now what would the prophets say about people who read the Bible like that?

9 JUSTICE IN THE GOSPELS

What Does the Good News of the Kingdom of God Have to Do With Justice?

SUBA PRIYA RABINDRAN

In the oppressive heat of a tin shed in Bhopal (Madhya Pradesh, India), a small group of *adivasis* (native tribes) have given up eating the very little that they have.[1] Their homes are gone, their villages are submerged, and this fast is their journey toward justice, toward a meager and mean "promised land"—a promised resettlement. Vinod Patwa, Chittaroopa Palit, Mangat Verma, and Ram Kunwar are frail, weak, and battered after twenty-nine days of fasting. Their failing eyesight waits to take in the beauty of justice.

They are the activists of the *Narmada Bachao Andolan* (NBA), the Save the River Narmada Movement.[2] Their villages have been submerged by large dams and destroyed by so-called development, and they are now refugees. It was a devised, calculated, and planned calamity rendering millions homeless—merely collateral damage. For many like the NBA activists, injustice is near as they wrestle with its muscle and might every day to survive, to eat, and to just be.

Suba Priya Rabindran lives in New Delhi, India, with her husband, Rabindran Shelley, and their two children, Samyuktha and Harsha. You can contact her by email at priyarabi@gmail.com.

Freedom and Justice in the Kingdom of God

Freedom and justice are two sides of the same coin. God's kingdom is God's justice: God's will being done "on earth as it is in heaven" (Matt. 6:10). "When that happens, justice comes. And with it comes freedom."[3] Similarly, John 8:32 states, "You will know the truth, and the truth will make you free," which is followed by verse 36, a very pertinent proclamation: "If the Son makes you free, you will be free indeed."

Christ's Sermon on the Mount is the fountainhead and core articulation of the justice of God. In the account in Matthew's Gospel, Christ extricates himself from the crowd and moves up the mountain to address his followers. What flowed out of his mouth that day has never ceased, and will never cease, to challenge humanity.

Jesus begins, "Blessed are the poor in spirit, for theirs is the kingdom of heaven" (Matt. 5:3). This is a startling opening statement, for kingdoms never begin with the poor and the lowly; they don't even end with them. Kingdoms never have space for the poor and empty. Poverty, both economic and spiritual, has never been viewed as a blessing, but rather as a curse. Jawaharlal Nehru, the first prime minister of independent India, speaks of the "continuous lack and ever-present insecurity" of poverty: "There was poverty and the innumerable progeny of poverty everywhere, and the mark of this beast was on every forehead. Life had been crushed and distorted and made into a thing of evil."[4] This is no pleasant spectacle. It certainly doesn't sound at all like a blessing.

Yet here is the Messiah of the poor and the empty (not of the powerful and the mighty) asserting their ownership of God's kingdom. He topples the social order of his time: he snatches the kingdom of heaven from the circles of the influential and the powerful and hands it down to the poor. In Matthew 23:25–27, Jesus lashes out at the Pharisees and calls them "hypocrites . . . full of greed and self-indulgence." In Luke 11:42, he accuses them of neglecting "justice and the love of God," for love of God and injustice can never pair up.

In the perplexing hours before his crucifixion, Christ traces power back to the source that confers it. In John 19:11 he says, "You would have no power over me unless it had been given to you from above." Power, in other words, is from God. Yet Jesus the Son of God transfers the power of the kingdom of heaven from the powerful to the poor. Mary's Magnificat (Luke 1:46–55) also clearly illustrates this transfer of power: "He has brought down rulers from their thrones but has lifted up the humble. He . . . has sent the rich away empty" (vv. 52–53 NIV). Jesus goes on: "Blessed are the meek" (Matt. 5:5). The "meek" essentially translates to the gentle and humble in spirit; Mary's Magnificat calls them "the humble." Christ further affirms that "they [the meek] will inherit the earth."

The message of Jesus here has profound political implications. "Theirs is the kingdom of heaven" declares a finished and fulfilled purpose, but the phrase "they will inherit the earth" implies that work still needs to be done. It is passages like Psalm 24:1, which proclaims that "the earth is the LORD's and all that is in it," that become a compelling call for the followers of Christ to demand justice in the distribution of the resources of the Lord's earth. In these Scriptures we receive our summons to open doors for the poor to have their full share of God's bountiful creation. Jesus' ministry likewise sounded the radical call of God's kingdom to bring God's justice into every aspect of our lives. Jesus' kingdom message manifests a new pattern of relationships that clearly illustrates God's concern for justice. The kingdom message challenges us to rise out of silence, complacency, neutrality, and inertia into compassionate political action. As Archbishop Desmond Tutu says, "If you are neutral in a situation of injustice, you have chosen the side of the oppressor."[5]

Salt and Light

In Matthew 5:13, Jesus addresses us as the "salt of the earth." Salt has innumerable functions: it permeates, penetrates, interacts with the medium, blends, preserves, and makes food palatable. But salt must travel to be effective. It must come into contact with the medium in which it is needed. Similarly, our place as "salt" should not be limited to dining tables, or in jars lining the shelves of our congregations. As salt we must be shaken into the world; we must make contact with the realities of "others." We must, like salt, dissolve ourselves in the "absolute, relentless, endless, habitual, unfairness of the world."[6] And it doesn't take much salt to make a difference—

too much salt, in fact could result in a Dead Sea,[7] unable to support life in its splendor.

Our job is not to be caustic and abrasive; it is to be peaceful, yet potent—a tough proposition. To borrow from McLaren, being salt is "doing justice"[8] by confronting endemic and systemic injustice. It is a call to invest all we possess—time, talent, resources, knowledge, our very beings—to create a more just world where it is possible for the impoverished and the silenced to inherit the earth.

In Matthew 5:14 Jesus adorns us with the mantle, "You are the light of the world." But in John 8:12, Jesus also says, "I am the light of the world." This may sound peculiar, but it is similar to the moon reflecting the sun's light—in this case, we reflect his light and righteousness. This reflected light dispels the darkness of inequity, dishonesty, and deceit—the breeding grounds of injustice. Light is also a form of power—power to create better social structures; to guarantee justice for the marginalized and the oppressed and rights for women and minorities; and to eradicate oppression and racial discrimination. Light possesses the power to create change because the source of our light, and therefore our power, is from above. Being light also calls for an inner righteousness of the spirit, for it is this righteousness that will bring to "light" the very hidden and embedded roots of injustice. This light targets the fundamental causes of injustice rather than its particular manifestations only.

This concept of light also calls for a visible resistance. In every locality, we need to be persistently vocal for a more democratic, just, and fair world. There are a million ways to do justice—pledging our minds, garnering our resources, refusing to be manipulated, and digging and tunneling for truth and justice if need be. We need to pledge to do whatever it takes. As Luke 12:1–3 suggests, light must reveal the concealed, expose the hidden, and make known the things that tear our world apart; it is then that justice will come.

Corporate Christianity and Justice

"Corporate Christianity," a form of Christianity that keeps injustice at a safe distance, buries its guilt in charity—a little bread, a few boxes of medicine, cookies after the bombs have been dropped, aid, donations, large grants, and so on. It needs these impotent acts of charity to silence its conscience. It comes out smelling sweet as it wipes away the stench of death and horror with which it had been soiled. Corporate Christianity, like everything corporate, loves largesse—more crowds, more money, more power, more wars. For corporate Christianity, wars are the "will of God." It blesses the guns, and then sends money to provide bread for the widows and orphans of war!

But Christ sends his followers out like sheep among wolves (Matt. 10:16). The night is dark and the wolves roam freely, but he refuses us permission to continue sitting in our pews and worship concerts. Are we willing to "come out" as Christ wants to, and be the "sheep" of nonviolent dissent? "Instead of fighting against each other," Brian McLaren says, "you must fight with each other, against injustice, for the good of each other . . . vulnerable without weapons."[9]

Even to do this little is mighty enough. Christ compares the kingdom of heaven to yeast—a little works through the whole dough. Jesus also compares the kingdom of heaven to a mustard seed—a profound organic comparison of what the kingdom's subjects must be. The seed must grow; it must provide shade; it must harbor life; it must resist gales and storms; and on its branches birds sing songs of liberation and redemption. The anthem of justice begins from the seed of the kingdom.

Servant Leadership—The New Road to Justice

How do we stall the armies of injustice? Jesus teaches us to train a new army (Matt. 20:25–28) of servant leaders that will build up the poor against entrenched systemic injustice. Jesus juxtaposes the gentile leadership of lordship and authority with his leadership of suffering and service. The greater—those more empowered and equipped—should serve the less empowered and equipped ("Whoever wants to become great among you must be your servant" [v. 26 NIV]). This model is time-consuming and difficult, but it is also time-tested. It is a labor of love.

Is this a call to renounce everything and become a slave? No, it has a profound message of justice and equity. It bestows the greatest dignity to the people in the margins. It tells the world that the poor are

89

endowed with power to steer their lives and to lead. It is a call to rise above charity. It is a call to a different kind of service—it is a call to educate, empower, enable, and assist. This servant-leadership model creates leaders, not followers. It is only this army that can stall the armies of injustice. Sustainable, indigenous development—that which is strategized and sustained by the community, not "imported"—is slow growth, but it is the sort of growth nature intends. As Amartya Sen puts it, "Greater freedom enhances the ability of people to help themselves and also to influence the world."[10] That's what happens when the last become first—they influence the world. That is the truly remarkable justice of the gospel of Christ.

READING THE EPISTLES FOR JUSTICE

How Would Early Christians Have Understood Justice as Written about by the Apostles?

SYLVIA C. KEESMAAT

On September 14, 2001, George W. Bush declared in the National Cathedral in Washington, D.C., that the task of America was to rid the world of evil. Given that calling, it was no surprise that the initial title of the U.S. mission in Afghanistan was "Operation Infinite Justice." "Infinite" because that is the scope that would be necessary to rid the world of evil, and "justice" because the word suggests that those who are the perpetrators of "evil" will get their just desserts. "Justice will be done." Bush's comments were breathtaking in their arrogance, but they were also unsurprising. In a world where violence

DR. SYLVIA KEESMAAT is a biblical scholar, home-schooling mother, and gardener. In her spare time she is adjunct professor in Biblical Studies at the Institute for Christian Studies and the Toronto School of Theology. With her husband, Brian Walsh, Sylvia is coauthor of *Colossians Remixed: Subverting the Empire.* They live on an organic solar-powered farm in Cameron, Ontario (www.russethouse farm.ca).

is praised as the pathway to peace, it is not surprising that a mission of military violence could be seen as the way to bring justice to the world.

Imagine you are a first-century Jew living in Galilee in the year AD 50. You can't remember a time when the Romans didn't occupy your land. They have always been there, taking the best of your crops, cutting down your trees for weapons, demanding the little money you manage to save up, terrorizing your villages, provoking the young men, taking liberties with the village girls, trying to destroy all hope of a peaceful and joyful future.

But you know they can't destroy all hope, because you believe in a God of justice. Every week you pray the Psalms and tell the stories of old, and you know the promises that your God will come in righteousness and justice to destroy your enemies and restore his kingdom of peace and justice in the land.[1]

Of course, the Romans try to tell you that they bring justice as well. They even have a goddess, Iustitia, whom they claim to worship.[2] But you know better. You live in one of the small villages that has resisted Roman rule, where the coming of Roman "justice" is something to be feared. You know what Roman justice really looks like. It was Roman justice that caused Herod, friend of the Romans, to order John's head to be brought in on a platter. It was Roman justice that caused the Roman governor Pontius Pilate to wash his hands of a man he thought was innocent and hand him over to be crucified. You know that these are the typical ways Roman justice plays out in the daily lives of those who live under the wings of the Roman goddess Iustitia.

But there is something else you hope for as a Jew in the first century, because you are also a follower of Jesus. You know that Jesus promised justice, and you have been trying to figure out what that looks like. Now that he is gone, you and the others who follow him have been trying to remember all that he told you. But it is so hard. Everywhere you look you see scorched earth from the last time the Romans conquered your village. Very few trees are left. Your crops have been taken from the exhausted land, where the Romans did not burn them.

Everywhere you look you see grinding poverty: there has been a famine and you have so little. You see farmers work as slaves for rich landowners who refuse to pay them. You watch as families decide which child will have to starve to death. You try to share with those who have nothing, but you have nothing yourself.

And everywhere you look there is violence. There is the violence of Rome. There is the violence of those bandits who are fighting against Rome. There is the violence of those in your village who serve Rome and abuse the villagers. There is the violence of those who are desperate, who have nothing, and who have nothing to lose from violence.

One day you hear a message from the other followers of Jesus in your village. The apostles sent a letter to you and it will be read aloud that evening in your Christian gathering. You are very excited. Will this letter have anything to say about the terrible injustices faced by your village? Will it give you some hope about the coming justice of God?

Almost the whole community has gathered as the carrier of the letter arrives that evening. You are glad to see that it is Luke, who had stayed with you while gathering stories about Jesus. The leader calls for attention, and Luke begins to speak:

"Paul, called to be an apostle by the grace of God, who revealed to me his Son, Jesus the Messiah, along with Peter, an apostle of Jesus Christ, James, a servant of God and the Lord Jesus the Messiah, Jude, his brother, and John, the servant of the Lord, peace and grace to you all."

This is quite a beginning. All of the apostles who regularly write to the churches have come together to address you and your fellow suffering saints of Galilee. What would they have to say? Luke continues:

"We have put aside our differences and come together to write to you because of the urgent need of your community in Galilee. We have heard of your suffering, the injustice and violence that you are undergoing. We have also heard of your faith and endurance, news of which has gone out to the whole of the world. We want you to be assured that the good news is this: in the gospel the justice of God is revealed, through faith for faith" (Rom. 1:16, 17).

93

Here Luke stops and looks up over the parchment he is reading. "The apostles asked me to make clear that when I say the Greek word *dikaiosyne*, I mean both Hebrew words, *sadiqah* (righteousness, covenant faithfulness), and *mishpat* (justice). Perhaps I should just say "God's saving justice" to capture the complete sense of *dikaiosyne*. I know that in this situation of utter injustice that you find yourselves, nothing but God's saving justice will be good news." (It should be noted that the Greek word for justice and righteousness is the same: *dikaiosyne*. A first-century Jew would hear overtones of both justice and righteousness in this word. As a result, in every place where the word *righteousness* occurs in the Epistles, the translation could just as accurately be justice.)

Luke looks down and continues reading. "We want you to know, believers in Galilee, called to be saints, that the saving justice of God is for all of creation. Indeed, God has reconciled all of creation to himself in the death of Jesus (1 Cor. 5:19; Col. 1:20). That is why he calls you to bring the good news of the gospel to all creatures (Col. 1:23) and to be the saving justice of God yourselves (2 Cor. 5:21), so that all of creation will be renewed. Do not think that only you yourselves become new from the gospel. No, wherever anyone is in Christ, there is new creation—all of creation is made new by those who are followers of Jesus (2 Cor. 5:17; Gal. 6:15)! And creation knows this; it is eagerly waiting for us to be revealed; eagerly waiting for the followers of Jesus to take up their task of tending it; eagerly waiting for the new heaven and the new earth where we will look after creation in our resurrected bodies (Rom. 8:18–23). Then, when all of creation has been made new, purified like gold, we ourselves will live in a world where justice will be at home (2 Peter 3:13). Know, therefore, that when you work for the healing of creation, you are living lives that show God's healing love for all of creation.

"As we wait for that day, brothers and sisters, we know that there are those among you who are suffering greatly. We ourselves have suffered in the same way: for the sake of the good news of Jesus we have been hungry, been beaten, been naked, seen the imperial sword flash over our heads, and been imprisoned. We want you to know that we count everything an honor for the sake of the gospel. We are willing to be shamed for the sake of the gospel.

"In the household of God, it is important that you care for those who have been tortured, those who have been abandoned, and those who have been shamed. Spend your time with those that are considered beyond respect, welcome strangers into your homes, share with other members of the community, and remember the poor, the orphan and widows, those with no access to land or money (Rom. 12:13; 2 Cor. 8–9; Gal. 2:10; 1 Tim. 5:9–11; James 1:27–2:6; 1 Peter 3:9). I, Paul, have made it my main ministry to collect money from the churches I visit in order that by their generosity to the poor, the harvest of their saving justice will increase (1 Cor. 16:14; 2 Cor. 8–9; Rom. 15:25ff).

"We are concerned here with equality, my friends, not with favoritism (2 Cor. 9:13–14; James 2:1–13). What matters is not the hierarchy of the world but the gifts of God. There is no longer Jew or Greek, slave or free, male or female among you, for you are all one in Christ (Gal. 3:28). No longer do we limit the gifts of God to those whom the world recognizes, but rather we each minister according to our gifts: whether Gentiles, slaves, or women (Rom. 12:3–8; 16:1–16; 1 Corinthians 12; Phil. 4:2–3; Col. 4:9).

"We know that some in the church have more than others, and we urge you to live together in such a way that no one is fed while another goes hungry. Did not Jesus offer up his body and blood for us? When you eat the Lord's Supper do not eat as the world eats, so that some go hungry and some are drunk, or you will be judged along with the world (1 Cor. 11:20–32; cf. Jude 12)!

"We urge the rich to beware! 'Listen! The wages of the laborers who mowed your fields, which you kept back by fraud, cry out, and the cries of the harvesters have reached the Lord of hosts' (James 5:4). Who are those laborers who have worked for you, but do not have a living wage? Pride in riches comes from the world (1 Tim 6:17; James 2:1–7; 1 John 1:16), but know this, that those who abide in God's love demonstrate that love in word and in deed; you do not have that love if you see a brother or sister without food or clothing and refuse to help (James 2:14–16; 1 John 3:17–18; 4:19; also 1 Tim. 6:17–19). Remember that God has chosen the poor in this world to be rich in faith and heirs of the kingdom (James 2:5; 1 Cor. 1:26–29). No matter where that brother or sister is, in your own community or across the world, if they are in need, you are called to minister to them.

"Be comforted, our children. Know that if we fall short, if we are unable to practice this justice, we have an advocate with the Father. Know that if we confess our sin he is faithful and just and will forgive our sin and cleanse us from all injustice (1 John 1:9). Know that if we cry out in our difficulties, the Spirit will also cry out on our behalf and work in us to enable us to walk as children of the light (Rom. 8:23–27; 1 John 1:5–7). Take comfort in these words.

"We know that comfort is sorely needed by your community. We have heard of your poverty, we have heard about the way in which all of creation has been ravaged by your oppressors, and we have heard about the suffering you endure at the hands of your enemies. We urge you, brothers and sisters, to hold firm with patient endurance, for endurance produces hope and hope will not disappoint you (Rom. 5:3–5; James 5:7–11).

"Above all, beloved, remember that in the face of violence the follower of Jesus responds only with love. Indeed, the justice of God was this: while we were still enemies, Jesus died to reconcile us to God, so that we might live for justice (Rom. 5:10; 1 Peter 2:24; 1 John 4:10, 19). So you too are called to love your enemies, welcoming them and providing them with food and water (Rom. 12:13–21). Indeed, following the command of our Lord, we call you to bless those who persecute you (Rom. 12:14; cf. Matt. 5:44; Luke 6:28; 1 Peter 3:9). After all, what does it matter if you give your body over to be burned, or if you hand over all of your possessions, but do not have love? Love provides the patience and the kindness that make it possible to love even those who persecute you; indeed, love covers a multitude of sins (1 Corinthians 13; 1 Peter 4:8). The commandment is this: those who love God must love one another (1 John 3:14–24; 4:7–27; 2 John 5). If, however, we give ourselves over to revenge or anger, we do not love, for anger does not produce the saving justice of God (James 1:12–20; 1 John 4:1–12). In the kingdom of the crucified Lord, who died at the hands of the enemies that he forgave, mercy triumphs over judgment (see Luke 23:32 and James 2:13).

"Remember this, brothers and sisters, even if we are like sheep led to the slaughter, nothing can separate us from God's love: not the death brought by the Romans, nor the imperial sword, nor the famine or the nakedness that they bring, nor the persecution that they inflict; no part of the rule or power of the most powerful nation on earth will be able to separate you from the love of God (Rom. 8:35–39).

"Work then, with patience, to hasten that day, when God will bring the new heaven and the new earth, that earth, as we said, where justice will be at home (2 Peter 3:13). Remember that what you build will be tested with fire on the day, and know with confidence that our work is not in vain because we will all one day be raised with new bodies on the new earth (1 Cor. 15:51–58; 2 Cor. 3:10–14).

"Greet the saints for us. Know that God's grace and peace will strengthen you, as we wait for the revealing of the kingdom of justice of our God."

As Luke finishes reading, you realize that everyone around you shares in a feeling of amazement. First of all, you are astounded that all of these apostles have put aside their differences to send a letter to your community. And secondly, you can hardly believe their words. Here they are, telling you that God's kingdom proclaims justice, not just for you yourselves, but for all of your land, for the very ground under your feet. All of it will be renewed when Jesus returns. This is a message of justice that you can really relate to. Good news indeed!

But you are also puzzled. You've spent a lot of your time hating the Romans. A lot of your time. And these apostles, who have no small differences between them, have put aside those differences to call you to bless your enemies, even to provide them with food and drink! You feel that perhaps you must have misunderstood. But when you ask Luke he points out what you knew to be true. Jesus had died at the hands of his enemies and had offered them only forgiveness. Jesus had died while we were yet sinners. Jesus had offered up his body and blood for the likes of us. And Jesus calls us simply to follow him: to offer the forgiving justice of God to those who are our enemies. This part of God's justice is a lot harder for you to take. But you know that you cannot pick and choose the bits of God's saving justice that you like. This kingdom demands your all, even the justice of God that calls you to give up on violence and begin to love those whom you hate.

97

Things haven't changed all that much, have they? We still live in a world where creation is sacrificed to war and to farming methods that will eke out every last dollar. We still live in a world where the rich look down on the poor, and where the lives of many are sacrificed for the wealth of a few. The words of the apostles have to change very little to apply to our lives today.

But there is more. We live in world where the forgiving justice of God is hardly proclaimed anymore, even in churches. We prefer punishment, and we prefer justice through violence. The radical Word of God, however, is one of forgiveness, peace, and love.

A reporter asked Bono about the title of U2's album, *How to Dismantle an Atomic Bomb*. "How *does* one dismantle an atomic bomb?" the reporter asked. "With love," replied Bono, "with love." How does one undo the radical evil, the radical violence, the radical injustice of the world? "With love," the apostles tell us, "with love."

SECTION THREE

JUSTICE

IN THE U.S.A.

11 MY NAME IS LEGION, FOR WE ARE MANY

Exorcism as Racial Justice

ANTHONY SMITH

And he was asking him, "What is your name?" And he said to him, "My name is Legion; for we are many."

Mark 5:9

"I stood my ground against Mista Charlie," said my childhood pastor at Mt. Zion Baptist Church in Birmingham, Alabama. He was retelling a story of the prejudice of the local police. He narrated, as only a good call-and-response preacher can, the seemingly indiscriminate way they picked up a young black man off the streets. In reality, he was a young man who was respected in his community, but he fell prey to the unfortunate indignity of DWB (Driving While Black). DWB occurs when you are in the vicinity of a crime and happen to fit the broad description of the suspect: young and black.

What I am about to share with you is mostly unknown to many in North America. There is a code word in the black preaching tradition for a racial imperialist and the larger "power and princi-

ANTHONY SMITH is the "Resident Emerging Theologian" of the Charlotte cohort group and also serves on the National Coordinating Group of Emergent Village. He facilitates a blog, *Musings of a Postmodern Negro* (postmodernegro .wordpress.com).

pality" of racial injustice that pervades our social landscape: *Mista Charlie*. Mista Charlie is any individual or systemic manifestation of racial imperialism. It describes both the most overt forms of racial imperialism and the more pervasive unconscious habits of racism. Mista Charlie is a power that sustains and emboldens the habits and legacies of racial injustice. In language more faithful to the Bible, the task of Christians in our day is to learn to cast out demons, for we must see this gospel habit of naming, casting out, and restoring the body politic from the sickening effects of Mista Charlie as seeking justice. This will require us to name and cast out everyday habits that keep Mista Charlie in power.

With this in mind I call your attention to the story of Legion in the Gospel of Mark. When reading this story it is my hope you will see the analogy between Mista Charlie and Legion. They have something in common: they are both personal and social manifestations of the powers run amuck.

This story is a popular story of exorcism, and it is also the most detailed episode of exorcism in the Gospels. We are given names, places, and a cinematographic description of the scene. Jesus jumps out of the boat to encounter a man screaming and cutting himself in a graveyard. His demons even talk to Jesus, begging him not to send them out of the country where they had found a comfortable place, for they knew Jesus had the ability to name and cast out demons that were oppressing people. The Gospels present the reality that demonic oppression was profoundly connected to Roman occupation; hence the name of the demons who were possessing the man was "Legion," a unit of Roman soldiers. In his book *"Say to This Mountain": Mark's Story of Discipleship*, scholar-activist Ched Myers gives light to Jesus' campaign of healing/exorcism in first century Palestine: "As a healer/exorcist, Jesus attends both to the pain of individual bodies and to the roots of repression/oppression in the body politic."[1]

The prophetic task of postmodern Christians is to properly name and cast out the demonic legacies of racial imperialism in our collective imaginations and habits. This will require that Christians creatively learn to practice a form of exorcism that may be required to cast out Mista Charlie from our body politic. The story of Jesus and the demoniac provides an excellent avenue for us to imagine this justice. In his book *Hearing the Whole Story: The Politics of Plot in Mark's Gospel*, scholar Richard Horsley gives us an illuminating postcolonial reading of Jesus' exorcisms:

> The series of episodes in which Jesus exorcises demons and the discussions of the significance of Jesus' exorcisms in the Gospels indicate that precisely in his practice of exorcisms God's kingdom is defeating Roman rule. Discernment of this has been blocked primarily by our isolation of Gospel stories and sayings, but also by our inability to understand the phenomenon of demon possession in historical cultural context.[2]

The contest is played out in the personal confrontation between Jesus and Legion:

> When the demon is exorcised, it is possible for it to be identified. Its name is Legion. The original hearers would have recognized immediately that "Legion" referred to Roman troops. For in their recent experience, Roman legions had burned the villages around such towns as Magdala and Sepphoris and slaughtered or enslaved thousands of their parents or grandparents. Moreover, in a series of military images, Legion is "dismissed" to enter the "troop" of swine, who then "charge" headlong down the slope as if into battle but are instead "drowned in the sea," suggesting not the lake but the Mediterranean Sea, whence they had originally come to conquer the people.[3]

Jesus' kingdom contest against the enslaving and oppressive powers of Rome in the person of Legion is a story of both liberation and healing.

But before Jesus "dismisses" the Legion of demons from the region we encounter a person who engages in habits that suggest he has internalized the larger Roman system: He lives among the dead; he cuts himself. This signifies that he has internalized the violence wrought against his own people by the Roman imperialist system. Here is some gospel truth: our everyday lives are formed, pressed, and oppressed by larger realities.

When Jesus is done with the man, the Gospel says that we find him clothed and in his right mind. When dealing with the reality of imperialism today, we speak primarily the language of democratic

103

liberalism, as if the mechanisms of procedural democracy alone, however important and beneficial, can cure our body politic of the demonic. Jesus' exorcism of the Legion, however, was political in a different way: he brought healing to the effects of empire on a local community, where people interact with each other. According to the Gospel story, the formerly possessed man went on to live a true, free, and beautiful existence.

In our own day, when discussions arise regarding the continuing presence of racial imperialism, we keep it within the arena of individual intentions and personal prejudice. Unlike Jesus who confronted individual and systemic injustice in one episode, we reduce our racialized habits to the purely personal. The recent responses in 2008 to the so-called inflammatory Africentric preaching of Rev. Jeremiah Wright bears this out. His preaching, which has a long- standing presence in the black church tradition, was dismissed out-of-hand as "aberrant" and unbelievably labeled "racist." I can imagine a scene where Jesus jumps off the boat of our current global moment to confront our world and asks: "What is your name?" To which I think the demon would respond: "My name is Mista Charlie; for we are many."

How do we break out of being "possessed" by racial imperialism? How would Jesus, if we were to bring the demoniac's story into our context, exorcize us? What everyday habits and beliefs would we be healed from as racial imperialists?

I believe a piece of the puzzle is provided in the work of Brooklyn College scholar/activist Melanie Bush. In her book *Breaking the Code of Good Intentions: Everyday Forms of Whiteness* she describes what she calls "cracks in the wall of whiteness":

> Moments also clearly exist when there are openings that can increase awareness about the processes and patterns of racialization, racism, and inequality. . . . Locating "cracks in the wall of whiteness" helps to uncover and affirm hope and optimism about the possibilities for challenging the vast historical inequalities and injustices systemically structured throughout our society and sustained by dominant ideological narratives that reinforce and reproduce racialized patterns.[4]

Professor Bush points to the many ways our bodies and minds are disciplined by the metanarrative of racial imperialism, a disciplining that renders one silent, indifferent, or blind to the legacies of racial injustice and inequities. To break through this narrative of Mista Charlie, she lists a number of "cracks" or "mechanisms" through which we can begin to prophetically gaze at our habits that sustain and maintain Mista Charlie's hold on our lives. In concert with Bush's "cracks" or "mechanisms," I will list the "catechism" of Mista Charlie.

1. *The naturalization and mystification of poverty, wealth, and inequality.* Many people think that racial inequality is a problem but surrender to a fatalism that says, "This is the way it will be." They will ask, "Didn't Jesus say that you will always have the poor among you?" as if God has ordained that there will always be poor people. We "naturalize," or think that poverty is simply a fate for some people. Some commentators suggest that this Gospel reference to the poor speaks more to the location of Christ-followers, meaning that a community of Christ-followers should always be among the poor, never hermetically sealed off from them by political, social, and economic boundaries set up by the powers.[5]

2. *The invisibility of racial dominance.* The invisibility of racial dominance hides the unconscious habits, both collectively and individually, of white privilege. "Whites assume that there is a common American experience; however, for them race relates only to people of color."[6] Many whites do not see themselves as "raced." In their minds they are just people, normal people who do not understand (sometimes willfully so) what the big deal is about race. "By acknowledging racism, yet detaching themselves from its consequences (unintentionally or otherwise), whites participate in allowing inequalities to persist."[7] In my experience the invisibility of racial dominance, intentional or unintentional, can lead to a general apathy about North America's racial history. The deep empathy required to immerse one's self into the history of racial dominance is blocked off by invisibility.

3. *The rigid control of words.* "The rigid regulation of discourse is a third mechanism that reinforces and reproduces racialized patterns within the organizational structures of society."[8] The narratives that govern our understanding of the history of our communities, the metanarratives that hide continuing legacies of inequity and the God-sanctioned language of dealing with race make it extremely dif-

ficult to look at the underside of the American Dream. Subversive narratives that call out the dark side of American history and the continued effects of racial imperialism are labeled as relic-language. We fail to look with empathy, for example, at the massive amount of wealth and resources transferred by the Federal Government to whites in the form of land grants and educational benefits after WWII and the concomitant alienation of people of color, which fostered the creation of white-dominated suburbia and the creation of the black ghetto. Our restricted table of language used to narrate North American history in a prophetic way is deeply impoverished when our dominant storytellers come exclusively from among the privileged.

We stand in an imperial graveyard. Our body politic has habits that render it nearly impossible to get at the deep terrain of racial privilege, dominance, and vast economic inequities that persist along racial lines. We scream in privileged agony, cut ourselves off from the painful history of others, and are unable to be chained to a profound practice of repentance. What would it look like for us to be clothed and in our right minds again? We would all strive to see and acknowledge our own complicity in the persistence of racial inequality. We would recognize our own privilege and not take it for granted. We wouldn't attribute our successes solely to our "work ethic" and "rugged individualism," but would see the racial dynamics that play into the success of some and the struggle of others. When Jesus is done with us, we would enter into a zone of racial justice tread thus far only by a few.

If we believe the kingdom of God to be an alternative reality soaked with justice, love, and mercy, then we will give prayerful, liturgical, and habitual attention to Mista Charlie. He is, after all, *our* national demon. As Jesus once told us, some demons can only come out by prayer and fasting. This will require a discernment and passion that can only come from a risen Savior who has triumphed over the power of sin and death.

JUST LAND

What Are the Key Justice Issues for Native Peoples in the U.S.?

RANDY WOODLEY

> Tax collectors and other notorious sinners often came to listen to Jesus teach. This made the Pharisees and teachers of religious law complain that he was associating with such sinful people—even eating with them! (Luke 15:1–2 NLT)

Why were the Pharisees so *furious* with Jesus? After all, they were themselves dedicated to giving alms to the poor and feeding the hungry sinners. But there was one key difference: Jesus "ate with sinners." This one simple act of Jesus sitting down at the table and eating with them granted a new sense of dignity to hungry, hopeless people, and it enraged the Pharisees and teachers of the Law.

The Pharisees needed the poor, hungry sinners in order to exercise their sense of "mercy." Feeding the hungry and giving alms to the poor gave credence to their ministry. By sitting at the table with these poor folks, Jesus showed his acceptance of them as equals. To

REV. RANDY WOODLEY (PhD, Intercultural Studies) is a Keetoowah Cherokee Indian descendant, ordained minister, author, teacher, theologian, poet, and activist. Among his writings is *Living in Color: Embracing God's Passion for Ethnic Diversity*. He and his wife, Edith, cofounded Eagle's Wings Ministry (www.eagleswingsministry.com) and Eloheh Village for Indigenous Leadership and Ministry Development, where they encourage and teach indigenous leadership and ministry. The Woodleys have four children and reside in Newberg, Oregon.

the hegemonic Pharisees, this truth was too much to bear. After all, without the qualified leadership of the dedicated Pharisees, how could anyone ever hope to find God? Social classism needed to be imposed.

The dynamics of this paradigm are painfully familiar to Native Americans, especially when it comes to dealing with Christians. Christians, particularly white Christians, require Native Americans to be poor and needy. By necessity we must have the worst health, the highest infant mortality rates, the lowest life expectancy, the worst living conditions, the least education, the highest unemployment, the highest teen pregnancy and suicide rates in the land. From a missionary point of view it is essential for us to be pitiable. Kipling scratched the surface of this in a poem when he coined the phrase "white man's burden." My friend Brian McLaren refers to this as the "excessive confidence of European peoples." If we were to become "equals" where, but the reservations, would all our youth groups go for affordable short-term mission trips? One can't go to Mexico or Central America every year! Do I sound cynical? Perhaps. But I think you can find some truth through my cynicism.

The key justice issues facing Native Americans today are many—economics, social inequities, the criminal justice system, political prisoners. (Like Nelson Mandela in South Africa, there are real Indian political prisoners in the U.S., such as Rocky Boice Jr. and Leonard Peltier.[1]) Injustices toward our people are *legion*, and they even include the way almost every church and mission agency still maintains and plants paternalistic, culturally hegemonic churches on our reservations.

But none of these issues can be effectively dealt with until we are invited to the table. I'm not even sure if Natives want others to do justice *for* us until they can do justice *with us*. You see, there are many things about us you need to know.

I was teaching on racism to a predominantly white seminary class when one young man raised his hand in desperation. "Just what do you want from us?" he demanded. I felt it was a fair question, and perhaps by now you are asking something similar. In order to begin to reverse the ravages of a brutal U.S. government and an American Christian colonial past; in order to start to expose the true history of this country as it relates to the theft of our land, the extinguishing of our cultures and the genocide of our people (wrought in part by the willing participation of American Christianity); in order for all sides to heal and for justice to occur: (1) we (Native Americans) need an open invitation to the "table" where we can participate as your equals and (2) you (non-Natives, but particularly whites) need to stay seated at the table when we say things that are painful and even offensive to hear.

An Open Invitation to Equality

When Jesus sat at the table with people in desperate physical and emotional need, he sat as one of them. We don't know much about those mealtimes, but it is unlikely that he sat at the "chief seat" or that he "lorded over" them. Jesus simply sat at the table as one of the people. His mere presence demonstrated equality and conferred dignity to those needing affirmation. Jesus must have fit in well, because his enemies accused him of being a "drunkard" and a "glutton."

During the recent "State of the Black Union" panel, Jesse Jackson referred to the Civil Rights Movement as a time when black people fought not for their freedom but for their equality. Using his metaphor, freedom only gets you to the playing field; equality is when you have a level playing field. As Native Americans, we do not have a level playing field. Our accumulated "capital" (lands, money, education, health, etc.) has all been stolen and still we are expected by Western Christians to show up "ready for the game." We are in many ways where African Americans were in the pre–Civil Rights days. An open invitation means that there will be a commitment on the part of Christians to continuously invite us to participate equally at the table, even if it means a sacrifice on the part of others to get us there.

White Americans can afford to get up from the table whenever things become uncomfortable. They are not required to go through the anguish of hearing our stories. They get to go back to the privileges afforded them by colonialism while Natives must return to the conditions relegated to us by that same colonial process. It hurts to hear our stories; they are sometimes even too tough for us to bear. So sometimes we laugh. We want others to be there to cry with us, but we also want them there when the pain is so tough that we all start laughing—even when we don't understand why. This is the way relationships are made. It takes time together as equals.

You also need to stay at the table because you need *us* more than you realize. We are a part of the body you shouldn't ignore. We have special giftings and understandings without which, the Scriptures say, you are incomplete. And we need to be needed for who we are—not as tools used out of a sense of duty. You need us for who we are—in all our strengths and in all our attributes given us by the Creator. If we don't become fulfilled in Christ, the whole body will suffer. While there are many ways the dominant Western church is suffering as a result of our absence, I will mention just one, which is perhaps the most important: the land.

The Land

Western Christianity, including its American version, lacks a good theology of the land. (A stolen continent is not really the best location in which to build such a theology.) First Nations view land as alive, and something with which we are in relationship and covenant. All of creation is viewed this way. We see ourselves not as over and above nature but simply as a part of it and as participants in covenant relationship with it and the Creator. This covenant relationship between God, the people, and the land is the source for our Native American spirituality.

When we speak of living with the land, the preposition *with* should be understood as paramount. One can live *on* the land and still ignore or even abuse it. Yet living *with* the land implies a harmonious relationship, a partnership between human beings and everything else: soil, rocks, water, trees, wildlife, birds, insects. This understanding of a relationship with the land is the overall framework we have inherited from our native forebears and that which we have incorporated into our Christian understandings and beliefs. We have a deep sense of the "groanings" of the earth, as St. Paul puts it.

American Christians usually see the land as a commodity. They see it from their sterile economic paradigm, not the richly relational biblical paradigm. Yet, from the standpoint of good stewardship, there is a need for a renewed sense of relationship and partnership with the land. In other words, living *with* the land means one views the land as much more than mere dirt. This broader view of the land seems to be the natural view among most indigenous peoples.

Even Christian environmental activists view the land differently than we do. I once accompanied such a group to protest mountaintop coal removal. The wonderful people who were exposing this evil gave logically persuasive speeches and called for action to stop the plunder of the land, yet I could only feel a deep sense of grief. While I applaud their efforts, I can't understand why I never heard or saw anyone weep or mention our natural relationship with the land.

In addition, we need to understand that humans are "walking earth." We also are the earth in which the Spirit dwells. When we die our bodies make a beeline back to the dust. The Creator has given native peoples the sensitivity to understand the simplicity of these things, and to value the land as a result. Conversely, we believe the dualism found in much of Western theology is odious to the Creator and a breach of this sacred covenant.

Indigenous people see a good earth that has been created by a good God. Scripture substantiates this view. God walked the earth in the garden (Gen. 3:8), and he still inhabits every inch of it (Ps. 139:7–12). The land is sacred in part because all living things are made to live on the earth (Genesis 1–2). First, man is made from the earth (2:7); sacred space is made and then given to humans (v. 8); and various ethnic groups are given places on earth (Acts 17:26). Land is made even more sacred because it is Jesus—the Creator-Son—who created the earth (John 1:3, 10; Col. 1:16; Heb. 1:2). Jesus became an earth-being and walked the land (John 1:14). Jesus promises to come back to the earth (Matt. 24:30), at which point it will become renewed for eternity (Rom. 8:21).

A theology of land is central to understanding the Creator, the cosmos, and our place. This relationship between the Creator, human beings, and the land is as sacred as anything else in Scripture. In my experience it has been difficult for the Western mind to understand these things. For First Nations, America is the holy land. Non-Natives need us to help them understand this relationship with the earth so they can learn to live in harmony with it.

Currently, a shift in the Western worldview is occurring at several levels. An increasing number of Euro-Americans have been successful at living "greener" lives. As an indigenous person and a Christian, I applaud all attempts at restoring what I consider to be a more natural view of creation and more natural ways to live with Mother Earth. Yet one vast difference between First Nations and the Euro-American worldview is the latter's emphasis on the individual above community. As First Nations followers of Christ, we believe that by forming and maintaining community, by practicing the way of Jesus, and by using the land for its intended purposes, we can bring about healing and even new blessings to the land. By restoring harmony, the land returns to the purposes for which the Creator intended it.

A range of practices will help us restore that harmony between the Creator, people, land, and all of creation, including praying to the Creator, loving one another, building sacred communities, practicing our traditions and ceremonies, reinstating natural wildlife, growing our own local foods, sharing resources (especially with the poor), doing justice, living more simply, living in peace and sending out messengers of good news to others, and telling the truth about what happened in this land—the good and the evil, the beautiful and the repulsive. It behooves us as Native American followers of Jesus Christ to encourage and participate with communities that follow these practices.

In a real sense, the Indian nations have "married the land" (*Beulah*), which Scripture speaks of in Isaiah 62:3–5. America's indigenous peoples love the land because we know it, because it is beautiful, and because it supplies our needs. It is a gift from the Creator. Each portion of the land has an important history. Many Native American nations have covenant stories with the Creator concerning their own land. We would like to welcome you, the strangers to our land, but for this to happen correctly the land must first be returned to us. What other conclusion could a Christian reach except that they should return that which has been stolen? What could it mean for the land to be returned? Aren't these the kinds of questions that deserve to be considered together, around a table of fellowship, among equals?

In sitting at the table with those in deep need, Jesus gave them the gift of community. This is the same invitation he extends to everyone. Perhaps the first gift of community is listening; simply by listening to others we impart dignity, which can be a powerful healing force. And healing can occur both ways. At the table we all realize that we are needy and gifted at the same time, and we all have stories to tell that relate to one another. At the table we can bestow a sense of dignity to one another. And if we can sit together in equality, Jesus will be sitting with us.

13 JUST ELECTIONS
What Is the Most Pressing Voter Issue Facing Our Democracy Today?
BART CAMPOLO

For a guy who likes both politics and writing as much as I do, I don't write very much about politics. Part of the problem is that I am a neighborhood minister in an American ghetto, so politics for me usually has more to do with competing drug dealers, jaded cops, and harried social workers than with big-time issues and elections. Most of the problem, however, is that life on the street has broken so many of my political ideals that I only have one left to write about.

When I first arrived in Cincinnati, I tried hard to convince my ghetto neighbors to get more involved in the democratic process. But I finally lost one too many street-corner debates about whether such a thing has ever even existed in this country. Down here, I learned, even folks who vote know better than to think that it actually gives them a voice. Down here, everybody knows that when it comes to American politics, the only thing that really talks is money.

Dictionaries define democracy as the free and equal right of every person to participate in the system of their government. In theory, that participation generally involves informed individuals voting for

BART CAMPOLO is a veteran urban minister and activist who speaks and writes about grace, loving relationships, and social justice. Bart is the leader of The Walnut Hills Fellowship, a motley little faith community in inner-city Cincinnati, and the executive director of the Evangelical Association for the Promotion of Education, which supports innovative mission projects around the world.

those representatives and ballot initiatives that best express their political wills, and guarantees that the interests of the poor will be protected by the sheer preponderance of their numbers. In an "advanced" society like ours, however, it is generally understood that the vast majority of voters are strongly influenced by highly sophisticated, openly manipulative, and incredibly expensive campaign technologies available only to those who can afford them. Under such circumstances, in the absence of systematic restraints, financing a campaign easily outstrips voting as the most effective expression of individual political will, and participation ceases to be free and equal. All of which is just another way of saying that when it comes to American politics, the only thing that really talks is money. Or, to be more specific, campaign money.

So then, on behalf of all those poor and oppressed people whom we emergent types keep saying God's justice is all about, whose participation in our mutual government continues to be relentlessly undermined and manipulated by technologies they cannot afford to influence, I hereby assert that for we who call ourselves true followers of Jesus, there is only one voting issue of ultimate significance: campaign finance reform. It really is that simple. If we can get the private and corporate money out of American politics, every other good thing that needs to happen becomes possible. Our friend Jim Wallis is fond of saying that politicians are the people who lick their fingers and stick them up in the air to see which way the wind is blowing, and that social movements are how we change the wind. But I am increasingly convinced that until one of those movements radically transforms the way we finance our elections, the wind blows where the money blows it.

At this point in history, I wonder if I need to cite many examples of the ways private and corporate money influences our leaders to act against the interests of the vast majority of Americans, let alone the interests of our brothers and sisters around the world, or if the real work of this chapter has less to do with describing the problem than it does with demonstrating that solving it is not impossible. After all, does anyone still doubt that our energy and environmental policies are largely determined by oil and manufacturing interests, or that our gun policies are largely dictated by the NRA, or that our farm policies are designed by a few huge agricultural corporations?

Does anyone still believe our tax codes and torts laws and economic regulations are not unfairly tilted in the direction of our wealthiest and most powerful individuals and companies? Or that this unfair tilt is not directly related to the well-documented fact that those same individuals and companies are the primary financiers of the campaigns of the "public servants" who write these codes and laws and regulations?

No, virtually everyone involved—and most especially our elected officials themselves—knows very well that our present system of government falls far below the standards of a true democracy. Unfortunately, the essence of the problem is that the people best positioned to change the rules for the sake of the common good are, by definition, obliged to a status quo that unfairly enriches their friends and unjustly ensures their power. They may loudly proclaim democratic ideals, but in reality these oligarchs of America cannot dare to imagine a political system that actually offers free and equal representation to every American, regardless of their wealth. In biblical terms, "They promise them freedom, but they themselves are slaves of corruption; for people are slaves to whatever masters them" (2 Peter 2:19).

So then, if we who would pursue democracy in the name of justice cannot trust our elected officials to imagine—and enact—a truly free and equal political system, then we must dare to do it ourselves, while there is still time. Really, this is the ultimate form of Christian political advocacy, wherein the advocate seeks to work himself or herself out of a job. After all, it is one thing to be a voice for the poor and the oppressed. It is quite another to make sure they have a voice of their own.

Close your eyes and visualize an election where every candidate who meets a basic standard of viability receives a small but equal amount of public financing for his or her campaign, and is prohibited from using any other money, including his or her own. Of course, these candidates don't need vast sums, not only because their campaign lengths are limited but also because no television or radio advertising is permitted. Instead, each candidate is provided with free airtime to lay out his or her positions on a common set of issues, and invited to participate in a variety of broadcast debates and forums designed to reveal their true character and their best ideas. Now add such bells and whistles as reasonable term limits, the outlawing of professional lobbyists, and increased opportunities for organizing additional political parties, and prospects become even brighter. On such a level playing field, voter power is restored and candidates with superior organizational and leadership capabilities are most likely to succeed. It's a crude vision, perhaps, but you get the idea.

Now open your eyes and understand this: even if we work out all the details in the best ways possible, nothing even remotely like that vision will ever happen in this country unless and until we voters entirely circumvent our elected officials by changing the rules directly through nonpartisan ballot initiatives. In a very real sense, such initiatives are our last hope for taking back our country from entrenched elites who have broken faith with the poor, and from multinational corporations that have lost touch with the long-term interests of humanity for the sake of the short-term interests of their shareholders.

Of course, even if we positively transformed campaign finance at the state level in all fifty states, it would still take a constitutional amendment to fix things at the federal level where they matter most. Given that our status quo–addicted Congress is essentially incapable of passing such a politically selfless amendment, it would seem at first glance that our democracy is doomed. Remember, however, that state governments have many ways of influencing federal policy, including the redrawing of congressional districts. Imagine the enormous public outcry that would arise against legislators who openly flout the will of their constituents in all fifty states, and a two-stage voter revolution suddenly seems more realistic.

Of course, even as we organize the ballot initiatives that will launch that revolution, we can and should also choose those candidates most committed to campaign finance reforms that empower voters over private and corporate donors, so long as we recognize that even they are inherently incapable of delivering the kinds of sweeping changes most necessary for the establishment of a democracy tilted toward justice. For that, we true believers will have to find a way to talk louder than all that money long enough to shut it up for good.

I know this chapter doesn't include many Bible verses, but I trust the others will make the case that whatever helps us more rightly use power in our relationships with other people—and especially in our relationships with the least of these—is worship to God, a joy to the Holy Spirit, and a genuine way of following Jesus. Because you have both the means and the education to read this book, God knows you have the power to help move campaign financing in this country closer to where it belongs. Here in Cincinnati, my ghetto neighbors are depending on you to do just that.

14 JUST LIBERALS
What Are the Strengths and Weaknesses of Liberal Politics in Light of Biblical Justice?
HEATHER KIRK-DAVIDOFF

When I was growing up, I didn't really distinguish between Christianity and liberal politics. They were both important to my family, and whenever someone tried to separate them, whenever someone suggested that Christianity didn't necessarily entail support of civil rights at home or abroad or government efforts to remedy economic inequality, my parents pushed back. One memorable Sunday was a case in point. Our city was about to vote on a referendum that would have made it illegal to discriminate on the basis of sexual orientation in the housing sector. During the worship service at the Presbyterian church my family attended at the time, the minister reminded the congregation to vote and commented, "I urge you to vote with your conscience."

My father would have none of that. To the surprise of the rest of the congregation (and to the mortification of his children) my dad stood up, pointed his finger at the minister, and said, "It's a sad day

HEATHER KIRK-DAVIDOFF is the Enabling Minister of the Kittamaqundi Community, an independent church in the tradition of Church of the Savior, located in Columbia, Maryland. She is the mother of three kids, the author of two books, and the partner of one husband. To learn more about Heather's ministry, check out www.kc-church.org or www.kirkwoodassociates.org.

in this church when our minister can't take a stand on an issue as important as this one." The shocked minister sputtered something out about how he, of course, was strongly in support of the referendum. Only then would my father sit down and allow the service to continue.

Now that I'm a minister myself, I can look back at that encounter and laugh a bit, grateful that no one yet has pulled a stunt like that at my church. But I'm also grateful to my parents for making it clear to me early on that being a Christian means taking a stand on behalf of those who have been excluded or marginalized. Jesus, they taught me, was doing exactly that when he shared his table with tax collectors and prostitutes, when he talked to Samaritans and embraced lepers. He was showing us what it looks like to share the love of God who is the Creator of us all—"red and yellow, black and white, we are equal in his sight." Following Jesus' example, we should ensure that people have equal rights and protections according to our laws, and we should advocate for the advancement of human rights abroad. In addition, we should follow Jesus' example in serving "the least of these"—those who cannot fill their basic needs on their own—and advocate for economic policies that ensure everyone can work for a living wage, with decent working conditions, and access to health care and safe housing.

Civil rights, equal protection, and economic justice aren't just the particular interests of my family. These are core principles of American liberalism. It was the air I breathed as a child, and it wasn't until high school that I learned that there were people besides Jesus who wrote and taught about this way of shaping our public life.

The History of the "L-Word"

Most of us learned in our high school civics classes that the United States is a "liberal democracy," which is to say we have an elected, representational government in which the rule of the majority is tempered by a constitution that protects the rights and freedoms of individuals, including minorities. The idea of constitutionally protected individual rights originated with Enlightenment thinkers such as John Locke and John Stuart Mill who argued against the so-called divine right of kings, asserting instead that God created all people to be equal. Those words and principles inspired the founders of our country, and continue to inspire Americans across the political spectrum today.

In the context of our liberal democracy in the United States, "liberalism" emerged as a political ideology, reaching its high point with Franklin Delano Roosevelt's New Deal and Lyndon Johnson's Great Society. Maury Maverick, a New Deal–era congressman from Texas, summarized this kind of government policy as "freedom plus groceries." Advocates for the government policies proposed under Roosevelt and Johnson often used an expanded sense of the "rights" our government should guarantee. Our citizens, they argued, not only have "negative rights" that protect their freedom but also have "positive rights" to the basic necessities of life.

Christianity taught me to care about the needs of other people, but John Rawls taught me how this compassionate ethic can shape a political system. Rawls's classic treatise *A Theory of Justice*[1] was one of the toughest things I had to read in college, but it made a lasting impression on me. Rawls theorized that government should be designed by people who imagine themselves to be in an "original position," that is, standing outside the system, without knowing anything about their economic status, race, gender, or ability. Rawls believed that from this "original position" everyone would prefer a political system that not only guarantees our freedom but also minimizes social inequalities. If we thought any of us could be poor, we would make sure the government keeps the poor from total misery.

Rawls first published *A Theory of Justice* in 1971, a time when liberalism as a political movement in the United States was already starting to splinter and wane in influence. My parents, whose lives were profoundly shaped by the Civil Rights Movement and anti-war protests, didn't hesitate to call themselves political liberals. But by the time I came of age politically, the term "liberal" had been used as a pejorative so many times that it had become an embarrassment. Now, many of my political allies use the term "progressive" instead, but our basic commitments have much in common with the liberals of the previous generation: a commitment to civil rights and equal protection under the law, and a commitment to economic justice, including access to affordable health care and the guarantee of a living wage. A significant addition is my generation's passion for the "positive rights" to clean air, clean water, and affordable, sustainable sources of energy.

I think there is great congruence between the root concerns of modern American liberalism and the predominant themes of biblical justice in the Old and New Testaments in part because they both rely on seeing beyond the physical realities of this world. I learned as a child how Jesus told his disciples that by serving "the least of these"—the people who were hungry, or who weren't adequately clothed, or who were imprisoned—they were actually serving him. As a college student, I learned from Rawls to imagine that I could have been born to any mother, in any community in the country. In seminary, I heard a similar call to imaginative identification with those at the bottom of the social order in the Hebrew Scriptures. God told Moses from the burning bush that he had heard the cries of the enslaved Israelites, and demanded that Moses tune in as well. Ever since, Jews have been commanded to identify themselves with the enslaved, saying each Passover, "God brought us out of Egypt with an outstretched arm." Each of these imaginative exercises breaks down my sense of separation from others who are less fortunate than I am, and encourages me to take action on their behalf.

While it may no longer be politically beneficial to embrace the term "liberal," these concerns are as central to our political life as ever. For one thing, economic inequality is an even greater concern for the United States in 2009 than it was when Johnson called for the creation of a "Great Society." According to the U.S. Census Bureau that measures inequality using a tool called The Gini Index, over the forty years of my lifetime economic inequality has steadily increased in the United States. Despite the unprecedented growth of the U.S. economy since 1960, only the top 20 percent of families have seen an increase in income over the past twenty years. The bottom 80 percent of families—the vast majority of the U.S. population—actually lost wealth as the economy boomed.[2]

The persistence and growth of economic inequality in our country begs the question of whether liberalism goes far enough in addressing the concerns that it acknowledges should be central to our political life. While liberals like Rawls are quite comfortable with inequality as long as it doesn't get too extreme, there are calls throughout Scripture for much more radical economic remedies. According to Leviticus 25, every fiftieth year was a "Jubilee year" when debts were cancelled, slaves were freed, and other actions were taken that redistributed income and leveled out economic inequalities. The earliest Christian communities lived according to an even more radical economic ethic. According to Acts 2:45, members of the early church "would sell their possessions and goods and distribute the proceeds to all, as any had need." We're a long way from that model now, and it's hard to imagine how we'd get there from here. Maybe that's exactly the problem.

Training Our Imaginations

Before we admit either the inadequacy of liberal politics or the impracticality of biblical justice, it seems to me that we should reconnect with the acts of imagination that lie at the heart of each. This isn't necessarily easy. The more separated and stratified our society, the harder it becomes to imagine the lives and the struggles of those who are different from us. It's impossible to see Jesus in the hungry person if we never even go to the neighborhoods where the hungry people live. And when we feel stretched economically ourselves, as many American middle-class families do, it's easy to forget that there are people much worse off than we are.

The remedy for the failure of our imaginations, therefore, cannot be a simple invitation to engage in the sort of rational abstraction Rawls suggests. Unless we have some knowledge of the conditions of the least fortunate in our society, such an experiment is impossible. And until we have relationships with the least fortunate, such an experiment will never really occur to us.

In order to build communities shaped by compassion, we have to act differently together, not just think differently on our own. This insight has led me to appreciate some of the most pointed critiques of liberalism by contemporary Christian thinkers. Theologian Stanley Hauerwas, together with Alastair MacIntyre, argues that liberal societies provide insufficient basis for learning the virtues on which human community depends. A framework that is fundamentally concerned with protecting individual freedoms does not encourage the practices that lead us to place a high value on compassion, connection, and community.

Here's where the church plays a crucial role. The church I serve is located in a middle-class suburb less than twenty miles from downtown Baltimore and some of the most destitute neighborhoods in our country, but the two communities are separated by a gulf of fear and ignorance that is hard to bridge. Now, due to a decade-long church-to-church partnership, almost every member of my congregation has a significant relationship with a poor person in Baltimore. These relationships not only give us opportunities for direct service but also affect the government policies we support and the candidates for whom we vote. Churches throughout our community are taking the next step and joining with each other in faith-based community organizations, advocating together for increased public support of affordable housing, support of the public schools, and more.

I've come to see that my father was on to something when he stood up in church and embarrassed his children more than thirty years ago. Vague appeals to "vote your conscience" don't make a difference. Abstractions don't change people's lives. Without a sense of community, liberalism makes no sense politically. The emerging church has been driven, in part, by a desire for a religious life that is more organic, more community led, and more engaged and relational. Liberal politics work best when they take on a similar shape.

JUST CONSERVATIVES

What Are the Strengths and Weaknesses of Conservative Politics in Light of Biblical Justice?

JOSEPH MYERS

Teach a man to fish and you feed him for life. Really?

Some of you might be wondering the same thing I did when asked to write this chapter: "Social justice? I'm a conservative; what do I know about social justice?" However, as I read through the preceding chapter I had to smile. The similar family experiences are uncanny. Of course, there are huge differences, yet Heather's description of the connection between faith and politics rings true on the other side of the aisle too. And I realized that while passive opinions on social justice and practices can create a knowledge that corrupts, they can also give a distinct perspective that can be helpful.

I grew up in a conservative family. Not much was ever directly discussed about politics. It was assumed that if you were in the fam-

JOSEPH MYERS is a multiprenuer, interventionist, conversationalist, reframer, and thinker. He is the author of *The Search to Belong: Rethinking Intimacy, Community, and Small Groups* (www.languageofbelonging.com/the-search-to-belong) and *Organic Community: Creating a Place Where People Naturally Connect* (www.languageofbelonging.com/organic-community). Joseph owns a consulting firm, FrontPorch, which specializes in creating conversations and strategies that promote and develop community.

ily and practicing the faith, you were a conservative through and through. I didn't differentiate my faith practices from a conservative political framework until I was out of college and developed a friendship with someone who was a politically liberal Christian. Until then, faith and politics were one and the same for me.

Conservatives are defenders. They see themselves as the defenders of truth, responsible justice, fiscal sustainability, and "the American way of life." When you combine this with conservative faith practices you get defenders of holiness, righteousness, and "the *Christian* American way of life." The mantra "God helps those who help themselves" is a sweet sound to the conservative's soul, yet it is a dead end in any serious conversation about social justice. Furthermore, no matter how hard you search, you won't find that saying in Scripture, and especially not in Jesus' teaching.

In Luke 10:29, an expert in the Law (obviously a conservative) stands and interrupts Jesus. He asks, "Who is my neighbor?" Jesus responds with the story of the Good Samaritan. This story speaks to conservatism in at least three ways.

First, it speaks to an essential conundrum of the heart. A man is beaten bloody and left for dead, and the next two characters to enter the stage are forced to decide between remaining holy or showing compassion. If they show compassion and help the poor man, they will be "unclean" for touching blood. If they decide to pass by, they remain "clean" and "holy." They decide to practice holiness instead of showing compassion, for they are defenders of what's right, pure, holy, and clean. Next to enter the story is a Samaritan man who had heard how "unclean" he was his entire life. He doesn't have the same concerns. For him, getting some blood on his clothes is a matter of being human, neighborly, and helpful. He chooses to help the hurting man.

Conservatives struggle most with this holiness-versus-compassion dilemma because our conservative religious belief systems teach us to choose righteousness over compassion, truth over helpfulness, and responsibility over sharing hope. It is this struggle that keeps us from dancing at the prodigal's return. It is this smug holiness that lets us pass by on the other side of poverty. We defend our actions by holding to "truths" that sound noble but demote compassion to a slave of our righteousness.

"Give a man a fish and you feed him for today; teach a man to fish and you feed him for life," for example, sounds noble and right, but it denies the fact that the man needs to be fed today. It doesn't allow for a learning curve so the man can grow his competency to fish and provide for himself. It also doesn't take into account the fact that on many days the fish just don't bite, or that a factory upstream dumped toxins in the stream that killed all the fish, and these things are not in the fisherman's control. Emerging conservative practices must give compassion its true place.

The story not only addresses the choice to show compassion; it also addresses the way compassion should be shown. The beaten man is nursed enough so the Samaritan can get him on a donkey and off to a place of care. Such care requires sacrifice, inconvenience, and generosity. Like the Samaritan, we must be willing to act, if necessary, without regard for reason, strategy, and time commitments.

But the story offers yet another insight. The Samaritan takes his newfound neighbor to a place of healing, pays his way, and then *leaves*. He gives enough help to be helpful and not so much help to be harmful. Within a Christian approach to politics, this practice has been difficult. Our call to love unconditionally often drives us to love too much.

There is a condition, it turns out, to unconditional love. The condition is that to love truly you must stop short of loving too much. The Samaritan helps the man get to a point of sustainable health, and then leaves. He doesn't stay around too long, and he doesn't offer too much help. Healthy compassion has this strange component that doesn't seem to belong; it sets certain boundaries and believes enough in the ones being helped to let them sustain themselves after we have done our part. The compassionate neighbor wants to rescue others from the first indignity of being wounded and abandoned, and from the second indignity of being made dependent or co-dependent. Moving forward, then, we must find compassionate, sustainable, and healthy solutions to the justice issues of our time, informed by Jesus' wise parable. We can't let our concerns for religious "holiness" become an excuse for crossing to the other side of the street; we must be willing to get dirty—"unclean"—in the messes created by human evil. We must make the tough spontaneous choice of interrupting our own well-laid plans and inconveniencing our tight personal agendas. And we can't go on creating "solutions" that in turn create new cycles of unhealthy dependence and codependence; we need to remember that even our Savior's love would not allow him to stay too long. The Samaritan story, it turns out, has something to say to both liberals and conservatives, and in that way, it calls us to move forward together in the path of justice and compassion.

16 JUST FAMILY VALUES

How Can Christians Advocate Justice for Non-traditional Families?

PEGGY CAMPOLO

Editors' Note: When we think about justice in our families, there are so many issues to consider—domestic violence; male domination and sexism; child abuse and neglect; childrens' rights; divorce; the availability of care for mothers and children; child labor; and the isolation and abandonment of the elderly. All of these issues are profoundly important and we wish we could devote a chapter to each one. The issue of justice for non-traditional families also deserves consideration, especially here in the United States, and especially in the aftermath of several decades of "culture wars." While opinions on human sexuality differ widely among our contributors as well as our readers, advocate and activist Peggy Campolo asks us to extend our concern beyond "traditional family values" to the way we value non-traditional families.

In 1976, President Jimmy Carter called for a conference on the family, which finally took place in a storm of controversy in 1980. In reaction to the conference, the religious right made opposition to homosexual rights—especially the right to marry—a cornerstone of their political efforts throughout the '80s and '90s. In 2004, Republi-

PEGGY CAMPOLO is an advocate for the civil rights of her GLBT sisters and brothers and their full inclusion in the church. A graduate of Eastern University, Peggy is a member of Central Baptist Church in Wayne, Pennsylvania. You can contact Peggy by mail at P. O. Box 565, Wayne, PA, 19087.

can strategist Karl Rove used ballot initiatives against gay marriage in key states to energize evangelical Christians to vote, ensuring the victory of George W. Bush.

"Traditional family values" became a code word overnight, used by those who wanted to reserve the term "marriage" not only for the union of one man and one woman but also to deny homosexual couples and their families many basic civil rights. The U.S. Government Accountability office cites 1,138 rights enjoyed by heterosexual couples that are denied to homosexual couples and their families,[1] including:

- the right to claim a partner's Social Security benefits;
- the right of gay couples who are poor to request food stamps and low-cost housing;
- the right to benefits for partners of gay veterans;
- in many states, visitation rights for partners or access to the ill partner's medical records; and
- the right to file joint income tax returns.

Several years ago at a gay rights rally, I met Betty, the mother of three young children. Her partner Gail was a professional woman making a very good salary. Both women wanted Betty to be a stay-at-home mother. However, this was not possible because the couple was not legally married. Therefore, neither Betty nor the children were covered as family members under Gail's medical plan. Betty's story is a powerful example of justice denied. It raises the question: how should Christians see "family values" as matters of justice? The campaign for "traditional family values" has done much to deny civil rights to homosexual people. It is also responsible for much of the hurt and humiliation gay, lesbian, bisexual, and transgender people must endure.

Television personality Rosie O'Donnell, a lesbian with a spouse and three adopted children, realized that there were not many places where a non-traditional family like her own could enjoy a family vacation. In 2003, Rosie and her partner Kelli O'Donnell hosted the first of their Rosie O'Donnell Family Cruise Vacations. A documentary film about one of these cruises shows some very non-traditional families enjoying themselves and talking openly about how much it meant to be having fun together in a place far from those who disapproved of them and called them names. Then, when the cruise docked in the Bahamas, an angry crowd met the ship, shouting harsh words and holding signs that let the vacationing families know they were not welcome. Bible verses on the signs made it look as though the protesters were Christian people. Some families did not leave the ship, but those who did had to deal with sobbing and frightened children.

The same "traditional family values" that deny justice encourage scenes like the one on that dock in the Bahamas. Consider Fred Phelps, the Baptist minister, who in 1998 drew national attention when he and his group picketed the funeral of Matthew Shepard, the young gay man who was beaten, tied to a fence, and left to die in Wyoming. Phelps regularly takes members of his family and church all across the United States to picket at the funerals of homosexuals, carrying signs that say things such as, "Matt is burning in hell" and "God hates fags." Many Christians who would not dream of emulating the picketers in the Bahamas or being part of Fred Phelps's group nevertheless struggle with the question of how they will define "traditional family values" and how they will vote on laws that define the family. It is not surprising that it is difficult to define "family values" when those at the White House Conference on the Family could not agree on even a definition of what constituted a family.[2]

In the Bible, there is no one definition of marriage or family, but rather there are many arrangements, including polygyny, Levirate marriage, arranged marriage, and what we now call "traditional marriage." However, in Ephesians 5:21–33, we find verses that give us some sense of what a Christian marriage should be. The relationship that should exist between a husband and wife is compared to Christ's relationship to the church: Christ loved the church so much that he died for it.

Christian marriage is a lifetime commitment between two people, each of whom seeks to help the other become all that God intended him or her to be. Today, increasing numbers of Christians are becoming convinced that marriage does not have to be between a man and a woman, but can be between any two committed people.[3] In my more than twenty years of ministry and advocacy for GLBT people,

I have seen *real* traditional family values like love, sacrifice, and commitment lived out by many couples whose lives are made incredibly difficult because they are not permitted to be legally married.

Sometimes I think it is the people who are *against* gay marriage who demean marriage when they reduce it to "plumbing" and baby making. As important as these may be, marriage is much more. It was so much more to my friends Randy McCain and Gary Eddy when they made a lifetime commitment to each other sixteen years ago. They were Christians, and wanted to establish a Christ-centered home. Randy had felt God's call to the ministry as a little boy and, in the early years of his committed relationship to Gary, he was minister of music at a Presbyterian church. The pastor knew that Gary was Randy's life partner, but told them to not talk about it. Feeling that his silence was shaming a wonderful and holy relationship, Randy grew increasingly uncomfortable. Then one day, a visiting preacher who knew his situation tried to make him feel better.

"Don't worry about it," he said. "Whose business is it what you do in the bedroom?"

Something in Randy snapped as he replied, "My relationship with Gary is no more all about what we do in the bedroom than my parents' fiftieth anniversary celebration was about what they did in the bedroom. They celebrated their love for each other and their family. Gary is *my* family, and that is why I must let people know about our relationship. I am not single. I am in a loving, monogamous, Christ-centered relationship with a man I love dearly."

After that, it was only a matter of time before Randy shared with the church the truth about his relationship with Gary, and that truth ended his ministry there. For love of Gary, Randy risked never again being able to minister in word or song. At times he thought he would die of the pain of his loss. *But God had other plans.*

In his living room twelve years ago, Randy started a Bible study group that grew into a small church. It was Gary's living room too, and having seen what a church had done to Randy, Gary wanted nothing to do with any church at that painful time. But for love of Randy, he set his own feelings aside and willingly helped carry their living room furniture to the spare bedroom on Saturday nights and set up chairs for church on Sunday. Gary's affirmation of Randy's call to the pastorate resulted in the birth of Open Door Community Church, a "grace place" in Sherwood, Arkansas, where all are welcome. It has its own building now, having long ago outgrown the McCain-Eddy living room.

I know many gay people who have been denied the privilege of adopting children, and others who have waited years to welcome home a child. Often people who are not straight are asked to take children who are "hard to place," and many of them do so willingly. Jeff Lutes and his partner Gary Stein always knew they wanted to adopt and parent children. Jeff was raised in a strong Southern Baptist home. Gary was raised in two religious traditions by a Catholic mother and a Jewish father. Like his parents, he is deaf. Gary is an excellent lip reader, and the couple communicated this way until Jeff learned American Sign Language.

Early in their committed relationship, Jeff and Gary felt called by God to adopt a deaf child since they had the communication skills to meet this special need. Niko, their first son, is deaf. He bonded with them immediately when they met him in China. Jeff and Gary then fostered five children before adopting two Hispanic children: son Trei, who is deaf, and daughter Jolé, who is hearing. Gary and Jeff like to say they have "a very traditional Gay-Deaf-Jewish-Catholic-Baptist-Chinese-Hispanic" family. But it isn't "traditional" enough for those who make the laws of their state.

Justice is denied this very special family because legally these two parents cannot be married to each other. Nor can they adopt their children as a couple. Legally, they can parent together only because of a loophole in the state law, created for a single or widowed *straight* parent who marries someone who wants to adopt his or her children. Jeff *or* Gary must first adopt as a single person, then after a specified amount of time, the other is permitted to become a legal parent.

There is a great difference of opinion when it comes to gay marriage, much of it emanating from the religious community. Yet, in Scripture we find a Jesus who defines the family in spiritual terms that he sets above biological relationships. When asked to pay attention to his mother and brothers, Jesus declares that those who do the will of God are his brother and sister and mother (Matt. 12:46–50). And even while dying on the cross, Jesus took time to create a new family for people he dearly loved, declaring that his mother and his beloved disciple John were to be, henceforth, mother and son (John 19:26–27).

Justice requires that we find a way to respect and affirm the rights of both the large majority of families created in the traditional way most of us know best and those families created by the marriages of God's GLBT children. Justice also requires that we find a way to do this without forcing those on either side of the debate about gay marriage to compromise what they believe is right.

My suggestion is that we adopt the model presently in place in the Netherlands, where civil rights are granted by the government to any couple, gay or straight. After the required civil ceremony, the marriage may then be solemnized in a religious ceremony if the couple wishes. Some churches or synagogues would marry gay couples, and some would not. As a true Baptist, I believe that decisions as to who churches will or will not marry should be made on the local level, thus preserving the autonomy of the local church. However, in the case of more hierarchical denominations, a decision would be made binding all the churches of that denomination. The important thing is that *the state* would not decide who could and could not get married in the church, and no religious group could impose on fellow citizens their version of "traditional family values," nor could they withhold basic civil rights from those who did not agree with them.

I have heard many pastors say that they feel uncomfortable when at the end of a wedding ceremony they must say something to the effect of, "And now, by the power committed to me by the state of Ohio, I pronounce you man and wife." Could we not have justice for all by separating the spiritual blessing of a marriage from the civil rights granted by the state?

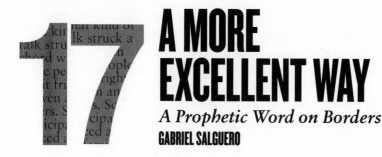

17 A MORE EXCELLENT WAY

A Prophetic Word on Borders

GABRIEL SALGUERO

We Are Here! Toward a Genuine Conversation

My wife, Jeanette, and I took Jon-Gabriel, our two-year-old son, to his first movie, *Dr. Seuss' Horton Hears a Who!* As we sat through my son's first visit to a theater, one powerful scene made me think about immigration. The powerful refrain shouted by the people of Who-ville, "We are here! We are here!" almost ended unheard. In many ways the people of Who-ville reflect the multiple sides of the national debate on immigration. Both sides are shouting, "We are here!" but this means radically different things for the host and immigrant cultures. The push-and-pull factors of globalization are interpreted in drastically different ways.[1] Immigration, as a manifestation of globalization, is a multi-sided story. The ways that host and immigrant cultures wrestle with questions of economics, survival, law, and human dignity are often worlds apart. All the

GABRIEL SALGUERO and his wife, Jeanette, pastor the multicultural Lamb's Church in New York City. He is the director of the Hispanic Leadership Program at Princeton Theological Seminary. Gabriel is an executive member of the Latino Leadership Circle and a PhD candidate in Christian social ethics with a focus on postcolonial studies at Union Theological Seminary.

while, followers of Jesus are torn: which narratives should frame our discussion?

Before we as Christians launch ourselves into the national debate, we must be willing to wrestle with all of the issues at stake. The easy way out is to label and ignore the other sides as radical, hateful, lazy, and any other word that prevents us from talking. To move beyond fruitless debate, we must do the hard work of caring and becoming informed. Immigration dialogue is not about clichés and bumper stickers. The words of God to the prophet Isaiah are clear: "Come now, let us reason together" (Isa. 1:18). Only after we have grappled with the complexity of the issue can we suggest another way.

A Thorny Road: Navigating Dominant Narratives

Fear from all sides frequently overheats our dialogue about immigration.[2] Certainly the conversation should have emotion because the lives of real people are in play, and not simply theories or policies. Still, if there is going to be an intelligent and meaningful dialogue about immigration in the United States, we need cool, clear, and honest talk, realizing that while an overwhelming majority of U.S. citizens believe there should be immigration reform of some kind, we share no clear consensus on what it should look like.

Several major narratives drive the debate on borders in the United States. I call them the *cost-enforcement* view, the *welcoming-reformist* view, and the *extremist* view. The multiple voices often collapse into a cacophony that leaves matters worse and groups embittered. If we are going to move from "chaos to community,"[3] we need to articulate our own narrative well and understand the narratives of others equally well.

The *cost-enforcement* perspective on borders raises concerns about economic advantage and legal fairness, including the following:

- *Personal security/economic strains.* The close to twelve million undocumented immigrants are eating up our resources, taking our jobs, and placing an unsustainable strain on national resources, leaving more people competing for fewer resources.

- *National sovereignty.* Doesn't every nation have the right to determine its national boundaries?
- *The rule of law.* If we provide a legal path to citizenship for undocumented immigrants, are we not rewarding lawbreakers?

In terms of economics, experts still dispute the impact of undocumented immigrants on the national economy in general and on low-income native workers in particular.[4] Some published studies indicate that undocumented immigrants put great strains on the economy, while others indicate they are in fact an economic asset. Either way, all agree that the influx of undocumented immigration has a mix of positive and negative repercussions for the U.S. economy. These complex impacts can't be ignored.

Regarding national sovereignty and the rule of law, all agree that national governments have a duty to maintain law and order. Some Christians, in light of Paul's argument line of thinking in Romans 13, see authorities as having a divine mandate to prevent anarchy and defend their own citizens.[5] Others hold this national responsibility in tension with a global responsibility. While a national government's number one priority is the plight of its own citizens, does it not also have a responsibility regarding the human rights of non-citizens?

The *welcoming-reformist* view emphasizes the human rights of non-citizens:

- *Global inequities.* Lack of food, employment, and safety drive people from their home countries to seek better opportunities for themselves and their families.
- *Family separations.* Many undocumented immigrants are separated from their citizen children during deportations. And about one-third of undocumented immigrants are brought into the country as children by their own parents.

The welcoming-reformers say that immigration is never far removed from global inequalities; we must deal with larger dysfunctions in the global system before we can resolve immigration challenges.[6] Border issues are inseparable, welcoming-reformers say, from international trade treaties like NAFTA and CAFTA. These treaties can adversely affect employment opportunities for workers both inside and outside the United States, resulting in incoming undocumented workers and outflowing jobs.[7]

Various *extremist* groups often bear an ominous resonance with Pharaoh's words in Exodus: "Look, the Israelite people are more numerous and more powerful than we. Come, let us deal shrewdly with them" (Exod. 1:9–10).[8] Perhaps Geraldo Rivera is correct: when an extremist sees the word *Hispanic*, he feels "his panic."[9] The fear exhibited publicly about Latino(a) immigrants also applies to Haitians, West Indians, Asians, and many other immigrant groups as well.[10]

Just recently while talking to my friend Fred I realized how this view affects many Latinos like us directly. Fred said to me, "I never leave the house without identification, even if I'm going for a jog. I'll put my license in my socks or jogging pants." I told him I do the same. I wonder how many Anglo citizens are afraid to leave the house without identification. Even though Fred and I were born in the United States, we fear being detained without recourse to our families or lawyers. I wonder how many of our professorial colleagues also wrestle with that real fear. When extremists dominate the debate, fear spreads.

"But I Say to You": How Might Jesus Legislate?

If we put the extremist approach aside as unproductive, we are left with two dominant narratives on immigration, and there seems to be a stalemate between them. Jesus is famous for steering conversations beyond either/or binaries. In Matthew 5, for example, Jesus challenges us repeatedly to create new ways of seeing things. We have a choice whether we, as followers of Jesus, will allow the either/or narratives to frame our responses to immigration. Will we provide a prophetic and just alternative? As Craig Wong has suggested, we need a new approach, a third way on immigration.[11] Fortunately, Christian *Unitedstatesians*[12] have some viable existing models for navigating this difficult terrain.[13] Although the Scriptures do not provide specific or simplistic policy recommendations, they do provide helpful narratives for pioneering a better way. Perhaps, under their guidance, we can affirm the legitimate concerns of both the cost-enforcement and welcoming-reformer camps.

When narratives are in tension, one time-tested Christian response is to seek the *summum bonum*—the highest good, or the "more excellent way" (1 Cor. 13). This more excellent way of love and justice requires a deep shift and a rereading of our shared biblical narratives so that we can learn to listen to them anew as pilgrims, strangers, and sojourners.[14] For example, Abraham and Sarah's life unfold in an immigration story, beginning with these words: "There was a famine in the land . . ." (Gen. 12:5). Similarly, Jacob's family is divided and reunited in a famine-related immigration crisis: "And *all* the world came to Egypt to buy grain from Joseph, because the famine was severe everywhere" (Gen. 41:57 TNIV, emphasis added). Many immigrants today are modern-day Abrahams, Sarahs, and Josephs, driven to today's more prosperous and secure first-world Egypts by many types of famine: food famines, employment famines, opportunity famines, and famines for justice created by corrupt and tyrannical governments, comprising what has been called an "anthropological famine."[15] As people of faith, the Scriptures invite us to see immigration not only through the lenses of economics and politics, but also through the stories of the Bible, including Jesus, whose family was forced to flee Herod's genocidal regime to take refuge in Egypt for a time. Inspired by the Revelation 7:9 vision of harmonious racial and ethnic diversity in the kingdom of God, Christians should not be limited by nationalistic concerns alone; instead, we should advocate for new and more just laws both in the U.S. *and* in the émigrés' countries, since all people live within God's circle of care. Enlightened by a higher Scriptural perspective, we see immigration as an issue that is fundamentally about human life and global community. All national considerations must be informed by this higher mandate for Christian love and justice.

As well, the biblical theme of wisdom versus simplicity, so evident in the Book of Proverbs, will challenge us to look more deeply at U.S. foreign policy and its effects on the people of the world. For example, if we argue that we should simply build bigger fences to keep people out of the United States without first wisely exploring the complex impacts of CAFTA and NAFTA on Central and South America, we will foolishly prescribe a cure without diagnosing the root causes of "famine in the land." And not only do we have a biblical call to wisdom as we seek to diagnose the problems and prescribe solutions, but we also have the biblical call to justice, which requires us at every turn to see "the alien and the stranger" as people with dignity and value before God. Our concern for our neighbor, brother, and sister does not end at our nation's borders. Dr. Martin Luther King, Jr.'s assertion that we live in a "one world-house" rings as true today as ever.

Regrettably, many U.S. Christians fall into the temptation of global myopia and amnesia. The explicit or implicit U.S. endorsement of military dictatorships in Latin America and elsewhere cannot be divorced from the massive flight from Latin America to "El Norte." The use of transgenic subsidized U.S. corn can't be separated from the migration north of tens of thousands of farmers from Central America. The reality of unfathomable foreign debt in developing countries can't be considered in isolation from the continuing influence and power of transnational organizations like the World Bank, the International Monetary Fund, and the Inter-American Development Bank. We must, in faithfulness to our call as Christians, open our eyes wide and face the ways in which our own nation's past and present actions have helped create the immigration challenges we now face.

Imagine a profoundly Christlike immigration reform that recognizes the complicity of multinational organizations and U.S. foreign policy in the destabilization of global economies and the displacement of poor workers to our south. Acknowledging that "there is famine in the land" would move us to a deeper sense of justice that recognizes the futility of merely building fences and deporting families, without also recalling the biblical concept of "the year of Jubilee" (Deuteronomy 15), in which paralyzing debt is forgiven and the land is able to rest and be restored. Imagine a Christlike immigration reform movement that understands there is no such thing as love without justice, for "[love] does not rejoice about injustice" (1 Cor. 13:6 NLT).

The Revelation vision of people "from every nation, tribe, people, and language" encourages us to consider immigration reform from the perspective of global ecclesiology (Rev. 7:9). Edgardo Colon-Emeric is correct to say, "The Church has no citizenship test!"[16] The eschatological vision of Revelation reminds us that we do not ask about citizen status for the breaking of the bread or baptism. It invites us to a deep shift in understanding the *catholicity* of the church: we are not just a community of resident aliens, but also a *parroquia*—an assembly of illegal aliens.[17] C. René Padilla implicates a nationalistic and nativist ecclesiology in arguing for a global church: "People everywhere need to recognize that all of them without exception share a common humanity and have the same human rights."[18] When we see the Revelation vision, we can no longer ignore the human faces of those dying in the desert between Mexico and the United States or in large cargo vessels from Asia. They aren't simply "the undocumented": they are our brothers and sisters, documented in the Lamb's book of life; when they die, part of the church dies. This eschatological, ecclesiological vision is the highest and most hopeful form of *e pluribus unum*: out of many, one. We as the people of God welcome and honor the "other" that Empire seeks to keep out.[19] The *shalom-reign* of God does not have borders, nor does it require a Green Card or a Z-visa.

To have this new vision does not blind us to economic interests or the need for national borders.[20] But it liberates us from having these as our only concerns, and it calls us to the more excellent way of justice and love. When asked, "Should laws be disregarded?" a postcolonial faith responds, "No." But when the law leads to more harm than good, we remember Jesus' bold assertion that the Law was made for humanity, not humanity for the Law. The law of the land (Rom. 13:1–7) doesn't exempt us from the law of love (Rom. 13:8–10). We submit to authorities in as much as they do not violate the great commandments of loving God and global neighbor. We respect borders, but we claim there should always be room at the inn for those strangers who travel among us, even if we have to help pay the way, like the Good Samaritan did for his unnamed guest. Hospitality is never cheap, but neither is inhospitality, especially when we remember the words of Christ: "I was a stranger [*xenos*] and you invited me in" (Matt. 25:35 NIV).

A JUST WORLD

SECTION FOUR

JUST PERSPECTIVES

How Can We Become
Just Global Citizens?

ASHLEY BUNTING SEEBER

When I was in junior high, I was convinced I was going to be President of the United States. I remember telling my friends, "I feel it in my bones!" My, how things change. . . . I loved (and still love) the United States of America. I was taken with our stories, heroes, hardships, and victories. Who doesn't like to hear about a group of revolutionaries founding a new nation based on new principles in the eighteenth century? Or about liberating Europe from an oppressive regime in the twentieth century? That was big stuff then, and it's big stuff now. Those stories mattered, and affected people's lives so much.

Then in high school, I read Isaiah 13–37, where God reprimands both Israel and the nations around it. Here my NIV Student Bible explained the "international relations" of the time. That insert ended with this question: "What do you think Isaiah would say if he were writing today about such superpower countries as the United States and Russia?"[1] That question floored me, and it was only the first of several over the next few years to do so.

ASHLEY BUNTING SEEBER and her husband Kilian live in Geneva, Switzerland, and are members of the Evangelical Lutheran Church of Geneva. Ashley is pursuing an MA in the Bible and Postcolonial Studies at the University of Sheffield in the UK. She enjoys running, traveling, cooking, and being a news junkie.

My first trip off the North American continent was to Thailand (which I highly recommend) while teaching for a summer. It seemed as though Thailand was changing a lot: the beautiful landscape was being covered with Pepsi and Coca-Cola signs, and new malls were being filled with fast-food chains. On a short trek in the northern region, a small village tribe hosted our group for a night. The villagers dressed in (what we thought was) traditional attire and danced. We thought it was great. But then I heard one of the villagers talking to a fellow trekker. "What did he say?" I asked.

"He said they never really dress or dance like this," my fellow trekker replied. I was perplexed. *What do you mean they never really do this?* I thought. *Then why are they doing it?* It dawned on me that this was part of the village's income, and that they did this to earn a living wage. Next I wondered when they actually do their traditional dances, or if they still do them at all. *Where did their culture go?*

Thai culture is incredibly rich, but Thai people were abandoning some of their most precious rituals, practices, and even food for ours. I bet nine out of ten people anywhere would agree that Thai food is better than American fast food, but having an economy of scale means we can produce almost anything cheaper and more efficiently than anyone else, and we therefore put a lot of people out of business.[2] We've also made American music, fast food, and fashion *cool*, and although this may delight shareholders and pay salaries, there are others who simply resent American pop culture blasting through stereos and popping up in malls throughout the globe. The only value indigenous cultures seem to have today is for the tourism industry, but even there, cultures have to accommodate to Western tastes if they want to pay their bills. These cultures are going extinct because their people are forced to abandon them in order to make a living.[3] I started to wonder, *What would happen if the U.S. loved Thailand as it loves itself?*[4]

My next trip off the continent was to Bosnia and Herzegovina (also to teach, and also highly recommended), where I got to hear the Bosnian take on things. Some Bosnian friends explained that they *loved* Bill Clinton, who supported the NATO efforts that brought peace to their region. When our team asked what they thought of then-current President George W. Bush, our friends explained their concern that our military action in Iraq wasn't for the good of the people, but rather for American interests at the expense of the Iraqi people. At that moment, it hit me: *If Jesus is Lord and no one else, why do we allow ourselves to do what no other country is allowed to do?* I remembered that, ironically, it was us who stopped Iraq when they invaded Kuwait. Several Bosnians also lamented that since they've been under capitalism, their communities have grown apart because everyone is competing against each other. It seems that neither communism nor war could undermine their communities, but capitalism has left them weak and estranged. *Why is my way of life so detrimental in Bosnian eyes?*

When I moved to Geneva, Switzerland, I met incredible diversity and was intimidated by how much I didn't know. Geneva is one of those places where the world goes to do business. Thirty-eight percent of this city-state's population is non-Swiss;[5] it hosts headquarters of many international organizations (like the WTO, the Red Cross / Red Crescent, and the World Council of Churches) and most of the UN agencies (like the WHO and UNICEF).[6] Needless to say, I learn a lot about being a good neighbor just by living here. I've met people from countries I'd never heard of, and for better or worse, I know there's no way they haven't heard of mine. *Why is it that everyone else knows more about the world, and my own country, than I do?*

I dearly loved my history classes and teachers, but often it seemed that by the time we got through the Revolutionary War, the Civil War, and the two World Wars, we had little time left for our country's recent history. We leave our classes at the end of the school year having just covered our victories in WWII or the Cold War, and I wonder if this is one of the reasons we still think we're the world's heroes. We don't know about the injustices we've supported in other countries,[7] or how we've made sure that the international financial and economic scales are tipped toward us.[8] *Do we as a country see ourselves clearly?* Perhaps more to the point, it seems we (I) have had a hard time moving on from those heroic days to actually being heroic in our generation in ways for which other countries are truly grateful. My British friend Paul illustrated this point well when I told him about this book: "Yeah, that sounds great," he said, "but what would American justice look like? Would it be restorative justice, or retributive justice? It seems Americans are focused on retributive justice more than anything else, on punishing people for their wrongdoing." *Do we even know how to seek distributive justice, to love other countries as we love ourselves?*

I sure don't. A year ago, at the age of twenty-four, I went to the Amahoro Africa Gathering in Kampala, Uganda. After the conference, most non-Africans went on field trips. I went to Nairobi, Kenya, where our group visited Kibera, the second largest slum in Africa. As we walked through Kibera, God kept asking me, "Ashley, can you find me here in Kibera? Can you find me in the faces of these little kids and their parents?" But I just wanted to get out of there, and get as many people as possible out of there with me. A few hours later, I tried to start a conversation about how to get people out of Kibera, but my friend Marius responded with a story instead: Marius' class pulled money together to get one of their classmates an apartment outside of the slum where he grew up. But living in the apartment drove him crazy; he only stayed in it for a month. "How can you live like this?" he asked his classmates. "It's too quiet, and I'm too far from my family and friends." I realized that although Kibera felt like hell to me, it is *home* for the almost one million people who live there. The goal is not to leave Kibera but to *transform* it. I'm sure there are some who want and maybe need to leave Kibera, but the presence of God and his kingdom are as real in Kibera as anywhere else. And although I can think of ways to help, I'm better off listening to the people who live there, who really know, and supporting their efforts.

So how can we as Americans live as just global citizens? Knowing the U.S. is a superpower, what would God say to us? What would happen if we listened to how other countries, both our allies and our enemies, see us? What would happen if we loved other nations as we love our own? If Jesus is Lord and no one else, what's stopping us from loving other nations? What can we do to help other cultures and societies (not just our own) thrive? How can we listen for ways to be helpful?

There are a few things I can do. I can keep making friends in Geneva so I hear their stories, even if I'm asked to explain why the U.S. is the way it is. I can stay involved in Amahoro Africa so my friends Claude, Kelley, Marius and others can explain things to me *again*. And I can be active in my truly remarkable church, which helps me live out these lessons I'm learning. Our Brazilian pastor, Lusmarina, makes our services challenging, we have members from every continent (except Antarctica, of course), we join with the Ecumenical Prayer Cycle in praying for every country once a year, and we sing songs from all over the world with the help of our music minister, Terry.[9] Although it's by no means easy (oh, do we have our differences!), it makes us better people because we have to choose between not talking to each other or starting the long process of learning about each other. And we choose the latter.

But what can *every* U.S. citizen do to make our country a better neighbor?

1. *Get to know the world in your hometown.* Get to know your neighbors from different countries or your neighbors across town, ask them questions, and try foods you haven't tried before. You can help refugee families resettle in the U.S.; it's not easy, but it will give you a glimpse at life lived differently. Try the International Rescue Committee[10] or Catholic Social Services.[11]
2. *Take five full minutes and look at a map or globe.* We're not alone.
3. *Travel.* I know money's tight, and I know you don't have enough time off work. But try to travel outside the U.S. at least once in your lifetime and then as much as possible. Talk to people. Hear their stories. Remember that life doesn't *have* to be the way we're used to. Most of all, spend time appreciating the culture around you simply for what it is, and not for what we as tourists want it to be.
4. *Read news and information from varying sources.* Here are a few:
   • From an Arab perspective: http://english.aljazeera.net/
   • From South Africa: http://www.mg.co.za/[12]
   • From Germany: http://www.spiegel.de/international/
   • From France: http://www.france24.com/en/
5. *Pray the news.* Just as you pray the Scriptures, pray as you read or watch the news. Ask God for help in understanding, for God to intervene, and for God to help you sort through information and get to what matters.

6. *Pray for the world.* You can follow the Ecumenical Prayer Cycle[13] yourself or as a group. The link provided in the endnotes includes what to pray about and sample prayers you can follow. No doubt you'll pray for countries that some consider our "enemies," but that gives us a chance to love our enemies and pray for those who persecute us.[14]

7. *Support world geography curriculum in your schools.* If you're a parent, help your child with his or her geography homework— you'll be amazed by what you'll learn. If your local high school doesn't have world geography classes as part of the social studies curriculum, petition your school board.

8. *Say, "I don't know," instead of making generalizations.* We should say this not only when we don't know the answer to a theological issue but also when we're not familiar with a global/international issue. "I don't know" doesn't mean we're giving up on learning; it means we're open to learning.

9. *Ask, "I wonder what 'So and so' is thinking?"* Whoever "So and so" is, it's never wrong to put yourself in someone else's shoes and imagine what they're going through. *I wonder what Ban Ki-Moon thinks about the U.S.? What does North Korea want, exactly?* The next step is actually finding out.

10. *Read the following chapters, and invite some friends to read along with you.*

JUST WEALTH

How Is the Poverty of the Poor in the Global South a Matter of Justice for the Rich in the Global North?

DARÍO LÓPEZ
Translated by Elisa Padilla

Just wealth? Recent statistics on poverty in the world indicate that one billion (that's one thousand million) human beings live on less than a dollar a day and that two billion, eight hundred million (2,800,000,000) live on two dollars a day. True awareness of this issue, however, is not merely a simple knowledge of the condition of the material misery in which millions of human beings find themselves nor an expert use of cold statistical data. For those who consider themselves disciples of the Lord of Life, who is just and loves justice, true awareness means committing oneself to finding answers to the following questions: What will the poor of the world

DARÍO ANDRÉS LÓPEZ was born in Bellavista, Puerto de Callao, Lima, Perú. He studied fishing engineering at the Universidad Nacional de Callao, Missiology at the Seminario Evangélico de Lima and at the Facultad Evangélica Orlando Costas in Lima, and got his PhD in theology at the Oxford Centre for Mission Studies in Oxford, England. He served as national coordinator and General Secretary of the Asociación de Grupos Evangélicos Universitarios del Perú (AGEUP), which is affiliated with IFES. He also served as President of the Evangelical National Council of Perú from 2000 to 2004 and was a member of various important commissions linked to the Peruvian government. He has written several books on theology, missiology, Pentecostalism, human rights, evangelical faith, and political action.

eat and where will they sleep today? Do they all have access to a job and worthy salaries, or are they exploited with impunity so that the rich accumulate more wealth?

Asking oneself these kinds of questions leads to other, more critical questions such as: Does just wealth really exist? Or is a good part of it the product of oppression and exploitation of defenseless social sectors? Is there justice when so many live in subhuman conditions under the states that should protect them? What about the scandalous indifference of those who live affluent lifestyles, who believe—like the rich fool of the Gospel of Luke—that the life of a person consists in the abundance of his possessions (Luke 12:15)? Can wealth ever be just when current practices used to obtain and accumulate wealth—particularly in the case of multinational companies with headquarters in the North and extended branches in developing nations—only seek to secure profits and increase material accumulation, with the complacent approval of corrupt politicians and useless, pernicious bureaucrats that so abound in the Southern countries of our world?

Personal Sin

Are the enormous profits that rich people in poor countries obtain and the money they have in their bank accounts the product of just working conditions, respect for the dignity of the poor, and a strict compliance with the protection of workers' rights? The story of Zacchaeus (Luke 19:1–10), the rich tax collector accustomed to fraud and extortion allowed by the political and economic situation of his time,[1] serves as a good illustration of current practices of securing and increasing wealth, practices used by the wealthy to recover and multiply their investments in the shortest time and with the lowest operative cost possible.

This man Zacchaeus, who had become wealthy by exploiting defenseless people under the control of a voracious and oppressive empire, had accumulated a lot of unjust wealth. After his encounter with Jesus of Nazareth, he was willing to give back to those from whom he had stolen much more than what the Jewish law of that time required.[2] In Jesus' words, this act was a sign that "salvation has come to this house." Of course not all wealthy people would be willing to do what Zacchaeus did, and even less if they are accustomed to an easy life of luxury and wastefulness that treats the poor as disposable objects or as the social cost that must be paid to reach economic prosperity.

What does this story tell us about the current accumulation of unjust wealth? The most direct teaching is that the wealthy often use the unjust structures they promote and heatedly defend to exploit and oppress the defenseless. They justify their actions with hypocritical assertions such as: "The present labor legislation allows it"; "I am not breaking any law"; or "I have an unlimited respect for human rights." They ignore the fact that many of these laws are fabricated by the politicians they have helped to put in power or are the product of bribes and the purchase of political votes on the part of corrupt politicians who are concerned not about legislating for the common good but about swelling their bank accounts.

In other words, current practices like extortion and fraud, coupled with exploitation and oppression of defenseless social sectors, are one explanation of why the wealthy get wealthier every day and why poverty increases in the nations that depend on the wealthy economies of the world. Poverty in the countries of the global South is not the product of compulsively lazy and hopelessly incapable people who lack the imagination to generate wealth. It is the product of selfish people who use unjust structures to increase their wealth, buy support and votes to maintain their privileges, and continue their accumulation of wealth. They pay no attention to critical issues concerning the future of the human race, care for the environment, the exploitation of nonrenewable natural resources, or the slow death of millions of undernourished children for whom the future holds no promises other than the violence and death to which the lack of resources has condemned them.

Structural Sin

The previous section leads us to affirm the existence not only of personal greed and injustice but also of institutionalized injustice, or structural violence that directly affects the poor. Our response as Christians, therefore, should consist of not only simply denouncing peoples' individual sins but also denouncing publicly the social sin expressed in national and international policies that perpetuate the material misery of millions and are indifferent to the violation of human rights. Our response should denounce ancient structural sins like poverty, racism, and exclusion, all of which are part of our common history in most countries in the global South. Our practice must also take into account the radical transformation of unjust structures that allow the wealthy to get wealthier while millions of human beings must beg for their daily bread and struggle to survive on unfair salaries.

These unjust structures that favor the unjust accumulation of wealth implement economic policies that treat the poor as objects to be changed or subdued rather than people to be empowered to manage their own change. They favor the local elites and the foreign multinational corporations. They do not use taxation to limit the accumulation of wealth. They do not interfere with the flight of capital to the First World or offshore banks (where the wealthy cannot be taxed), and they permit the unlimited exploitation of natural resources in poor nations with no heed to environmental or community damage. All these policies explain the unjust distribution of wealth in poor nations and help create inevitable consequences of hunger, unemployment, exclusion, and unsatisfied social and political expectations felt by the majority.

On a global scale, unpayable foreign debts keep developing nations in perpetual slavery. They must struggle to invest their resources in paying the rising interest rates to international financial organizations like the International Monetary Fund or the World Bank so they will not be disqualified from international credit. These countries must also accept the conditions set by powerful nations, called Structural Adjustment, which require debtor nations to focus government spending on repaying their debt instead of on government programs to help the poor, such as health care, education, and infrastructure. This load of debt condemns the poor to misery, because the poor rarely benefit from the loans requested by their governments in the name of all their citizens. The political autonomy of countries in the global South is therefore quite relative since organizations and nations in the global North continue to hold the keys to international markets, wealth, and production.

International treaties like CAFTA and NAFTA are another way of ensuring economic benefits and control for powerful nations like the U.S. over weaker economies in poor nations. Moreover, the prevailing neo-liberal economic model excludes small states from interfering in the "free market economy" (free, that is, from limits on accumulation and selfishness). All of this adds up to an amazing rise of unemployment and underemployment; a collapse of public education and health-care systems; a widening of the gap between poor and rich; and an incredible growth of marginalized populations who lack basic services like electricity, water, plumbing, fuel for cooking, and decent housing.

A Common Missionary Agenda

On the basis of this description of personal and structural sin, we must articulate a common missionary agenda. Churches and followers of Jesus of Nazareth in both the global North and South must work together in the following ways:

1. We must ask ourselves if, in both our public proclamation of the gospel and civic responsibility, we are denouncing social and structural sin that serves to legitimize and justify the unjust generation and accumulation of material wealth.

2. We must evaluate if, as disciples of the God of Life, we are denouncing social sins like unjust trade, the justification of wars that are primarily motivated by economic interests, and the control of the natural resources of developing nations by powerful nations. We must evaluate if we are denouncing the passivity with which we tolerate the systematic violation of children's rights to life or the rights of defenseless groups such as undocumented or ethnic minorities.

3. We must all ask ourselves, particularly Christians living in the U.S., if we are critically evaluating the political platforms of our presidential and congressional candidates, particularly whether their proposals promote fundamental human rights like the right to a life with dignity—not only inside our national borders but also around the world.

4. We must become informed about the mechanisms that multinational corporations use to generate unjust wealth, such as the

use of factories that contaminate the environment, extremely low salaries for workers, and the denial of basic labor rights (such as the eight-hour workday, paid vacation, and social benefits).

5. We must stop buying products sold by corporations that abusively exploit the poor and do not follow a policy of environmental protection.

6. We must understand that in order to bring about change, it is not enough to donate dollars to organizations that work to alleviate poverty. We must work for equal opportunities for all and just trade between the global South and North. Until this is accomplished, very little will change for the poor and excluded. Wealthy Christians must reflect critically about the need for change in the structures that generate and perpetuate institutionalized violence, reducing the poor to a sort of "social garbage."

7. We must go beyond gaining awareness and denouncing injustice; we must engage in collective political action that promotes state policies more favorable to the poor. We must do so because the poor are neither faceless statistics nor an historical accident: they are human beings whose dignity does not reside in state policies nor in the crumbs offered to them as "charity" by the rich, but in their heritage of being created in the image of God. Material poverty is explained not only by individual sin but also by social and structural sin that allows and promotes the exploitation of human beings.

8. We, especially if we are wealthy Christians or Christians in wealthy nations, must renounce our indifference, and we must doubt the "sincere" and "objective" information fabricated by those who seek to cover up, distort, or accommodate reality to their petty political and economic interests.

The task ahead is not easy, but it can be initiated by simple actions that may not appear to be very effective or efficient at first: adopting a simpler lifestyle that puts a limit to luxury and wastefulness; visiting poor nations to learn about and meet poverty face-to-face; and maintaining civilian vigilance over politicians and the use of public funds.

Just wealth? In an unjust world like ours it seems difficult to affirm that wealth has been obtained in a just way, with respect for human dignity and without violating basic rights. When you take into account that the countries in the Northern Hemisphere control world markets and sources of production, and that the distribution of income in the Southern Hemisphere is unequal and corrupt, almost always favoring those who have political and economic power, it seems impossible that wealth could be accumulated by just means.

In the face of this reality, Christians in the global North must remember that the Lord's Prayer teaches that the material bread is not "my bread" or "your bread" but "our bread," the bread of communion with all human beings and of solidarity with those who are in a situation of social and economic disadvantage. Consequently, they must learn to share their material bread with their neighbor and be generous and sensitive to their brothers and sisters in the global South. They must understand that this generosity and solidarity also requires an active search for relationships of justice, respect for the human dignity of the poor, and the transformation of structures and systems that allow and perpetuate forms of institutional violence.

They must also ask themselves, as they see their pantry full of groceries and the unnecessary comforts and luxuries in their homes: Have my fellow human beings eaten properly today? Do they have a just and decent job and salary? What does the future hold for undernourished children without access to health care and basic education, who live in homes that lack basic services like water, plumbing, and electricity? What hope is there for those who work more than eight hours a day, are scarcely fed, and struggle with deteriorating health due to inhumane working conditions? In other words, it is not simply about practicing generosity and solidarity with those in worse economic conditions; it is also about generating changes in opinion and social and political actions in support of just commerce in the world, economic policies that lift up the human dignity of the poor, a just distribution of wealth, and truly equal access to the sources of production. For "the earth is the LORD's, and everything in it, the world, and all who live in it" (Ps. 24:1 NIV).

Bendice Señor, nuestro pan, y da pan a los que tienen hambre y hambe de justicia a los que tienen pan. Bendice Señor, nuestro pan.

Lord, bless the bread you have giv'n, and give bread to those who are hungry; give hunger for justice to those with bread. Lord, bless the bread you have giv'n.[3]

THE BUSINESS OF JUSTICE

PAMELA WILHELMS

Of the world's 187 largest economic entities, 100 are corporations.

Rhett A. Butler[1]

Only one institution is powerful enough and pervasive enough to turn these problems around . . . and it is the institution that is causing them in the first place: Business. Industry. People like us. Us!

Ray Anderson, Founder and CEO, Interface, Inc.

It was eight degrees as we got out of the car in downtown Denver on a night that demanded a very compelling reason to venture out. An annual fund-raiser gathered a mix of musicians, artists, social entrepreneurs, pastors, and business leaders, and focused on an organization that works to provide clean, safe water to villages in the developing world. During the evening, we learned the heartbreaking statistics of water access in the global South, the success of the proj-

PAMELA WILHELMS is a social architect, organizational consultant, and executive coach. She has worked internationally in both the public and private sectors developing the leadership capacity for profound change which maximizes individual and organizational potential on multiple dimensions. Leveraging the invisible social structures, she coaches leaders on systems innovations that will shift companies and drive a healthy regenerative economy. www.wcgsite.com.

ects the previous year, and the story of a particular village in Central America. An industrial plant belonging to an American company had dumped pollutants upstream of this village, harming its natural water source. So we pledged money and listened to these stories.

I switched gears quickly the next morning, flying to California for a meeting with a client. Heading down the hall to our meeting room, I glanced to the right and was met with pictures I will never forget. There, on this beautiful wall, were pictures of the company's operations in the same Central American country highlighted the night before.

Throughout the day as I led a group of executives through a session on systems thinking and cultural transformation, I was distracted by the newly-discovered systems issues at work in my own life. Systems thinking helps people see and map the "whole," the macro frameworks and connections that influence their work and strategies. Though I am considered an expert in this discipline, that day I was shocked by the unintended role I was playing in a complex system: by night I supported a not-for-profit that sought to remedy environmental and human harm inflicted by the for-profits I was coaching by day.

If justice as we've defined it is "the right use of power in our relationships," we must explore our roles in some of the most powerful institutions in history. The corporate boardroom is the earthly kingdom of power today, so in terms of our role in business—as leaders, employees, stockholders, and consumers (those with the most power!)—we must ask ourselves some deeper questions about our stewardship of corporate power. We have achieved much in the Industrial Revolution, but one of the unintended consequences is a pollution-based economy that will not sustain seven billion-plus people on the planet. We are living far beyond what our natural resources will support, and issues of justice are at the core of why we need significant change in all of our global systems. The shift from the Industrial Age requires new systems, models, and frameworks for a regenerative economy that will drive not just an economic bottom line but a triple bottom line: economic, social, and environmental prosperity. These economic, social, and environmental systems are inextricably linked together in a larger system, and each is crucial for the flourishing of life. Our current crisis has revealed the interrelatedness of the systems of our world: if our global economic systems are riddled with injustice, they harm our social systems,

159

and damaged social systems in turn undermine our economic systems, both of which depend on the ecological health of the natural systems that nourish us.

Those of us who follow Jesus and participate in the new economy of the kingdom of God must forge a new definition of wealth. Wealth for us can't be reduced to the single bottom line of profit; it must also include justice, love, relationships, and service, for in the economy of heaven these are the currency of greatest value; they are the basis of true wealth, not just for the individual but also for the commons, the collective. Guided by this deeper definition, we can re-deem (or re-value) business as a vehicle for meaning, purpose, reconciliation, economic independence, and the flourishing of life within God's abundant creation.

But we have created a false dichotomy in this country: the "for-profit" sector exists to make money and the "not-for-profit" exists to benefit the common good of society. Seeing this false dichotomy, a global movement is transforming the for-profit business sector, and it is tied directly to this biblical call to justice. The successful companies of this new Post-Industrial Revolution will be those driven by missions that create both economic and social value, make a difference for the common good, and leave the world a better place ecologically.

From a Mechanistic Worldview to Living Systems

Is there justice in business? Or is justice only a "non-profit" human activity, and business is business? When looking at the business of justice, we must examine the economic assumptions of the modern Industrial Age that helped create the incredible gains of the Industrial Era, including the following:

- Economic growth is always progress.
- Natural resources are unlimited.
- Reducing processes to their smallest tasks increases efficiency.
- Capital and physical assets are our most valuable resource.
- Opportunity for individual accomplishment is the backbone of capitalism.

These assumptions greased the machinery of the Industrial Age, but had unintended negative consequences that have left us in severe global crises. Our current systems, lubricated by these assumptions, are perfectly designed for the results currently being manifest in the world markets, both positive and negative.

For the past couple of decades, however, business in the Western world has been shifting away from the mechanistic frameworks of the Industrial Age to new frameworks in support of the Information Age. Globalization has brought an interdependence we have never known before and demands both new structures and new metaphors to understand those structures. Increasingly, natural living systems rather than mechanistic systems have become the metaphors that frame how we live, structure, adapt, transform, and create. The writings of Peter Senge, Meg Wheatley, David Bohm, and many others have challenged our models of organizational structure. We are turning from seeing ourselves as functionary units in static social machinery to dynamic human participants within living, complex, adaptive systems. In this move to understand a deep ecology in organizational systems, we are learning from the world that sustains life for us, and from which we have become so disconnected. In the mechanistic mind-set, we valued economic growth at the expense of that which nourishes us, but as Gaylord Nelson said, "The economy is a wholly owned subsidiary of the environment."[2] As a result, we come to see every environmental injustice as a social injustice as well.

In the Industrial or Modern Era we became impervious to the concept of the "whole." But now, we must rewire our brains to get the bigger picture of the "we," the commons, the collective. Guided by systems thinking, we must see the whole as greater than the sum of individual parts. This expansion in our thinking unleashes new energies in the business sector. The biggest lesson of my life in corporate change is that we are intrinsically relational beings: when we are in relationship to our core values and the people around us, and when we are focused on the higher values of the common good, we come to life and perform at extraordinary levels.

My work over the past fifteen years, reframing leadership and organizations in the context of living, dynamic systems, has profoundly reshaped my understanding of Christ and his message. I now see a deep ecology at the heart of what Jesus calls the kingdom. I see how he uses living systems as metaphors throughout the Gospels. I see in these stories not only metaphors for growth, transformation, healing, and redemption, but also a radical challenge to rethink leadership: in complex, adaptive, living systems, we who lead must use a different kind of power in new and different ways. The leader must shift the power dynamic from a "power over" hierarchy to a power-as-service model that engages the collective intelligence and the power of the commons. In this context, power is used not for win-lose competition, but for the common good, so all can excel.

Revealing the Core Human Need for Meaning and Purpose

While working with organizations and leaders from every continent, what has become clear to me is the core human need in any culture for meaning and purpose. Healthy systems demand that people understand what they uniquely bring to the ecosystem of the company. People are more productive when they are working from their gifts, talents, interests, strengths, and passions. My experience has taught me that when people learn more about themselves, they start to ask those deeper questions: "So what are these gifts for?" "What is my time on the planet about?" *Those* questions help people come alive, put a sparkle of hope in their eyes, and always have an element of justice. People value themselves more and begin to "show up" in new ways. At a deep level, we are created to seek justice, love mercy, and walk humbly with our God, and when we are able to do that as part of our day in commerce, sales, or production, we discover a deep and abiding joy. As David Whyte says, "Work is not a static endpoint or a mere exercise in providing, but a journey and a pilgrimage in which the core elements of our being are tested in the world."[3]

Aesthetics, Justice, and *Shalom*

The great joy of my work is that I have experienced the beauty of wholeness, a glimpse of the beauty of *shalom*, in organizations that

162

discover purposes much larger than themselves and much higher than the single bottom line of making money. When individuals get clear about their giftedness, then bring that to the collective, and an organization starts to dream about the redemptive potential of business, that organization becomes a living organism that carries a deep sense of the aesthetic.

By "the aesthetic," I mean a fuller sense of beauty on multiple dimensions: emotional, physical, spiritual, and intellectual. When you hold a deep sense of what the aesthetic brings, you start to tap the reservoirs of the soul. The mechanistic mind has so neatly masked our vision for the aesthetic, but companies are bringing in poets, musicians, visual artists, and many other creatives to help people break out of the mechanistic frameworks. The most successful companies of this century are recognizing the link between economic success and the fuller experience of being human. As the aesthetic warms and waters human communities, seeds of justice begin to germinate.

The culture comes alive, energy becomes palpable, and people awaken to the reality that there is something vital in the human spirit, something sacred that reflects the image of God in which we were created. Business should be a place where the best of human creativity, collective intelligence, learning, and growth come together to allow everyone on the planet to be engaged in meaningful work, have clean water, and enough to eat. That is a picture of beauty, and an expression of the kingdom and justice of God. We now need to experience the deep shifts or conversions that allow people to see what is possible.

I know and work with many companies that exhibit this beauty of justice, at least in parts of their organizations. I won't claim perfection in any of them, and neither would they. But they're talking about ways that industry can help reduce global poverty and eliminate toxins in production and recovery. They're exploring how to return everything we produce and consume to the environment, not as toxins in landfills, but as resources for life and for the future. They're helping their companies, their industries, and their supply chains to shift from consumptive and destructive ways of doing business to creative and constructive ways of participating in a regenerative global economy.

Nike, for example, has learned from past mistakes and is becoming an ethical leader in its industry. As a publicly held, multinational corporation, Nike works to bring the best products to the world of sports. But they're not just asking how to improve the single bottom line. They're asking new kinds of questions: How do we use our strengths and our core business to make the world a better place? What do sports bring to the world, especially the world of the less advantaged? How can sports create a more just world? They've discovered research showing that young women who have been involved in sports are more likely to seek higher education, to bring more to their communities, and to not be abused. They've created a business line called Considered which contributed much of the clothing used in the 2008 Olympics; the products in this line will be given a bronze, silver, or gold label based on their sustainability rankings according to a number of important criteria. Nike's goal is that every product qualifies for at least the bronze level by the fiscal year 2011. And the company has declared a goal of zero waste, zero toxicity, and 100 percent recyclability across its entire product line by 2020. Inspired by one of their maxims, "It is our nature to innovate," Nike has drawn together creative people committed to a triple bottom line, thus creating a better future.

Seventh Generation is helping transform the household cleaning industry by creating non-toxic products. It derives its name from the Iroquois saying, "In every deliberation, we must consider the impact of our decisions on the next seven generations." Gregor Barnham, the Director of Corporate Consciousness for Seventh Generation, once told me, "With every design, if it doesn't have that level of beauty—designing for the deepest moral good, the deepest aspect of justice—we have a corporation without a soul. It doesn't have at its core a deep sense of the spiritual. People don't recognize that we have been 'de-Godded' in our culture." Barnham understands that we've been mechanized to the point that we don't see the deep, just work of God in our everyday exchange of goods and services. But when we connect people with work that is important to the soul, we build our recognition of the divine.

The current economic crisis has exposed injustice and dysfunction in our economic systems. But we can't simply blame Washington and Wall Street: government does not exist without us voters, and Wall

Street does not exist without us consumers and investors, employers and employees. We have more power than we realize, and the time has come for us to exercise that power through what we buy, how we invest, how we define wealth, how we steward our resources, and how we lead and manage our businesses. We are all in the business of seeking and doing justice.

JUST ECOLOGY

*What Demands of Justice
Does the Planet Make upon
Followers of Christ?*

LYNDSAY MOSELEY

Delio's voice was barely audible but the excitement was unmistakable: *"El tigre! El tigre!"* Looking in the direction of his extended arm and pointed finger, I drew in a quick breath as I saw it swimming across the Cuyabeno River, still brimming from twenty-three inches of rainfall the night before. Only its head was visible above the flowing water as it moved across the current. Its dark and determined eyes seemed startled by our presence, but it had come too far to turn back. I stared intently as it swam past the tip of our canoe to the flooded banks of the river on the opposite side, finally pulling itself out of the water onto the bank. Flexing, bending, and shaking water from its spotted hide, the creature sent a quick glance our way before disappearing into the shadows of Ecuador's pristine old growth rainforests and ancestral lands of the Siona tribe.

As a widely recognized leader in the creation care movement, **LYNDSAY MOSELEY** is an editor of *Holy Ground: A Gathering of Voices on Caring for Creation* and coauthor of *Faith in Action: Communities of Faith Bring Hope for the Planet*. In 2005, Lyndsay helped launch Sierra Club's national faith partnerships program after serving on staff with the National Religious Partnership for the Environment. Lyndsay was recognized by *Sojourner's* magazine in June 2008 as an emerging Christian leader. She lives in Washington, D.C.

"Did you see that?" someone whispered gleefully into the silence. "We just saw a jaguar!"

"I can't believe it!" someone else said as our voices rose in clamoring excitement. "I just put away my camera!"

I sat grinning and shaking my head in a mix of disbelief and delight. Delio, a Siona shaman and our host, had spent the last few days sharing his vast knowledge of the flooded rainforest like a proud father. He took us around by boat and on foot to show off its treasures: beautifully colored toucans, parrots, and kingfishers; frogs, snakes, and caiman; a three-toed sloth and all but one of the species of monkeys native to the area; and pods of rare and threatened "pink" freshwater dolphins that frolicked in the river while we fished for piranha in the glow of the sunset. And then we saw a jaguar in a chance encounter with one of the rainforest's most elusive and endangered creatures. Like the river around me, my heart overflowed as I thought about all I had seen.

We had come to the Amazon with an organization called the New Community Project to learn about not just the diversity of life in the rainforest but also its vulnerability. As economic interests clash with fragile ecological systems, rainforests and the wildlife and indigenous populations that depend upon them are destroyed at alarming rates. In eastern Ecuador, the rainforests exist above large deposits of oil. As one of the poorest countries in South America, Ecuador's government has been and continues to be under tremendous pressure from international debts. Ecuador contributes only 3 percent of the world's total oil supply, but oil revenues account for almost half of the country's gross national product. As a result, the government has encouraged oil development in sensitive areas with historically few environmental protections. The U.S.-based company Texaco was said to be the first company to discover oil in this region and ran operations there from 1972 to 1990 when Ecuador instituted environmental protections.

I recall the stark expression of sadness in Delio's eyes as he pointed out the oil sheen on the water one afternoon, and the only hint of anger I ever saw in this otherwise peaceful man as he stood over the source: unlined storage pits filled with bags of toxic sludge buried from a previous oil spill less than thirty feet from the water's edge. After Delio's persistent requests for a second clean-up effort, oil companies had hired Siona men to dig up the contaminated dirt and leaking bags and relocate them. The Siona men earned ten dollars a day, received no information or training for handling toxic substances, and were given only a pair of gloves to accomplish the task. Rainforest residents—humans, plants, and animals alike—rely upon the river for all of their water needs. Naturally, many of them are getting sick with illnesses that challenge the shaman's ancient medicinal wisdom: various cancers, spontaneous miscarriages, dermatitis, infections, headaches, and nausea. He tells us this situation is pervasive in the region.

Since 1950, more than 50 percent of the world's rainforests have been lost. More than 20 percent of the Amazon has already disappeared, and estimates suggest annual loss of twenty thousand square miles per year. At this rate, the entire Amazon could be gone within fifty years. Economic forces drive the other primary threats to the rainforest as well, including the quest for timber, cattle grazing, coffee, and cocoa. As roads are built to move equipment into the rainforest and products out, "settlers" follow looking for jobs and access to land to improve their own livelihoods.

This massive deforestation and the impacts of development—air and water pollution, soil erosion, extinction of plants and animals, and the decimation of indigenous tribes—damage or destroy the fragile ecological systems that support life in the region. Scientists estimate that we are losing more than 137 species of plants and animals every single day because of rainforest deforestation, and there are only five hundred members of the Siona community alive today in Ecuador and Colombia combined, a small fraction of the size of their community just a generation ago.

⸺

Delio's son started the small outboard engine, and we began our three-hour journey out of the Cuyabeno Reserve. I settled back into my thoughts with the hum of the motor in the background and the cool wind on my face, occasionally dodging low branches and letting all that I had learned sink in. Three hours later, we climbed out of the canoe and loaded our belongings into the waiting van. From my open window, I smiled and thanked Delio for the last time.

"Bye, bye," he said, beaming a beautiful smile in our direction. "Bye, bye." This was the only word I ever heard him speak in English.

As we pulled away, I felt sadness and a nagging frustration well up inside, interrupting my exhilaration and joy from the journey. Soon we were driving along the dusty road away from the Cuyabeno. A large oil pipeline followed along the road, and I realized that of all the things I witnessed in the Ecuadorian Amazon, the ugliest and most destructive had my human fingerprints all over them. Every year, 40 percent of Ecuador's oil exports go to the United States to feed our voracious appetite for fossil fuel. As an American, I feel complicit in the disappearing rainforest, the retreat of the jaguar, the catastrophic loss of plant and animal species, and that twinge of incredible sadness in Delio's eyes.

In the introduction to this collection, Brian McLaren writes that the Bible has more to say about justice than we ever imagined, in part because we have been trained to focus on other things. This is precisely the case when it comes to pursuing justice in our relationship with God's creation.

Rather than seeing plants, animals, rivers, and mountains as essential components in a larger, interdependent web of God's creation, we have gotten carried away with the anthropocentric, mechanistic Enlightenment worldview; we act as if these elements of God's good creation are merely objects or "raw materials" to be exploited and manipulated for human gain. Since the time of the Industrial Revolution in the nineteenth century, our failure to see the whole of God's creation from a biblical perspective, coupled with increasingly powerful technology, has allowed us to cause irreversible damage. We clear-cut forests, drill pristine wilderness for oil and natural gas, blow up entire mountains in the quest for cheap coal in Appalachia, fill streams and rivers with our toxic wastes, and dangerously accelerate global warming by spewing carbon dioxide into the earth's atmosphere. In our wake, we leave behind a trail of decimated ecosystems, polluted air and water, depleted soils, diseased or completely destroyed forests, and innumerable species increasingly in danger of extinction as their homes are destroyed.

As followers of Christ we must recognize, in humility, that God declared every part of creation to be "very good" for its own sake, independent of its value to human beings. Psalm 24:1 declares, "The earth is the LORD's, and everything in it" (NIV). Psalm 104 celebrates God's attentiveness to creation: "How many are your works, oh LORD! In wisdom you made them all; the earth is full of your creatures. . . . These all look to you to give them their food at the proper time . . . when you open your hand, they are satisfied" (vv. 24, 27–28 NIV). And yet we find a surprising command in Genesis 2, which teaches that God places great trust in humanity by commissioning us to be stewards of all God has made, quite literally instructing us to "work it and take care of it" (v. 15 NIV).

Being stewards of God's wonderful creation begins with recognizing God's ownership, but it is equally important to understand the fundamental reality of our relationship with God's creation: we are all connected. How we live impacts the world around us. Decisions we make about the goods and energy we consume or how we handle our wastes can either help God's creation flourish, or bring about destruction. This is a fundamental scientific principle, also expressed in biblical wisdom. *Shalom* is a Hebrew word for *peace* found throughout the Old Testament. The vision of *shalom* is much richer than what our English word *peace* often evokes; it is nothing less than God's intent for creation from the beginning: a world teeming with life, flourishing in a state of physical and emotional health, each part relating to the whole of God's creation in peace, harmony, and abundant joy. It is a vision that calls followers of Christ together and gives us hope. We are learning the hard way, however, that we cannot experience God's peace and justice on earth if we disregard our relationship with God's creation.

Many Christians have been slow to embrace the biblical vision regarding ecology and justice. However, as we hear the cry of creation and understand that our own livelihood is tied up in its greater health and well-being, we may return to the Bible with new eyes and opened hearts. Jesus told his disciples that the greatest command is to love God and that the second is to love our neighbors as ourselves. How can we proclaim to love God if we are destroying God's handiwork for our own gain? How can we love our neighbors when our appetite for energy contributes to deforestation of their homes and habitats, or pollution of the water they drink or air they breathe? We must not ignore the reality that low-income communities and communities of color often disproportionately bear the burdens of our collective environmental choices. What about our nonhuman neighbors? The vision of justice in the biblical concept of *shalom* suggests that followers of Christ should consider all of God's creation as deserving of our love and care, not just our human brothers and sisters. If not, we are in danger of the final judgment reflected in Revelation 11:18: "The time has come for judging the dead, and for rewarding your servants the prophet and your saints and those who reverence your name, both small and great—and for destroying those who destroy the earth" (NIV).

What will it take? What can we do? Here are five steps we can take to bring about justice in our relationships with God's creation:

1. Repent. Shift your attitude from entitlement to gratitude.
2. Embrace God's love for creation by gaining knowledge of the plants and wildlife in your community, and discover and honor the ways you are intimately connected to them.
3. Learn about the threats to God's creation, especially the disproportionate impacts on those who Jesus called "the least of these."
4. Take practical steps in your own life to reduce your impact on the planet, God's creatures, and our human neighbors.
5. Call others in your community, including your family, church congregation, and community leaders, to join you on the journey.

JUST RELIGION

Why Should We De-colonize God's Name?

SAMIR SELMANOVIC

> Whatever is true, whatever is noble, whatever is right, whatever is pure, whatever is lovely, whatever is admirable—if anything is excellent or praiseworthy—think about such things.
>
> Philippians 4:8 NIV

Twenty-four years ago I entered the story of Christ, studied the Bible diligently, and loved Jesus passionately. I renounced the communist atheism I grew up with, abandoned the practices of Eastern religions, and—in order to be a Christian—was forced to leave my Muslim family home. Then, unexpectedly, fifteen years after my conversion and subsequent ten years in pastoral ministry, the Christian story as I had learned it began to trouble me. I found it less true, noble, right, pure, lovely, admirable, excellent, and praiseworthy than when I first believed.

I believe as firmly as ever that two thousand years ago, God visited us—in person. Through the life, death, and resurrection of Christ,

SAMIR SELMANOVIC, PhD, was raised in Europe in a Muslim family and served as a Christian pastor and community organizer in Manhattan during 9/11 and its aftermath. His book *It's Really All About God: Reflections of a Muslim Atheist Jewish Christian* will be published in 2009. He is a member of the Interfaith Relations Commission of the National Council of Churches and is the founder of Faith House Manhattan, a congregation led by a priest, a rabbi, and an imam. Contact: www.samirselmanovic.com.

God declared himself to be *for* us and *in* us. However, while I faithfully testified to the world about my encounter with the living God through Jesus Christ, something was gnawing at me—the possibility that God is fully present, alive, and well among people of other religions, or even no religion at all. If proven true or plausible, this possibility would dwarf all other issues of our theology and practice. It would mean that we would have to relearn how to be Christians *on earth* where we have to live, as Paul said, only "knowing in part."[1] We would need to learn to live as earthly citizens without the ill-founded comfort of being exclusive custodians of God's truth on earth which in effect puts us "in charge of God." We would need to embrace our status as creatures, limited and interdependent with other creatures, in the kingdom where *Another*, and not us, is the sovereign one.

Acknowledging and questioning our tendency to draw boundaries around God could transform the way we relate to God and treat one another. Does our account of God's decisive act of self-revelation through Jesus Christ among *us* necessitate God's *in*decisive acts among *them*, especially when we realize that "them" happens to be the vast majority of earth's inhabitants both past and present? Isn't something terribly wrong with a religion that, in order to explain God's saving presence within it has to resort to insistence on God's saving absence (or should we say damning presence) outside it?

From Dehumanization to Delight

Race, gender, nationality, political conviction, age, and countless other categories by which we differentiate ourselves from one another mirror diversity in nature. Differences are not merely a matter of fact, but a matter of principle of life. Diversity is a blessing. Interdependence is the way God wanted the world to be. When we insist that we are self-sufficient, or that particular characteristics—such as our race, for example—make us not only different but *truly* human, we imply that others are not truly human, and therefore create a justification for the dehumanization of others. Sooner or later this inevitably results in indifference, neglect, and violence. This is where devastating nationalist wars, such as the recent one in my home country, the former Yugoslavia, come from. This is why truths like the one expressed in Sting's cry that "Russians love their children too" so poignantly address Western fear and our inability to see the true humanness of *the other*. It is no different in religion.[2]

My contention is that the unwillingness to see God in *the other*[3] and to see the Great Commission as a two-way street where humility and inclusion are *the* method to teach about Jesus, is a grave tactical error of our witness in the world, a paralyzing dead end in our theology, a failure of our imagination, and a disheartening crisis of our identity.

I do not say this lightly. I became a Christian at great cost and am more passionately committed to Christ now than when I first believed. I am not a relativist. I believe that Jesus offers grace to every person of every religion through the example of his life, through his good news of the kingdom of God, through his unique revelation of the character of God as one who suffers with and for us, through his defeat of the powers of death through resurrection, and through his abiding presence in the Holy Spirit. In addition—or should I say *because of it*—I have come to believe that to deny God's full involvement and presence among *the other* not only mirrors disregard for Samaritans and tax-collectors (*the other* of Jesus' time) but also re-enacts Peter's denial of Christ.

Today, I *expect* God in *the other*: in their community, their practices, and their texts, just as I want *the other* to expect God in our community, our practices, and our texts. To me, this is a bottom line of *just* Christianity: that I refuse to break the Golden Rule while pursuing the Great Commission, to betray Jesus in the act of sharing him.

God does not create in order to abandon. "'Are not you Israelites the same to me as the Cushites?' declares the LORD" (Amos 9:7). In contrast to our propensity to exclude, God committed himself to including *all* of humanity by insisting, "'I act with steadfast love, justice, and righteousness in the earth, for in these things I delight,' says the LORD" (Jer. 9:24).

The love story between God and those of us who are a part of the Christian story is specific, unique, and passionate, but the focus of God's love is nothing less than the whole earth and all of humanity. To know God's love, my heavenly parent does not have to whisper in my ear, "I love you more than your sister." God is with *the other*, in *the other*, and for *the other*. In fact, God knows no *other*. For me, to grow as a Christian includes retraining my heart to "delight in these things."

Siding with the Excluded

Perhaps every generation should be judged by what kind of legacy it leaves for the next—including its theological legacy. The way we hold our beliefs is as ethically important as the way we treat the environment, the way we elect our governments, and the way we structure our economic policies. Our diverse religious worlds are colliding, and the Christian theology we are passing on to the future is simply not adequate for the experience our children are having.

We insist that while all religion excludes people, the gospel is different from all religion, and thus is an antidote to exclusion: We are accepted by God, not because we are better than anyone else, but because of Jesus, who was excluded for us on the cross. Other faiths, however, have their own way of addressing this reality, their own way of being one with each other and one with God. These ways, while foreign to Christianity, are true, noble, right, pure, lovely, admirable, excellent, and praiseworthy. As such, these religions and worldviews have a corrective and healing influence that Christian religion simply cannot supply either to the world or to its own adherents. Thus, Christianity *needs* the world as much as the world needs Christianity.

Moreover, we have huge, unanswered questions lingering above our Christian heads: How is the Good News good for those who have never heard? Are people who have never heard about Jesus— or have heard about Jesus in an inadequate way, or have very good (moral) reasons to reject Christianity—an experimental "control group" to demonstrate to the universe the superiority of salvation through Jesus Christ? Is their role in history to be a human sacrifice? Is the God of our current theology uncompassionate, uncreative, or incapable? We dodge these questions by relegating the repulsiveness of these notions of God to "mysteries of God." But these mysteries are bad mysteries: they are unjust and self-serving. They cast human beings as mysteriously expendable.

Imagine someone telling you that the island of Manhattan is under a siege by a viral disease and that the city authorities have organized *one* bus to leave the place. How could that possibly constitute good news for the citizens? Such "good news" is now a problem not only for those "who have never heard," but for those of us who have heard it a thousand times. Christian theology is suffering from a lack of compassion. My young daughters don't want to inherit a religion that hogs God and argues for a vacuum of grace in the rest of the world. If Christianity precludes them from finding God to be *with*, *in*, and *for* their friends, then they want to stay with *their friends*. They would rather get off the bus. They would rather be excluded like Jesus than exclude for the sake of Jesus.

God Our Stranger

To hold our faith commitments with passion, to be fully Christian and at the same time to stay fully open to what *the other*—and through *the other*, God—has to give us, might at first seem impossible. For centuries this issue has been hopping from footnote to footnote of Christian theology. Fortunately, in the last several decades, exploration of theologies of religions has been rapidly moving from the sidelines to center stage. Comparative religionists, thoughtful practitioners, and theologians from diverse Christian traditions have laid out different models of Christian identity that explore God's presence among *the other*, offering a deep well of insight into relevant biblical texts and providing breathtaking wisdom and inspiration.[4]

And not a moment too soon. A tectonic shift in Christian consciousness is well under way among regular folks, albeit underground. In the privacy and anonymity of filling out surveys, seven out of ten Americans, Christians included, agree with the statement that many religions—not just their own—can lead to salvation.[5] With token exceptions, one would not recognize these movements by listening to sermons, attending Bible studies, singing our worship songs, or reading our magazines. Our conscious, public group identity still seems to require an uncompassionate, uncreative, or unjust God.

Emerging Christianity openly argues that we should deal with our Christian hubris and stop dismissing the questions about the character of God and the goodness of the good news as irrelevant concerns. My daughters' generation is calling our bluff. A Christ-like course of action would be to cease boasting about inadequate answers to these legitimate questions and to cease presenting such answers as a scandal that people just have to accept, calling exclusion of *the other* "a mystery" and "an act of faith." These notions have nothing to do with the scandal of Christ and everything to do with the scandal of Christianity.

I am turning a corner here. I am venturing into the very territory where we used to think that "God is less," and I want to know whether this is so. If, as many present Christians claim, God's saving presence is not there, if those who have never heard have *really* never heard, that will compel me to advise my daughter to find some better news to live by. Our theology is at stake here. If there is no God on the outside, the inside collapses.

If, on the other hand, I find God there, among *the other*, whether as a cosmic Christ, a "seed of the word" in disguise within the concepts and practices of other religions, or in a form truly different from and foreign to Christianity, I will embrace my Christian story with renewed joy and passion. My faith in Christ will dwarf the religious fervor I had while living in a story that could only be true if all other stories were proven false. That is my definition of *just* Christianity: not only to concede but to celebrate the presence of God in *the other*.

We are in this together. All humans, no matter their religion, are God's beloved and are called to be God's agents on earth. How can we possibly repair the world if we don't learn how to be interdependent with *them*? And how can we possibly be interdependent with them if we call their light darkness? There is a line between light and darkness, but as Alexander Solzhenitsyn says, this line runs not between "us" and "them" but through the heart of every human being.[6]

Finally, without this shift in our thinking and practice, we will lose our love for God. Understanding our relationship and life with *The Divine Other* (the Holy One who will always confound us) is inex-

177

tricably intertwined with our relationship and life with *the human other* (the parts or aspects of humanity that also confound us). We exercise our relationship with God through our relationship with the stranger. That's why the Hebrew Bible says "love your neighbor as yourself" once, but says "love the stranger" thirty-six times. That's why, when Jesus was asked to expand on who our neighbor is, he answered that it was the merciful stranger, and not necessarily the people who are most like us.[7] That's why Jesus insisted in Matthew 25 that our relationship with *the other* is *the* way our relationship with God will be measured. That's why the God of the Bible often visits his people as a stranger, like the angels that visited Abraham and the wise men who visited baby Jesus. Strangers bring news. They are necessary. We are created to depend on them. To exclude the word and work of a stranger can mean rejecting the word and work of the Lord, for only strangers can see and tell us what we cannot see or tell ourselves, and thus bring a new whirlwind of love and passion into our own faith.

JUST CITIES

What Does the Call to Justice Mean for Life in Our Cities?

CHAD R. ABBOTT

I was crossing Ohio Street in downtown Indianapolis when I looked up to see James and Kate making their way down the sidewalk ahead. James was pushing his wife, Kate, in her wheelchair and waving to me, his pastor. Kate rode forward with her head down, hands pressed upon her temples, and I could tell from her body language something was not right. When we were finally close enough to speak, Kate immediately said, "They denied me my disability." She was in tears, covering her face as if to veil that side of our humanity that lives between hope and despair, not knowing which will win out. Kate continued: "I mean, I just don't understand. I am sitting here in a wheelchair, barely able to move, living in and out of hospitals, and they suggest I am not disabled." I told her I was sorry this happened to her, and she responded, "Maybe I ought to just jump out in front of traffic and end this thing. It would just make everyone else's life

CHAD R. ABBOTT is a clergyperson who has served churches in both New Jersey and Indiana. He graduated with a BA in religion and philosophy from Greenville College and a Masters of Divinity from Princeton Theological Seminary. In the wake of the U.S. invasion of Iraq, Chad coedited *Breaking Silence: Pastoral Approaches for Creating an Ethos of Peace* with Pilgrims Process, Inc. in 2004. He lives on the near east side of Indianapolis with his wife, Shannon, and daughter, Isa. When he is not reading or writing, you might find Chad on the frisbee golf course, riding his bike, or playing the saxophone with his jazz ensemble.

easier." My heart sunk as I tried to clumsily say something pastoral to support her, realizing full well that my growing up white, middle-class, and of able body, in the richest and most powerful country in the world, did not afford me the reality of knowing what it must be like to live in poverty, not have health care, or be denied disability when you can barely walk.

What is required of us who receive the cries of people like Kate in our world? In the congregation where I served James and Kate as pastor, an emergent United Methodist congregation (no, this is not a contradiction in terms) in Indianapolis, the answer we gave to this question came from Micah 6: "To do justice, and to love kindness, and to walk humbly with God" (v. 8). The justice we focused on attempted to challenge the root causes of systemic oppression, from racism, sexism, homophobia, war, violence, and socio-economics to our misuse of the earth. It is into this framework that people like James and Kate entered our community broken, abandoned, and looking for a faint whisper of hope within this harsh world of ours.

James and Kate came to our congregation after living several months in homeless shelters. They were trying to reenter the world after spending time in prison. Kate had barely survived being hit by a car, and both were alienated from anyone resembling their family of origin. Without any health care or an adequate social service system to help them rise out of their poverty, they turned to the church. Our congregation sat in the middle of a major thoroughfare between two homeless shelters within a couple of blocks in either direction. This same thoroughfare is also spackled with homes selling for $500,000 and new development condos starting at $350,000 apiece. While we were by no means living out justice, mercy, and discipleship perfectly, people like James and Kate began to experience hope for their desperate lives and, what is more, so did some of our more affluent Indianapolis residents. It would not be all that unusual to see a retired public health expert or someone from our mayor's office in worship sitting next to someone who has no health care because they live under a bridge, are an ex-con, or have been imprisoned for sleeping in our state-owned war memorial parks. I began to realize that to do justice in this context requires a great deal of courage, faith, friendship, and, perhaps above all, the ability to laugh out loud at ourselves and the sheer madness of life in our cities.

If indeed we are to agree with our introductory definition of justice being "the right use of power in our relationships with others" then, to be sure, those of us whose context is the urban landscape must begin asking the all-important question, "What does the call to justice mean for life in our cities?"

I once preached a sermon entitled "World History's Greatest Lie." I suggested in this sermon that we lie when we tell ourselves we are not connected to one another. (I have no verifiable evidence to suggest that it is the greatest lie in history, but it made for a good sermon title.) The dual influences of capitalism and rugged individualism, particularly in the West, has hypnotized us into believing not only that we do not need others to survive but also that we are fundamentally separate.

Theologians, sociologists, anthropologists, and social prophets have been trying to break us of this lie for generations. The book of Genesis begins by suggesting that creation itself is an intricate web of interdependency: light and dark, sun and moon, fish and animals, male and female, all of which rely upon each other to exist. Paul describes the church by referencing the human body and suggesting that we are connected like foot, hand, ears, and eyes, none of which could function without the others. Mahatma Gandhi suggests in his autobiography that "soul force" interlaces our lives. Jewish theologian Martin Buber suggests in his book *I and Thou* that when we construe life in objective rather than relational terms, we demonize others as objects to be exterminated and therefore cause suffering. Buddhist monk Thich Naht Hahn uses the term "inter-being" to suggest that all of life, from the birds to all human beings, represents a sense of interconnected energy, and that to destroy one piece of this life is to destroy it all.[1] These thinkers all suggest a similar theme: life is designed as a web of interdependency, and when we live as though this web does not exist, we cause suffering. While there is no location on earth that world history's greatest lie does not impact, it is within our urban centers that this lie is most visible.

Perhaps the best term to characterize the relationships of urban living is *transparency*. Life in a city is an eclectic mix of races, religions, social and economic backgrounds, music, art, theatre, housing, neighborhoods, and education. The density of living in close proximity to businesses, homes, hospitals, schools, and government agencies creates a dynamic intermingling of life experience, commerce, and social experimentation. In this intermingling of life, the injustices that exist within our social systems are less hidden, and stare us in the face as we walk by someone begging for change, see rows of homeless people sleeping under a bridge, or witness long lines at the nearest poverty prevention center. Whether we admit it or not, the transparent nature of our cities daily shouts out the desperate need for justice, therefore exposing the lie we tell ourselves that in spite of our common humanity and close proximity to each other, we have no need for each other. The city will not allow us to avoid this lie.

If the relationships we share in the urban context are ones of interdependency, then how can we demonstrate the right use of power and get to the root causes of injustice? I do not think we can answer this question without first engaging in conversation with those whom injustice directly impacts. There is a human face behind every system of oppression. I argue that the path toward justice must first travel through two doors: (1) friendship and (2) humility.

John 15:15 states, "I no longer call you servants, because a servant does not know his master's business. Instead, I have called you friends, for everything that I learned from my Father I have made known to you" (NIV). This suggests that friendship is an "incarnational" event. It is not like a servant relationship in which power is distributed over another, but rather like a relationship where there is, as a good friend of mine would say, "mutual delight." Living in a city and demonstrating a right use of power means establishing friendships that operate out of mutual giving.

To live justly through friendship in the urban context means that we dare not ignore the transparency of our lives. It means that friendship exists to tear apart the lines that would suggest we do not need each other to survive. We become friends with beggars, prostitutes, sinners, and kings. We share stories with the wealthy broker, tax attorney, city officials, and crack addicts. We even venture to mingle with our enemies. Establishing these friendships is not a suggestion that we become an accomplice to injustice by accommodating to all parties out of some misguided attempt to be politically correct. And it is most certainly not designed for us to demonstrate a sense of power over others. Simply stated, friendship is the core of the right use of power because it automatically assumes that God's image abides in all people and that no person is beyond God's saving redemption. Justice without friendship to both sinner and saint, poor and rich, enemies and comrades, will merely keep us believing in the illusion that we do not need each other.

A close companion to friendship in the endeavor to live justly in our cities is humility. When I think of the city and humility I am reminded of Jesus' entry into Jerusalem, "the city of peace," on what we consider to be Palm Sunday. In their book *The Last Week*, Marcus Borg and John Dominic Crossan suggest that on Jesus' day of entry, two processions occurred: one of imperial rule expounding imperial theology and one of humble servanthood displaying humility and grace to the outcast and the poor.[2] Pilate entered Jerusalem with cavalry, leather armor, and the banners of empire surrounded by the blind patriotism of a people controlled by the elite. Jesus entered Jerusalem on the other side of town on a donkey with the poor, lame, and outcast laying palm branches on the road and shouting, "Hosanna in the Highest Heavens!" His posture of entry into this city and its injustices was not one of arrogance, pomp and circumstance, or overwhelming power, but one of humility, trust in God, and compassionate friendship with those pushed to the margins. Through his mode of entry into Jerusalem, Jesus suggests that in the kingdom of God, we overcome injustice not through a top-down approach of control, domination, and violence but rather through a grassroots movement of friendship, solidarity, and hope that grows from the ground up.

In the end, justice begins to take root in our cities when we allow friendship and humility to guide our path toward solutions at the root of our systems. Such approaches are not overnight fixes, but lifelong endeavors of investing in people, communities, and creative solutions to the problems that push so many of our urban neighbors into despair. I don't know what will happen to people like Kate or our broken health-care system in the future, but I do know that were it not for the *people* of my congregation investing in her—humbly and through genuine friendship—she would have probably jumped out in front of that oncoming traffic a long time ago. It is from such humble friendships that a lifetime of justice work begins. The Kates of our world cause us to write letters to Congress, rally for affordable housing, design house gatherings in our neighborhoods to discuss how we might improve our educational systems, and to invest our lives in the lives of the poor.

For people who believe that urban injustice can only be solved Caesar's way—the powerful forcefully controlling and fixing the powerless—it seems like lunacy to believe that humility, friendship, and solidarity with the poor and powerless can make a difference. But watch Jesus ride into the city on a donkey. Hear the crowds cheer and shout their confidence in God. Maybe what is foolish from a human perspective turns out to be wise from God's perspective after all.

24

JUSTICE IN THE SLUMS

Urban Poverty as a Monument to Injustice

JORGE TASÍN

Translated by Elisa Padilla

The term *justice* carries a lot of weight in the conceptual universe of the Bible. Justice is an issue of faith because there is no genuine faith if a person who declares it does not support it daily and fully by actually *doing* justice. The Bible is very clear about this.[1] According to the Bible it is not even enough simply to believe in justice or have warm and positive feelings about justice; we must *do* justice. This is what the biblical text requires. This implies a daily and specific social, political, and cultural commitment that goes way beyond merely a personal attitude. Doing justice is not fulfilled merely by personal morality: there must be militancy for justice played out on the vast and complex stage of our world.

We must acknowledge that many of our churches still follow the long, Puritan-pietist heritage, with its primary focus on the individual believer's moral behavior before God. The emphasis that has been

JORGE TASÍN was born in Buenos Aires. He studied theology and worked for many years in projects related to helping people with addictions to drugs. He has written a couple of books on this theme, taught theology in several institutions, and works today in Sueñitos, a day-care center located in an area of extreme poverty in the city of Buenos Aires. He is married and has three young-adult children..

handed down to us from the seventeenth century, and that is currently in force, requires the Christian to live, as an individual, a life of personal morality according to the biblical precepts—no lying, no adultery, no drunkenness, and so on. But very little or nothing at all is said about the biblical mandate to be doers of justice in the diverse scenarios that make up our concrete social realities.

True, we live in a time of postmodern suspicion. We have turned the original Cartesian principle backward. Before, doubt was considered a needed step to reach certainty, but now, every certainty gives way to doubt. This condition of suspicion, inspired by the famous teachers of doubt—Marx, Nietzsche, and Freud, not to mention Kant and Lacan and their disciples—can make us hesitant to speak boldly and confidently about injustice, certain that some acts are evil and wrong and deserve passionate denunciation. Chastened by suspicion, some might say we must not be forceful or categorical about our outrage at injustice, or we risk being branded as intolerant, arrogant, pre-scientific, and even pathological. After all, our view of injustice is only that—a view, a subjective impression that can't be taken too seriously.

But in spite of that suspicion, the world hurts. What happens in the world causes pain, and there is something undoubtable and certain about that pain. I know, because I work every day in Ciudad Oculta, a *villa*, or "misery village," located on the city limits of Buenos Aires, behind the barrios of Mataderos and Villa Lugano. It is a place that hurts; every day it hurts. Pain is a reality: you can walk it, touch it, smell it, feel it. *If you want to understand, you must feel*, Gramsci used to say, somewhat contrary to dominant scientific thought. Ciudad Oculta is a place of shacks and narrow corridors marred by garbage, gunpowder, and drugs, a place of extreme poverty that is dominated by violence. The main perpetrators of this violence are young people between eleven and thirty years of age. They are the consumers of the new Argentine drug, the *pasta base* or *paco* (the residual waste of cocaine production that is smoked). They exercise violence against outsiders and against each other. They are who and what they are because of socio-economic injustice, of poverty, of state and institutional abandonment. They are victims of emotional starvation, of symbolic emptiness, of lack of affection. They get drugged and they hurt others; they steal and kill almost as

186

an instinctive reaction caused by felt and accumulated anger at their condition as pariahs, forgotten and denied. They believe no more, trust no more, wait no more; for here in the *villa*, the absence of resources is almost absolute; the institutions only represent an indifferent remoteness or a brief repressive presence, and the churches, barely and in the best of cases, offer a wind of weightless words emptied of any pertinent content.

Beyond probable subjectivities and in spite of suspicious academic discourse, in this place you can touch reality, walk it, feel it, know it beyond doubt. Today, just a few hours ago, while I participated in a support meeting for mothers whose children are hooked on *paco*, I unexpectedly found out about an episode of attempted suicide. Alejandrito, a thirteen-year-old, tried to hang himself on a rope from one of the wooden beams in his shack. His mother arrived suddenly and found him hanging, on the verge of asphyxia. Desperate, she tried to untie him, but her son reacted by kicking to prevent her from doing so. In spite of this she was able to save him. The neighbors, having been warned, called the medical service who revived him and calmed him down. He is now hospitalized in the emergency section of a nearby public hospital.

I know Alejandrito. With the rest of his family he participated in several years of recreational activities in a community center I helped to coordinate. Claudio, his oldest brother, came to get me at the place in Ciudad Oculta where I now work—a day care center— and we gave each other a meaningful hug. He immediately told me that Alejandrito wanted to see me, so the next day I went to visit him at the hospital. I took him a box of *alfajores* (pastries), hugged him, and tried to muster up the courage to tell him I love him, that what he did hurt me. The world, both as a whole and in its many parts, hurts as a result of what happens and what doesn't happen. Poverty is painful.

When I think of where and how Alejandrito grew up, I begin to understand somewhat his horrific decision to take his life. Ciudad Oculta is not the only epicenter of poverty or outright destitution in Buenos Aires, or even in the rest of Argentina. The most trustworthy data from 2008 shows that of its almost thirty-eight million inhabitants, more than ten million live in poverty and almost four million are homeless.

As for Ciudad Oculta, the first thing that must be clarified—due to the various prejudices, set phrases, and erroneous criteria—is that socio-economic destitution is not a natural nor spontaneous fact, but a *produced* result of economic, social, and political patterns. Extreme poverty is not an anomaly for the dominant system, but rather one of its unavoidable results. It is not an imbalance of the social model, nor a disruption or abnormality to be corrected, nor an unresolved matter. It is the inevitable consequence of a socio-economic system that is perfectly designed to ensure the progressive and constant enrichment of a few, the salvation of a few more that make up the so-called middle class, and the harm, destruction, and exclusion of many more—the majority. Alejandrito is one of those "many more." There are millions of Alejandritos condemned to misery. With the exception of a few rare cases, they have absolutely no chance to become socialized,[2] develop, grow, and live with a minimal degree of economic and cultural dignity.

Argentina is more than a poor nation; it is an unjust nation. It is today, as it was long ago—as always—a brutally and profoundly unjust nation, teeming with social, legal, economic, criminal, political, labor-related, sanitary, bureaucratic, and legislative injustice. The percentages for wealth distribution expose the continual and growing historical gap between the profits of rich and poor. The manner of wealth distribution favors the petty appetites of the dominant elite, made up of landowners, important business sectors of national firms, and pools of transnational corporations. It is done with the complicity of the mass media, the governments, and the guild of professional politicians, all of whom do their ugly work under the protective care of the forces of repression.

The other important thing to point out is that the immense majority of the more than twelve thousand Alejandritos who inhabit the overcrowded and irregular fourteen hectares of Ciudad Oculta do not wish to live there, or live as they do. What is more, when you get to know them and listen to them, you realize they detest the social and environmental conditions under which they lead their life. They complain about the filth, they lament the violence, and they suffer from the drugs and their consequences. They are afflicted by the lack of work. They hate living in this way and feel overburdened, fearful, and frustrated. At the same time, however, they lack the necessary resources—not only economic ones but also the emotional, social, and spiritual resources—to change the conditions they live in and the future available to them and their children. They live in poverty, endure it, bear it, and can't avoid it.

In Ciudad Oculta, like in so many other places where the world hurts, there is a noticeable absence of the church and of Christians. The worst part of it is that this absence of action is not understood as a betrayal of biblical values. In fact, in most churches it is understood that their task is to *preach* the gospel, hand out tracts, give sermons from the pulpit, and carry out different religious propaganda strategies. Most churches see themselves as walled, pristine gardens of Eden that are fortified and isolated from the corrupted social realities outside. They design themselves as proselytizing societies reduced to a liturgical experience whose dynamics go no further than life within their walls. They are communities that for the most part go unnoticed not only in society but also in their own neighborhoods. Simply put, they make no difference. They don't count for anything in the real world.

Their leaders prefer to apply themselves to ecclesiastical administration, pastoral counseling, and Sunday sermons that consist of unbearably light exegesis, distorting conceptual oversimplifications, and unacceptable divorces from reality. They seldom register any of the pain of the marginalized and dispossessed, there is no criticism of the corruption of government employees, there is no call to sociocultural participation, and there is no incentive to create change or get involved in social spheres. In other words, being a Christian is not understood as a way of actively getting involved in society to promote peace, justice, equality, and truth.

In our country we have had bloody dictatorships, wars, embezzlements, massacres, government and corporate corruption, torture, and kidnappings. This has all been only in the last thirty years. The national patrimony has been plundered without limit and there has been a growth of drug trafficking and consumption, family violence, racism, labor exploitation, prostitution, and child malnutrition. The educational system has collapsed and banks have stripped people's savings. In the face of these and other atrocities, either the church has remained silent or its voice has lacked the necessary force to be heard and considered. At the same time, while many citizens joined different associations—in defense of human and civil rights, environmental care, antiviolence, and unemployment benefits—and organized protests, conferences, marches, meetings, and demonstrations, the church has hardly ever participated officially in any of these.

The church does not, for the most part, say anything relevant or do anything constructive, does not get involved, does not contribute its voice or its body to denounce or mitigate injustice. Most leaders and pastors are concerned with strategies that will add more members to their communities rather than carrying out their prophetic task and servant commitment to defend those who are most vulnerable and poor. It is in this absence, this lack of involvement, this indifference, this inaction, that the gospel is tragically mis-defined and betrayed. This explains the church's damaged reputation among many of the flesh-and-blood people who cannot count on it to protect and safeguard their lives, rights, needs, and hopes.

It must be underlined: the social inaction of the church implies—whether consciously or not—a political stance. By remaining silent and uninvolved, the church tacitly supports the status quo and the powers of the moment. A Christian community is never politically innocuous or neutral. What it does or does not do in practice implies its position and its political message, since what is at stake is not its neutrality—such a thing does not exist—but the interests of those whom the church defends. Being doers of justice can only mean putting one's own body on the line in the concrete world on behalf of those who suffer injustice. Otherwise, worship services and sermons have no value; the church is left standing on the wrong side, across the street from God, on the side of the system and its injustices, as a wheel in the mechanism and an instrument of its destructive order.

JUST SUBURBS

What Does the Call of Justice Mean for Life in Our Suburbs?

WILL AND LISA SAMSON

There is no away. This is a phrase that gets tossed around a lot in conversations about creation care. Where exactly is this place called *away*? Is "away" somewhere near our suburban development, and will what we send "away" ever come back?

Central Appalachia is *away* for most people in the United States and the rest of the world. In a place far removed from the average suburban experience, mountains are being destroyed on a daily basis with blasts equaling the power of the bomb dropped on Hiroshima, all in an effort to mine the coal that powers our lights and washing machines and iPods. Left behind after the blasting and removal of coal are tons of rock and the sludge from washing the coal. Left behind are the people whose water tables and houses have been destroyed by the blasting, parents who cannot bathe their children in the brown goop that comes from their tap, families inundated with

LISA SAMSON is an award-winning author who has written over twenty novels. Her most recent novel, *Quaker Summer*, received a starred review from *Publisher's Weekly* and was nominated for a Christy Award. **WILL SAMSON** is a PhD student in sociology at the University of Kentucky where he is working on research in the areas of sustainability and Christian community. They, along with their three children, Ty, Jake, and Gwynnie, live in Lexington, Kentucky, as part of Communality, an intentional Christian community dedicated to living out the call of the gospel in tangible ways.

thick gray soot that gets into everything. But also left behind are systemic damages: tens of millions of pounds of heavy metals from mountaintop blasting that now pollute southeastern U.S. streams and rivers; sterilized lakes and fisheries that are an increasing reality throughout the U.S.; and toxins in the air that now affect people far from the Appalachian mountains, even in environmentally conscious cities like Asheville, North Carolina.[1]

The reason we still talk about coal as a "cheap" source of energy is because the companies that profit from our coal "externalize" the cost of cleaning up the residue of mountaintop removal mining. And we flip on our lights in our suburban home, never aware that issues of justice—human, economic, environmental—are as close as the switch on our wall. Even if you are reading by them in the comfort of a suburban home far away from the mountains of Eastern Kentucky, or in Wyoming or Colorado (also places where mountaintop removal is practiced), your daily life is tied to issues of justice. *There is no away.* If there is one phrase that should be part of a *Shema* of justice, a daily confession for all people of faith, whether in the suburbs or not, it would be the phrase, *There is no away.* And perhaps this is most important in the American suburbs, where many of us located ourselves to get away from questions of need.

We live in a time of unparalleled freedom of choice. At our grocery store here in Lexington, there are more than 140 different brand and scent combinations of deodorant. Many of us connect daily with people all across the globe through email and social networking sites. We have a kind of freedom to create our networks and choose our lifestyles that would have been unimaginable to all but royalty even one hundred years ago.

But has that made us more whole? And has that information caused the world to be more just? In some ways we have become more aware of issues of justice. Campaigns against human trafficking and the genocide in Darfur have been helped by modern communication technologies. But if we live in the American suburbs, we are not confronted daily with injustice, and removing global concerns is as simple as unsubscribing from an email list or dropping a Facebook group. The power to remove ourselves from questions of need is a relatively new, and perhaps short-lived, phenomenon; escaping some of the structural injustice in the suburbs may in fact involve more than leaving a Facebook group. As we write this, the American economy is in the grips of the double whammy of an acute collapse in our banking, lending, and insurance industries and a deep recession in our chronically unsustainable economy. *The Atlantic Monthly* recently asked if the American suburbs were on their way to being "the next slum."[2] Thus, even what we believe to be true about the suburbs, that they are a place for one to avoid the problems of culture, are not proving to be true. There is no *away*. But there is a "here." And we are in it. And God is at work where we are.

This is what the prophet Jeremiah was trying to get at in speaking to God's people as a kingdom was drawing to a close. In Jeremiah 29, he offers the familiar words, "For surely I know the plans I have for you, says the LORD, plans for your welfare and not for harm, to give you a future with hope. Then when you call upon me and come and pray to me, I will hear you" (vv. 11–12). These are words we love to quote, because we long for a future with hope. But back up just a few verses and see what the promise is predicated on: "But seek the welfare of the city where I have sent you into exile, and pray to the LORD on its behalf, for in its welfare you will find your welfare" (v. 7).

Your welfare and the welfare of your neighborhood are bound up together. This was the clear message to God's people, and it is just as clear today. In God's economy, there is no *away*. There is *here*, and this is where God invites us to join in. Thus we come to the central question this essay seeks to answer: What does the call of justice mean regarding life in our suburbs? What kinds of practices might we inhabit that would allow us to see God at work in our suburban neighborhood and to tune our hearts to beat in line with God's heartbeat of justice in the American suburbs? Without stooping to a list of ten easy, convenient, and inexpensive steps toward more just living or some such nonsense, we wanted to offer some spiritual practices that might help you live into questions of justice in the suburbs.

The first move, it seems to us, involves a shift from the kind of thinking that allows us to separate ourselves from the injustices of the world; we must move toward a model where we think *wholly*, and act *wholly*. Almost forty years ago the phrase "Think globally, act locally" came into vogue. That was a good concept for a world just coming to grips with globalization. But if the issue of mountaintop removal teaches us anything, it is that categories like "local" and "global" are not as viable anymore, given our immense ability to spread injustice. For us to answer the call to live justly in the suburbs, perhaps we need to move away from the distinctions that are going away in a globalized economy. Thus, human trafficking in Asia, environmental damage in Appalachia, and the child down the street left to fend for herself are all in our world of concern.

We use the phrase "wholly" as an attempt to get at the biblical concept of righteousness. As Brian McLaren wrote in a meditation in our book *Justice in the Burbs*, the word that gets translated "righteousness" in the New Testament is "a sturdy and social word that invokes fairness, integrity, right treatment, and equity in human relationships."[3] In other words, it looks at the whole picture. And so, as you consider life in the suburbs and how that relates to questions of justice, we would encourage you to connect into these questions by shifting your thinking to be more whole.

However, thinking about the big picture can be overwhelming. Lisa recently returned from Swaziland, where she witnessed firsthand the devastation of a generation by the AIDS epidemic. We don't know how to solve those problems. But there are problems right in our neighborhood, and these problems connect to global systems of injustice. Families suffer from generational addictions to substances and to material prosperity. That is why we are proposing that our commitment to a place be viewed as a long-term proposition. So much of our injustice is driven by consumerism, our need for the latest and greatest, our unquenchable desire to keep moving on up, in a race with the Joneses to find an even better neighborhood and "lifestyle."

But commitment to a place can represent the most radical change we can make in our hyper-consumeristic culture. In *The Purpose Driven Life*, Rick Warren suggests that people get away for forty days of purpose to recalibrate their lives. We would suggest that the problems of injustice require more than that. Perhaps what we need are forty *years* of purpose, a kind of commitment that would seem antithetical to our world of unimaginable choice.

In order to achieve the commitment to a place, however, we need to shift our congregations from providers of religious goods and services to communities of moral formation. The exciting thing is that this can happen in a whole variety of churches and communities. Many of us are aware of New Monastics that have created intentional living communities as a way to shape people toward connection with issues of justice, and we certainly applaud those efforts. But likewise, a pastor of a suburban megachurch in the Lexington area committed to riding his bike for a year to make his congregation aware of the issues of global climate change. This may seem small to you, but to his congregation of thousands it sent a powerful message.

And it becomes a powerful statement that there is no *away* when thinking about issues of energy consumption. Living near Appalachia, where mountains are literally blown up to get at the coal, we understand that. But did you know that if you live in Tampa, Florida, your coal comes from the same destroyed mountains? An important move toward connecting with energy injustice is simply learning where your energy comes from.[4]

Another simple move toward thinking and acting more wholly is to reconnect with our food. Many Americans are well fed, and the average food item travels over fifteen hundred miles to our grocery stores. Despite that, however, malnutrition is rampant. According to the World Health Organization, more people die from heart attacks, strokes, and Type 2 diabetes than are killed by war, famine, AIDS, tuberculosis, and malaria combined.[5] A simple step toward reconnecting with your food, and reconnecting the global and the local, is to plant a garden. It does not have to be much—it could be just a tomato plant. But most of us have no idea how hard it is to grow food, or to provide positive calories for our family.[6]

Finally, commit to biking or walking at least part of the time in your neighborhood. This is certainly practical because oil, as it turns out, may be running out sooner than we expected, and we are likely running short on time for innovative solutions. But the greater reason is this: there are things you will see at five miles per hour that you would never see at sixty.

And perhaps that notion—slowing down to see what God is already doing in your neighborhood—is the greatest suggestion we can make to you as you seek to engage with issues of justice and join in with God's work. There are many people engaged in seeking to solve global problems through global solutions. We have no idea how to do those things. But we have started by committing our lives, and quite possibly the rest of our lives, to seeking justice in Lexington, Kentucky, among a group of people seeking to do the same. All of these suggestions are ways to help you engage with the people around you, to bring the kingdom to your place, and to incarnate the love of Christ to your family, your neighbors, and the unseen people who get food to your table or electricity to your power outlet.

26 JUST COUNTRYSIDE

How Can Justice "From the Roots Up" Affect Life in Rural Areas?
SARAH FERRY

I have often been told that one of the primary causes of injury to farmers living in rural and impoverished areas around the world is falling out of their fields. For a long time I could not wrap my head around how this might happen. Based on my experiences as a child visiting my relatives' farms in South Dakota, I imagined the vast acreage full of soybeans and corn that stretched out to the horizon. The farms were large and flat; an injury from falling seemed impossible.

On my first trip to the Dominican Republic, however, I explored the work of the farmers living in rural communities, and I quickly realized that not only is it very possible to fall out of one's field, but it is a great danger. The poorest farmers are left with the worst land, land that is nearly impossible to work and yields very little. Most of this land is on very steep hills and mountainsides. The farmers must do their best to cultivate the little they can, while torrential rains flush their farms clean of the lasting nutrients in the soil. As I stood on a steep hillside with Juan de Los Santos in Zumbador,

SARAH FERRY is the evaluation specialist at Plant with Purpose (www .plantwithpurpose.org), which helps partner organizations provide environmental, economic, and spiritual programs to communities in six countries. Sarah lives with her husband in San Diego, CA, and likes to connect with God through gardening.

Dominican Republic, he pointed out to me the road at the bottom of his hillside farm. He said, "See just over there, on the other side of the road? That is where my farm has now settled. All the rains have washed the good soil off my farm, over the road and down that hill. It has been a very hard struggle to regain control of my land and to provide for my family."

In God's design for the world, soil was replenished, not depleted, and humans were able to depend on it for the abundant supply of their needs. Over the past centuries, humans have increasingly begun to miss the mark of God's original design, in which humans and nature work together to provide for one another. As humans began to assert a manipulative dominance over the land they were given, suffering began to occur, and those impacted most by it have been the world's rural poor.

One of the greatest causes of poverty around the world is deforestation. Large companies have caused tremendous deforestation by clearing land to raise cattle and for other purposes, but it is occurring in an even greater magnitude and at a faster pace at the hands of the rural poor themselves, who are trapped in a vicious cycle of deforestation and poverty. The poverty of rural farmers around the world drives them to seek out charcoal (made from wood), one of the most common income sources, to sell in the markets to fuel the homes of those in the cities. This heavy dependence on charcoal spreads deforestation at an incalculable rate.

Trees act as a sponge in the ground, absorbing water from the rains and distributing it to springs while keeping the ground moist. They contribute nutrients to the soil and their roots filter the groundwater, ensuring healthy, clean drinking sources from the nearby springs. Cutting trees to create charcoal only exacerbates the problem these communities face by drying out the land and debilitating water sources, depleting nutrients from the soil, and making the soil vulnerable to erosion. This causes poverty to spread wider still, as more and more farmers suffer from the degraded environment and experience decreased yields in their production. They too then join in the acts of deforestation in a desperate effort to survive.

This cycle, left unchecked, has created some of the most extreme poverty in the world. As I write this, I am returning from the border region between Haiti and the Dominican Republic, where the suffering in Haiti from deforestation has left farmers unable to farm, utterly broke, and starving. In some communities, the extent of deforestation has dried up the land, preventing the growth of any sort of edible vegetation, where neither bark nor leaves remain, and some desperate people are reduced to literally eating dirt just to curb their hunger. This image of God's children eating the dust of the earth is a powerful icon of injustice. This is the ultimate sign that humankind and the environment have disengaged from the relationship for which we were intended.

We cannot forget the voices of those around the world who struggle daily to survive with only what nature can provide them: those who are directly connected to the ecology of the land, and whose livelihoods come from their labor in the soil, trees, oceans, and rivers. If we are to engage in a conversation about a just environment, we must engage in conversation with those whose homes are among the trees, fields, and wilderness. Their transportation is their feet; their road is not paved. Their work is the land and their tools are their hands. They live *in* and *with* the land, not just *on* it. These are the rural poor.

But not all of the problems of the rural poor begin close to home. Some of their problems begin thousands of miles away—in our own country, in fact. Few of us in the U.S. realize how much the rural poor across the world are impacted by our government, especially through the U.S. Farm Bill. This bill enables the U.S. government to subsidize the costs of staple crops such as corn, wheat, rice, cotton, and soy. These subsidies essentially allow the largest U.S. farming corporations to sell their crops at a price lower than it costs to produce them, and these corporations are rewarded handsomely for producing greater quantities of these subsidized crops. The resulting excessive supply is then dumped into the world market, competing with the natural costs of farmers' crops abroad. In essence, the bill, through its subsidies of select crops, sets an artificially low world price for these products, and in turn economically devastates faraway communities and families who depend on growing and selling those crops in their traditional culture.

Pressured by this unfair economic advantage, farmers desperate to survive resort to practicing unsustainable agriculture and deforestation. When those desperate measures backfire—as they surely will—the farmers have no choice but to abandon their farms entirely.

The Mexican government estimates the flood of U.S.-subsidized corn into their markets has driven over two million rural farmers from their land since the mid 1990s.[1] Since many of these former farmers eventually enter the United States illegally, we could say that illegal immigration is a harvest of the political and economic seeds we are sowing. We can't blame the immigrant without also accepting our own responsibility.

So the U.S. Congress, U.S. agri-business, and voters like you and me are connected in one eco-economic system with a Mixteco farmer in Oaxaca, Mexico. His farm has been devastated, and he doesn't want to leave it, but unless we can seek justice, he will be forced to leave his family in order to provide for them: "I would like to have my main source of work here at my home. I don't want to emigrate. I don't want to be a day laborer or employee for a company where they exploit us. I say this because I have lived it and I have suffered and I see so many families abandoned. But if there are opportunities here at home, I can be with my family." His plight recalls the words of the prophet Isaiah (41:17–20):

> The poor and needy search for water, but there is none; their tongues are parched with thirst. But I the LORD will answer them; I will not forsake them. I will make rivers flow on barren heights, and springs within the valleys. I will turn the desert into pools of water, and the parched ground into springs. I will put in the desert the cedar and the acacia, the myrtle and the olive. I will set pines in the wasteland, the fir and the cypress together, so that people may see and know, may consider and understand, that the hand of the LORD has done this, that the Holy One of Israel has created it.

In my work at Plant with Purpose (also known as Floresta), a not-for-profit organization, we are working to bring about biblical justice for the land. As agents of God's reconciliation, we are seeking to reconcile the urban poor with the land, and the distant rich with the urban poor. We seek to reverse the vicious cycle of poverty and deforestation by promoting the restoration of our relationship with God, the Earth, and each other. Through our work and that of other organizations working in this area, new hope emerges in more and more corners of the world. Through reforestation, sustainable farming techniques and community development efforts, the poor

200

and needy are now finding water, there are now springs flowing where they had dried up, trees planted in the desert are flourishing, pines are growing in what was once wasteland, and people acknowledge that the hand of the Lord has done this, as Isaiah prophesied.

In nature there is no garbage, and nothing is thrown away because there is no away. Every part of God's beautiful creation has a purpose and a place, even after its primary or obvious purpose seems to have been served. For example, compost, a common element on rural farms, can become a kind of parable—albeit a smelly one—if we're paying attention. The farmer creates a pile of wasted remains of the harvest. Little by little, the earth's worms, insects, and microbes turn what was trash into the treasure of new soil, organically rich and useful to the farmer. This soil will support and nourish new life for the next harvest, renewing the land and making it even more robust than before.

This is the Lord's justice, to make good from all things and for all things to work together. All things are connected in God's world and no action—be it political, economic, or environmental—is without consequences far or near. But the parable of the compost reminds us that there is no "garbage" or "too late" for anything or anyone, including the poor or the earth. Everything can be changed for the better, so as to reveal God's justice and harmony on Earth.

I have seen this healing and renewing process happen to Juan de Los Santos, the farmer in the Dominican Republic. The steep, scarred hillsides and depleted soil of his farm have been transformed. Juan's hillside farm and the farms of his neighbors are flourishing again with crops of oregano, cilantro, green onions, beans, pineapple, and palms. These farms will continue to produce quality crops for years to come. Once they were impoverished, farming depleted land, but now Juan and his neighbors have experienced the justice of reconciliation. They have been reconciled to their land, and their verdant farms are now a shining symbol of the kingdom of God lived out on Earth. Justice calls us to see how we are all connected, the poor and their land, the urban consumer and the rural producer, the policies of the powerful and the plight of the poor farmer or immigrant. When we see these connections and make each relationship more just, we will join Juan de Los Santos and live justice from the roots up.

SECTION FIVE

A JUST
CHURCH

THE POWER OF ORDINARY

How Are Evangelicals in the U.S.
Awakening to Social Justice Issues?

SHAUNA NIEQUIST

Today is a very ordinary Tuesday around our house. The life of a writer and the life of a mama are, at least for me, each lonely in their own ways, so the list of people I'll see on a given day is a short one: my husband, our son Henry, his babysitter Lindsay, and, if I time it right, the mailwoman and the UPS man. Tonight I'm meeting with my writing group, so that adds a whopping three more faces to my well-populated day.

I did some chores this morning, thinking about the topic at hand: evidence that the evangelical church has become captured by the call for justice. I am my mother's daughter, and when a friend encouraged her to read Isaiah 58 every day for a month, her life changed and mine with it. I understand justice through the bars of that haunting and beautiful passage: loosing chains, breaking yokes, sharing food and shelter, and believing the words of the prophet that in doing so,

SHAUNA NIEQUIST lives outside Chicago with her husband Aaron, a worship leader, and their son Henry. She has worked at Willow Creek Community Church and Mars Hill Bible Church. Her first book, *Cold Tangerines,* is a collection of essays about the evidence of God and the extraordinary moments in our everyday lives. www.shaunaniequist.com.

we will raise up old foundations and light will break forth like the dawn. Lovely, muscular, life-shaping words.

As with most questions, the answer to this one presents itself to me in layers. The evidence of evangelical commitment to justice is clear and beautiful and unmistakable in the stories of organizations like World Vision, World Relief, Opportunity International, and Compassion International. One common thread that binds these organizations is that they, for many years, did the great work that they do largely separately from an American church that showed little interest in their convictions. They worked hard and thanklessly, doing the work all Christians have been called to do, far before it became popular. They involved experts and scholars and lawyers and doctors far more often than pastors, and it is to these and many other organizations, I believe, that we evangelicals owe a great debt. As we, individually and collectively, wake up to our responsibility, these organizations graciously allow us to join what they've been doing for a long, long time. They are, in many ways, the silent, faithful shoulders on which current evangelical activism stands.

Sojourners magazine is another beautiful example. My mother has been reading *Sojourners* for decades, and it kept her sane and gave her language to express her deep convictions when she felt as though she was the only Christian compelled by such things. Many of the best justice moments at our church, Willow Creek, have been inspired by one issue or another of *Sojourners* that my mom left on the counter so many days in a row that my dad had to read it.

Many of the brightest moments of recent evangelical social activism have come from the voices of pastors and the response of the churches they serve and inspire. Chris Seay, for example, had a vision for reclaiming Christmas as a fitting time to reject consumption and consumerism rather than reinforce them. He was joined by others to launch the Advent Conspiracy (www.adventconspiracy.org), which seeks to rediscover Christmas as a world-changing event for needy people around the world. Similarly, Willow Creek's Celebration of Hope, as detailed in a later chapter by my mother and Nathan George, offers lovely, compelling evidence of what happens when pastors use their voices to call their communities to life-changing and world-changing action.

206

It occurred to me, however, this Tuesday morning as I carried the laundry down to the basement, that the most compelling evidence for the evangelical church's progress is right within my view: the people who populate my everyday life are living and creating stories of justice even as I write. If the compelling work was begun by relief organizations, and has been continued by pastors and church communities, it has now become the daily work of passionate individuals, and, in my corner of the world, passionate women.

Lindsay, our babysitter, is thin and brown-eyed, a reader and writer. I can hear her talking quietly to Henry as I write, coloring with him, feeding him. She has just returned from several months in South Africa, serving a community devastated by AIDS and poverty. Her return to the States was inspired by the desire to learn, to gain a degree in International Development, and to return to South Africa, able to create change on a systemic level. In the mornings, she blows bubbles on the porch with Henry or takes him to the park, but while he naps she reads and writes papers about religion and politics globally.

One of the women in my writing group, Lori, and her best college friend, Jane, started a non-profit several years ago called Chosen Hope. It's an organization that serves children all over the world by inviting families and particularly children in western Michigan to provide school uniforms, basic hygiene items, and other essentials to children living in poverty. Neither woman had experience in the world of non-profits. One has three young children and the other a very full-time job, and Chosen Hope has been a learning process, an adventure, and an act of faith and obedience for both women.

Another writing group member, Ruth, is by her own description a stay-at-home mom from the suburbs. Ruth has the best hair of anyone I know—almost black, very tight curls that rise up around her head like a wild halo. She is the president of the board of HIV/AIDS Services in Grand Rapids. She leads trips to South Africa several times a year, speaks at colleges and churches, and reads voraciously about HIV/AIDS globally and locally. She is a mentor and connector for people who care about AIDS in our community and internationally, and builds relationships wherever she goes—with Christians and non-Christians, gay and straight people, people infected and affected by HIV and AIDS, and people who don't know the first thing about the epidemic.

She has been a valued volunteer at her church for many years, and when, for a moment, it looked as though the church's focus might shift away from these areas, she decided that her commitment to this cause was greater than a program or role. She found that this way of living and this constellation of relationships had become embedded in her life, and that they were not subject to organizational whim. The church, thankfully, has continued its focus, and one has to wonder how much an articulate, intelligent, courageous stay-at-home mom in the suburbs had to do with that.

What's remarkable about these women is, first, that they are women. These are the same people who were relegated to church nurseries or kitchens fifty years ago, and now they are on the front lines of the most significant global emergencies of our day. In my corner of the world, many of the most courageous, outspoken, gutsy activists I know are women, and I don't think that's a coincidence. Possible reasons abound.

My mother, who is an activist, believes that global poverty and AIDS will be addressed primarily by women because they are evils that affect families, and family is the territory women cannot as easily abdicate as men too often do. Traditionally, men devote themselves to struggles over land, power, and governance. Women, however, repeatedly rise up in the face of hunger and sickness. Another friend proposes that American women have become activists because in most churches, the power roles are still claimed by men, leaving strong, energetic women few options within the leadership of the church. So they look outside the church, and find many worthwhile challenges there. I don't know all the reasons, but I do know that the women I know are passionate, educated, active, and heeding the call of justice with creativity and wisdom and intuition that I believe the church has never before seen.

It is remarkable as well that I didn't have to look far for these women. These are not people I heard of from a friend of a friend, or urban legends, or myths. These are the women I see all the time, the women I talk with almost every day. This circle of women teaches me, pushes me, makes it necessary for me to find my own contribution and voice, and if friendship does a better thing than that, I don't know what it is.

These are normal (if normal exists) Christian women. They own homes and have children and busy jobs. They're not radical, except that they are. They're boundary-pushing, question-asking, solution-creating, Christ-bearing radicals, and this is becoming, of all things, ordinary. These stories are the norm, not the exception, in my corner of the world, and that seems like cause for celebration and, dare I say it, hope.

There will always be early adapters, crusaders, high-profile advocates. We need them, and they've raised awareness and opened a very necessary conversation. The greatest sign of hope, however, is not that early adapters and rock stars, metaphorical or otherwise, have given voice to these causes. The greatest sign of hope is that normal women in a normal town on a normal Tuesday are giving hands and feet and spirit and soul to making the world better and to answering the call of the prophets, the call for justice.

Praise God that having evangelical Christian women pursuing justice is becoming ordinary. Thank God that these stories are less and less shocking, and that the practice of passionate, intelligent justice in the lives of Christian people is becoming blessedly ordinary. Hallelujah for a creative, strong, gutsy tribe of women doing what they do, day in and day out, with grace and courage, and making it ordinary.

MORE THAN "JUST US"

Justice in African American Churches in a Post–Civil Rights Era

ALISE BARRYMORE

This is the Church of God in Christ.
This is the Church of God in Christ.
You can't join it.
You have to be born in it.
This is the Church of God in Christ.

Belonging and believing have been my struggle and my story. I began to believe when I was eight years old and I decided to become a member of the neighborhood church to which three generations of my family "belonged." It was affiliated with a Pentecostal denomination, the Church of G-d[1] in Christ (COGIC).[2] The above song was one of the first ones I learned. And while these exact words are unique to that particular denomination, it gives witness to an unspo-

ALISE D. BARRYMORE is one of the founding pastors of The Emmaus Community. She holds a BA from Yale University and an MDiv from McCormick Theological Seminary. She is currently completing her Doctor of Ministry degree, which focuses on spirituality. You can contact her at abarrymore@the emmauscommunity.org.

ken ethos and understood perspective among the African American Christians who have filled the pews of many a local congregation. We were convinced that G-d had made G-d's self known in a very particular way among African Americans and that both the legacy of that revelation and our unique worship style was to be treasured and passed on from generation to generation. We were not simply "born again" by way of faith. There was a sense in which church membership went well beyond mere participation; it was about kinship, affirmation, acceptance, and empowerment. To be Black and to be a Christian (in any denomination) was to be a part of the Black Church family.

The Black Church[3] has been, and continues to provide, a safe space for African Americans to gather for fellowship, to celebrate cultural feasts and fests, to discuss potential partnerships, to plan responses to systemic and individual racism, and to exercise authority and leadership. As men and women of African descent have been excluded from mainstream society and dominant culture because of the "accident of birth," Black people found a place to belong, free from intrusion and demonization, in the pews of the Black Church. Racial-ethnic identity was the sole prerequisite for one to reap the benefits of the larger group. In effect, we really didn't choose it, but were "born in it."

This connection to racial-ethnic identity and religious heritage was so intricately intertwined in my experience that my first image of G-d was not of a man with flowing blonde hair on the back of the paper church fans that were neatly tucked into the back of the pew (and were regularly used in syncopated harmony when the crowded sanctuary was heated by both the rays from the sun and the fiery presence of the Holy Spirit). Instead, as a child, I had imagined that G-d must have been the man whose portrait hung in the entryway of our church. His was the only one in the entire building, except for that of the deceased founding pastor. The man in the picture was Dr. Martin Luther King, Jr. And it was the 1970s.

Even after I discovered that Dr. Martin Luther King Jr. was not G-d Almighty, and that he had been assassinated five years before my birth, what he symbolized for my elders and leaders could not, and cannot, be minimized or ignored. He clearly articulated the appeals, ambitions, and aspirations of the Civil Rights Movement in the United States during the 1950s and '60s. His words, coupled with the actions of those who are unknown and those who have been widely celebrated, like the late Rosa Parks, represented a call to justice that was predicated on equal access, unfettered opportunity, redistribution of resources, and racial pride. His presence challenged the status quo, demanding rights and respect for the brothers and sisters from Mother Africa. He embodied a spirituality that took seriously the cognitive dissonance that arises when one's belief in a G-d-given human value is challenged by discriminatory institutional paradigms and individual practices of persecution that seek to eradicate that very same sense of dignity. In some respects the Civil Rights Movement, as embodied in Dr. King, was a seminal moment in the development of Black consciousness that became the incubator for the creation of Black Liberation Theology.[4] To be Black and Christian, whether in the pew or the academy, was to participate in the struggle for justice—a justice that demanded, and continues to demand, freedom from ideological, socio-political, economic, and cultural oppression.

It was this call and commitment to justice that was woven into countless sermons throughout my childhood. The invocation to work toward the creation of alliances and relationships that thrived in the midst of redistributed power was so consistent and so compelling, and the mandate to action so clear, that I was often unclear of whether King was alive or dead. His was a living presence among those who remained, a beacon toward the path of righteousness. In the end, his hopes became ours. His dreams became mine. Even before I was old enough to understand it all, his message became my charge.

Recently, however, I have noticed a shift occurring in the way in which I describe justice, a change in how I seek to live in a just way. To be sure, I am not convinced that it is normative for, or demonstrative of, many, most, or even more than a handful of African American Christian contexts. I recognize that I speak from a particular social location as an ordained, Generation X, female church planter who has strong commitments to a womanist theological perspective.[5] But I do sense that this way of envisioning and embodying justice is faithful to the legacy of both my racial-ethnic identity and my commitment to live faithfully in the midst of an ever-changing, postmodern context. Perhaps it may have application and relevance with those who have similar life experiences or who are kindred spirits.

Simply stated, justice can no longer be primarily defined by the *access* to comparable education, sustainable employment, and unrestricted address that was demanded in the 1950s and '60s. While the legal decision of the *Brown v. Board of Education of Topeka* (1954) made it undeniably clear that separate could not be equal, this flavor of justice is insufficient because Blacks or Afro-Americans may have been allowed proximity and encouraged to walk alongside those of other racial-ethnic heritages (particularly those of European descent), but little else changed in the relationship with those new acquaintances.[6] Power continued to rest in the hands of those who had previously controlled them. Justice demands more than proximity of the oppressed to the oppressor.

Neither can justice be primarily connected to *allotment*, the acts of compassion that result in food pantries, clothing distribution, emergency aid, and other demonstrations of benevolence. This display of justice was prominent during the Reconstruction period (1865–1877), and continues to be reflected in both the lingering talk of reparations and during crisis situations like those necessitated by Hurricane Katrina. Justice, thus displayed, although good and right and necessary, was then, and is now, erratic and connected to the wavering emotions of the benefactor. Therefore, relationships were linked to the ability and propensity of an unseen other. Not much had changed, save that a morsel of generosity had been extended; the powerless remained at the mercy of the powerful. Justice demands relationships where the empty are not forced to lag behind the full, straining for the scraps that may fall.

Lastly, justice in our contemporary context must exceed the *autonomy* of body and the *acknowledgment* of personhood. My ancestors rightly longed for this autonomy and acknowledgement during the days of the seventeenth, eighteenth, and early nineteenth centuries when chattel slavery was the standard in the United States, and they were important early steps toward justice. But for justice and freedom to be experienced actualities rather than mere theoretical possibilities, theoretical rights must be embodied in concrete human relationships, where people of different races know and feel in head

213

and heart that they are equal partners, working hand in hand to create a better future together.

In the end, my emerging sense of justice now must broaden beyond the concerns of my racial-ethnic history and heritage, wherein justice seemed to be defined almost exclusively in relationship to what the dominant culture could or should do for or to African Americans or how power was to be wrested from the closed fist of those who didn't look like us. Our focus was on justice for our people. But justice can no longer be about "just us." Justice demands that all, even those who were previously oppressed, become radically inclusive and relentlessly attentive to the other stories unfolding around us. Of course, this is not to say that African Americans should deny our commitment to our own story; neither should we refuse the leadership roles and responsibilities that our journey has uniquely equipped us to fulfill. In the spirit of the kingdom of G-d, where the last are made first and where priorities and privileges are often inverted, we must embrace the call to move from what has been perceived as behind to a place of humble leadership from the front.

Wherever I am invited to lead, I want to lead from the conviction that contemporary justice is not simply or mostly about civil rights for a particular group but about human rights for all. As such, justice must attend to the development and strengthening of relationships that transcend one's own group. That is, justice is built on racial reconciliation, not isolation or accommodation or integration. To be reconciled is to be in right relationship, in harmonious agreement, in active association. This reconciliation is facilitated and established when we envision and embrace the image described in the First Testament—"the wolf will live with the lamb, the leopard will lie down with the goat, the calf and the lion and the yearling together; and a little child will lead them" (Isa. 11:6 NIV).

When the influential relinquish their power and resist their proclivity to devour, justice begins to roll like a river. When the weak receive the power, but refuse to use it in the same way as the oppressor, justice begins to flow like a never-failing stream (see Amos 5:24). When we who are powerful allow and encourage the unlikely to take the forefront, and when we who count ourselves experts agree to follow them with confidence and joy, we do justice—mercifully and humbly—as G-d desires. When we intentionally change our pace to walk in rhythm with Jesus, who did not consider power and privilege as something to be grasped, we seek first the justice of G-d's kingdom. With Jesus, we humble ourselves and join the powerless and downtrodden in profound solidarity. Together we learn the joy of being persons in community, in the one true family—a family that is never "just us" but rather welcomes all people into brotherhood and sisterhood, because through Jesus, we have been born into a new way of being alive.

SUFFERING FOR JUSTICE

How Can We Anticipate and Pay the Price of Seeking Justice?
ANNEMIE BOSCH

When two opposing forces clash and somebody steps in between them to seek reconciliation, the reconciler often gets crushed.[1] This is what happened to Jesus. This is what the cross is all about. If we, like Jesus, seek first God's kingdom and justice, and if we choose to join Jesus in the ministry of reconciliation, there is no escape from the cross. In the way of Jesus, only the willingness to suffer injustice can overcome injustice, and only compassion can move us to suffer to ease the suffering of others.[2] So the pathway to justice and reconciliation will often lead us through a deep valley of suffering.[3] If we have the courage to take our stand between oppressor and oppressed, we will join Jesus as "in-between people," and at times, the experience may be crushing for us.

ANNEMIE BOSCH studied theology and teaching, tried to live love (in Bomvanaland and in Tshwane), and was always committed to promoting mutual understanding, acceptance, forgiveness, reconciliation, and justice among the people of South Africa. She and her husband David have seven children, twenty grandchildren and a great-grandchild.

216

The South African Context

I write as a follower of Jesus from South Africa. With my husband, David Bosch, and with many others, I was part of the struggle against a great injustice in our nation. But our experience in South Africa, though dramatic, is not unique. Any time people of any and no faith stand up for justice, there is a price to be paid.[4]

For three centuries, South Africa was ruled by a small minority of European descent. This ruling minority felt enormously threatened by their small size in comparison with the overwhelming numbers of "indigenous" Africans. Driven by fear, the Nationalist Government wanted to pre-empt racial conflict and protect their position of power and advantage by keeping the races apart,[5] so they devised the Apartheid Policy.[6] The Apartheid Laws, applicable only to those of darker hue, legalized the discrimination that had been part and parcel of South African society since the first Whites set foot on African soil. Inequity and injustice toward Blacks went from bad to worse. (It is important to remember that this also happened everywhere else Europeans colonized other nations.[7])

White South Africans, whether of English or Dutch descent, lived in a kind of constant, raw anxiety.[8] We were taught to live in perpetual fear of the three great "dangers": the Black Danger, the Roman Catholic Danger, and the Communist Danger. Whenever White South Africans thought they detected one of these threats, they went into defense mode, which meant attack mode, which meant that anyone who frightened an Afrikaner would have reason to fear for their own safety. Many people suffered horrible injustice because of White fear. Some of us, though we were supposedly the beneficiaries of Apartheid, knew we must join with our neighbors who suffered, to work with them against racial injustice and for racial reconciliation.

When We Stand Up for Justice

Many tangled plot-lines of fear and anger, offense and revenge, lead to situations of injustice. To free the future to be different from the past and present, we must struggle to understand the complex fears, reactions, motives, and stories that helped create current unjust con-

217

ditions in the first place.[9] What fears and desires formed us? Why did we think what we were doing was right at the time? Why did we think the other person was wrong? What kept us from understanding the suffering of the other? What beliefs or values in both our backgrounds led to our conflict? What pushed us to violate our standards of fairness and compassion? If we have honestly thought, prayed, spoken, and listened about these things, only then can we confront unjust systems in a bold, nonviolent, and respectful manner,[10] always trying to work for mutual understanding and reconciliation, always upholding the cause of the oppressed.

To my mind, God's justice is love made visible. God's healing justice is not like the "easy" vengeful justice of the world. It is not primarily retribution or punishment of those who are unjust, but seeks to overcome evil with good and fear with love.[11] This is not a sentimental feeling, but a love that involves strong and unequivocal nonviolent action, resistance, and witness against evil,[12] "a craving for justice."[13]

As many of us experienced during the Apartheid Regime, the upholders of injustice can be amazingly creative in squashing dissent to continue their regime.[14] The Special Branch Police,[15] for example, would often start by creating an atmosphere of uncertainty around and in you. They would do this by first asking your friends and relatives about you, sometimes over a period of years before actually confronting you. In this way they made sure you would hear about it and feel uncomfortable and insecure in the knowledge that they were watching you. Then any (or many) of the following things might happen to you:

- The tapping of your phone at home and at work[16]
- Reading of your incoming and outgoing mail[17]
- Discrimination on any level
- The curtailing of one or more freedoms—of movement, association, speech, conscience, or any other kind
- Exclusion from a group you belong to or want to belong to[18]
- Isolation and being pushed to the periphery, or simply being ignored
- Humiliation[19]

- Economic injustice
- Name calling[20]
- Being purposefully quoted out of context[21]
- Using unflattering pictures in the press or on TV in order to make sure that many who see them will get a negative feeling about you[22]
- Losing your job[23]
- House arrest
- Banning[24]
- Detention without trial[25]
- Physical abuse and torture
- Murder,[26] sometimes through arranged traffic "accidents"[27]
- The disappearance of family members
- Imprisonment and particularly solitary confinement[28]
- The petrol-bombing of homes and the burning down of property[29]

Each intimidation would leave its mark. Each could lead to bitterness and the seeking of revenge. However, we are reminded that revenge is God's, not ours. Should we retaliate, we would only create more violence, more anger, more injustice—because violence *always* begets violence.[30] As Gandhi said, following the "an eye for an eye" approach to injustice will leave the whole world blind.[31] God, through his love and forgiveness, can liberate us from this self-destructive attitude and gives us the grace to forgive. Humanly speaking, there is no way we can forgive such horrendous suffering as many who stood for justice had to bear. Yet, without forgiving, we can never find healing or hope.[32]

Those who suffer directly as victims of injustice and those who suffer because they call for justice need to be comforted and healed,[33] but not only these groups need comfort. Immediately after the first free and fair election in South Africa at the end of April 1994, Desmond Tutu, arms thrown wide, repeatedly called out, "We are *free*! We are *free*! White and Black, we are *free*!" His "we" included everyone, oppressor and oppressed. And to the multitude in Soweto (the largest Black "township" in South Africa) where I was privileged to be, he stressed the fact that even the perpetrators of injustice needed healing,[34] and that only love could conquer evil. For he knew that often the perpetrators were convinced that what they were doing was right. For example, those conscripted into the South African Defense Force during Apartheid were systematically brainwashed; as a result, many of them genuinely believed that what they were doing in the army was the will of God. They were fighting injustice, Communism, and terrorism, were they not? Clearly, they were on the side of God and "craving justice" (as the Zealots, in Jesus' time on earth, thought they were doing, when they wanted to call down God's wrath on the Romans for occupying their country[35]). Because of this conviction, a large number of conscripts still need healing today, fifteen years after the New South Africa was born.

Shortly after this "birth,"[36] the Truth and Reconciliation Commission (TRC) demonstrated something of God's healing justice. But despite the wonderful work the TRC did, neither perpetrators nor victims were sufficiently counseled. As a result, scarred by the past, many from each group were unable to take responsibility for the future of the nation. The former victims often adopted an attitude of entitlement, whereas the disempowered perpetrators retreated into their own, bitter little worlds and were only concerned for their own interests. Attitudes of entitlement and bitter retreat both led to further injustices, creating new wounds that continue to bring pain to our nation.

For example, many of the former victims and former perpetrators have looked for scapegoats. People who differed from the rest of us in any way have been singled out as targets for scapegoating. Foreigners have been especially vulnerable. In 2008, we had many outbreaks of brutal violence against "illegal immigrants," and as a result, new anger, new resentments, and new bitterness were born.[37] Anyone who tried to intervene to protect the victims would receive the same treatment as the victims themselves. Of course, South Africa is not alone in its xenophobia. All nations across the ages have vented their fears and anxieties on foreigners. No wonder the Bible bids us time and again to love the strangers in our midst and to treat them justly.[38]

At the end of June 2008 we saw a distressed Desmond Tutu on national television. As during the Apartheid times, he exclaimed,

"These people are created in the image of God! If you do this to *them*, you are doing it to *God*!" Many followers of Jesus shared his horror at what was happening, but too few tried to do anything about it.[39] Often this inertia came from ignorance, along with a lack of practical training in conflict resolution.[40]

Confronting Evil

If our hearts drive us to confront the evil of injustice, we may unintentionally add to the injustice unless we are guided by four principles. First, we must not seek suffering (or martyrdom) for the perceived "glory" thereof.[41] The prideful pursuit of fame and acclaim—even through suffering and death—pollutes our work and guarantees that it will have unintended negative consequences. As Paul said, we can give our bodies to be burned, but without love—without that pure motivation—it means nothing. Second, we must respect the dignity of those we confront for their injustice, and even in our boldness we must remain humble.[42] Even when we are convinced that someone's behavior is unjust, we must take care to not become judgmental.[43] In light of 1 Corinthians 10:12 ("if you think you are standing firm, be careful that you don't fall!"[NIV]), we would be prudent when confronting those we regard as unjust to remember the warning of Maretha Maartens: "The seed of the most horrendous wrongs lie hidden in the soil in us, ready to sprout the moment circumstances are favorable." Remember that our attitude will influence the reactions of others.[44]

Third, we must be sure never to use deceit, violence, or any other unjust means in fighting injustice. As Jesus said, we must move "like sheep among wolves"[45] and we should "be cunning as a snake and inoffensive as a dove."[46] Finally, we must pay attention to our own souls. Otherwise, we may become our own worst enemy by harboring resentment against those who wrong us, and thereby exacerbate our suffering one-hundred-fold.[47]

Compared to many of my friends, and to countless people whom I do not know but know about, I experienced suffering in a very limited way during the struggle against Apartheid. Yet I was terribly hurt when, for example, I was fired from my job in our denomina-

221

tion. The fundamentalist supporters of Apartheid policy urgently needed scriptural justification to bolster their credibility, so they were threatened when my husband and I criticized the Reformed churches for misinterpreting the Bible to defend the indefensible. After I was fired, I became bitter. My suffering was intensified since I believed that no good Christian should ever become bitter; my self-image disintegrated because of my self-recrimination. Those pastors hurt me when they fired me for speaking the truth, but then my own unhealthy reactions hurt me even more.

It took me three years of endless talks with friends who had *really* suffered, yet carried no bitterness, to process this loss of my credentials. I learned that all of them had gone through periods of resentment, but had discovered how "bitterness is the poison we take in the hope that someone else will die." My release came when I accepted the fact that, in spite of my faith and strong sense of justice, I was just as susceptible to sin as the next person. I needed the love of God, forgiveness, grace, support, and the time and insight of others to bring perspective to my views and be healed.

There are other ways we can hurt ourselves through our reaction to injustice. If due to fear of consequences, we hold our tongue and don't speak up for justice, we lose our sense of integrity. We allow our tormenters to hold us hostage emotionally, and we trade our integrity for safety. As a result, we are often filled with a disempowering kind of self-reproach. If, on the other hand, we lose ourselves in God and in the cause we are fighting for, our flagging hope and courage will be rekindled, "for if we are weak, then we are strong."[48] So, if you experience similar struggles in the cause of justice, be kind to yourself. We all make mistakes on the journey, and healing is a gradual process, but it does happen! And what a feeling of liberation and joy this brings with it!

Confronting Injustice Today

The poor, our enemies, and our earth itself suffer today through the injustice committed by citizens, big business, industry, or government.[49] If we confront their injustice, we will once more threaten those in power[50] and they will cry out, as the people of Thessalonica did when Paul and Silas visited their city: "Those who turn everything upside down are here. They are out to destroy the world and now they are here on our doorstep, attacking everything we hold dear."[51] They will not let go of power, profit, position, or possessions—"all that is dear to them"—without a fight. If they don't succeed in silencing the whistle-blowers by persuasion or threats, they will without doubt use other tactics, like making them hurt or "disappear." So if you challenge people in power about their injustice, don't be surprised if some kind of hardship comes your way.[52]

Jesus had daily fellowship with those rejected by his countrymen— the tax collectors, women, children, strangers, lepers, Samaritans. He lived a justice so totally alien to his tradition that he experienced repeated rejection, suffering, and ultimately death. "It is of such a man we are called to be disciples. And it is totally out of the question that we shall be his disciples without getting hurt ourselves."[53] It is equally impossible that we will suffer for the sake of justice without discovering we are blessed in the process—so, even in your suffering, be blessed![54]

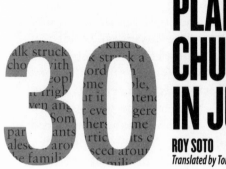

30 PLANTING CHURCHES IN JUSTICE

ROY SOTO

Translated by Tomas and Dee Yaccino

Latin America was colonized twice: once by the Spanish, and then again by North American missionary forces. We are forever blessed by the Christian inheritance of those faithful men and women who brought the gospel of Christ and opened the way for his followers to seek his kingdom. But we are also forever vexed by the unfruitful baggage they unintentionally brought with them. Those artifacts of religious colonization have created an exclusionary, condemning, and legalistic religious subculture full of odd behavioral norms and exclusive insider language that still reigns in the majority of our religious organizations.

More recently, yet another giant has arrived on the church scene, often referred to as neo-Pentecostalism. Since the 1990s this new Pentecostal movement has introduced a discourse of triumphalism, escapism, sensationalism, and prosperity in which it has condemned

ROY SOTO has served as the founder and pastor of Shalom Community Church in Fraijanes, Alajuela, Costa Rica, for ten years. He is also the facilitator for holistic mission (*mision integral*) for La Red del Camino for Costa Rica. He and his wife, Jesenia, have three kids, Amber, Naomy, and Roy Jr.

poverty as a curse. Its self-proclaimed apostles bear witness against poverty by showing off their riches and wealth. It grieves me that we Latin Americans would allow ourselves to be colonized all over again by whatever rising "chiefdoms" the wind and airwaves blow our way. The only difference between the original military colonization and the more recent religious one is that now instead of swords, the Bible is the weapon of choice.

My own background within evangelicalism taught me that the only way to do and be the church was largely anthropocentric and escapist. The only thing you had to do, I thought, was to get people into heaven. During my time in seminary, this became my main frustration—our theology offered excellent discourse but had no practical consequence on the streets and in our communities. I felt a call from God to be a connector in his kingdom, but I didn't dare tell anyone that I did not agree with this conventional style of doing and being church for fear of being hit by a bolt of lightning.

Finally in desperation one night I gave in and let God know how much I abhorred this kind of self-centered church and even told him to go ahead and strike me down with that lightning bolt if he wanted to. But instead, God gave me the opportunity to reread the Gospels and start a "*shalom*" community from scratch in the beautiful rural area of Fraijanes, Costa Rica.

Fraijanes of Alajuela was founded by a Catholic friar named James. Its name is a fusion of "Friar" and "James" in Spanish. The population consists of simple, hard-working, friendly people with few expectations in life. Its geographical distance from the city limits access to and from the community, and as a result, slows progress in every area, particularly affecting the quality of education, health care, and socioeconomic development.

Unlike many of the surrounding communities, Fraijanes possessed deep Catholic roots they were proud of, and their strong, traditional Catholic heritage kept them from "sharing their turf" with other expressions of faith. In fact, those who dared to try to establish any other type of faith community were often met with death threats and persecution. When we began ministering in Fraijanes, we suffered from a lot of antagonism, and we asked ourselves, "How are we going to establish a community of faith with dynamic, alternative theology and practices in such a hostile environment? How are we going to win the confidence and respect of this community in a way that serves as a bridge to establishing a community of love and faith?" The answers may not win the approval of everyone reading this, but in our case they worked. The best way we could answer those questions in our context was to create a community of such love, service, and justice that it would make our neighbors ask, "Why are they like that? Why do they do what they do?"

Soon after we arrived in Fraijanes, we went to the community leaders to ask how we could serve them—something they told us had never happened in forty years. The response of the main leader was, "Pick up the garbage in the streets and in the rivers because there is a lot of it." What a wonderful response! You see, Matthew 25:31–46 had created a divine crisis in our community of faith. It describes the separation of the goats on the left from the sheep on the right for reasons we had never really considered before. It seems that giving somebody food, visiting the sick and imprisoned, and clothing the naked is more important to God than the form of liturgy we had in the church itself. So our church decided to invest a majority of its resources in serving people to try to be the sheep on the right. This caused a lot of tears and opposition. Our church became known for picking up garbage and taking an interest in those who didn't have anything—not necessarily a very attractive profile for some churches. We were also known for being a church where everybody was welcome and resources were administered with justice.

As an alternative community, we began discipleship by facilitating conversations around the question, "What does *shalom* mean in our context?" We concluded that *shalom* would mean a holistic practice of the gospel incarnated in the reality of our neighborhoods. We wanted to show a different Christology from what people had previously known: not the traditional image of God the King sitting on a luxurious throne, voluntarily neglecting the pain of humankind, but instead, the incarnational image of God-with-us, consistently demonstrating that he experienced the same pain and needs as humans do. If we see God as the first missionary, coming among us in Christ, we know that God truly understands us and is incarnated in us now. When our neighbors see us building sidewalks, reforesting the watersheds, and serving them by burying their loved ones, they are not looking at mere humans; they are seeing Jesus serving in their midst.

At one point, the wife of a local farmer (and former antagonist) asked, "Why are you cleaning our pig pen and washing our pigs? Religious men like you aren't supposed to do things like that. Didn't God set you apart to do the things of the Bible?" Apparently the title "pastor" had been modeled poorly for her. We corrected her by saying, "Because Jesus would have done it for you." We simply lived the gospel in front of her. Maybe this would not be the most popular method among pastors who would prefer to not get their hands dirty, but it was effective; after a month, she came to the doors of our church with her husband, saying, "We want Jesus to wash us clean in the same way you washed our pigs clean."

The only way we were able to break with the old paradigm was by serving: getting our hands dirty with the garbage of our town, washing pigs, making coffins for those who could not afford one, and building and painting houses. Our focus has prompted many different reactions in many different settings, and I believe it has something to do with people's concept of "planting" churches. The idea often connotes constructing a building where there wasn't one before. The goal of church plants is to gather people who in turn become "the church." But the definition of *ekklesia* means something more than planting a building or congregating people together. It means having relationships with God, our neighbors, and creation in a personal, collective, and harmonious way.

We need to ask ourselves, "What are we really doing when we plant a church? Is there a secret to doing it in a way more in line with how Jesus would have done it?" How interesting that Jesus referred to those who were not yet in relationship with him as "sheep without a shepherd"—not as unsaved, unbelieving, or unrighteous outsiders. If we are sheep without a shepherd, then isn't the gay person a sheep too? And the alcoholic, Buddhist, Muslim, or agnostic? All of us are sheep, and our job is to create spaces and opportunities for those sheep without a shepherd to connect with *the* Good Shepherd.

We don't do this through some strategic planning mechanism modeled after the modern marketplace. We do it by breaking down the social, religious, political, and relational barriers that we ourselves have taken part in creating so that everyone has the opportunity to reconnect and restore the relationship with God that was there with man and woman in the very beginning. We have to understand that

227

the mission of Jesus and his kingdom is not that of one person, de-nomination, or missionary agency; his mission has a cosmic reach. Redemption and restoration includes *everything* that was affected by sin. The holistic mission of Jesus has saving purposes for everything and everybody, and brings justice and peace to all.

The church of the twenty-first century must be a "church in the heart of the community, with the community at heart." It is not the same thing to be the church *in* Fraijanes as it is to be the church *of* Fraijanes. Nor is it the same to be the pastor *in* Fraijanes as it is to be the pastor *of* Fraijanes. From the moment we entered the community—from picking up garbage, asking neighbors about their needs, getting their prayer requests, and building a sheltered bus stop so they wouldn't get wet, to becoming consultants and active participants in community decision-making processes—we intentionally inserted ourselves into the public life of Fraijanes.

The church must assume the role of the protagonist. The potential for the church to be the determining factor in social reconstruction is great. The church that reflects upon the community's situation and social life becomes a two-way vehicle for transformation: to itself and to the community that surrounds it. People were transformed when they turned to Christ, and they in turn helped us attain a new type of ecclesial life. Then, as people in our community began to follow Jesus, through practical discipleship their ears became attuned to the cries of the people around them.

One result of this two-way transformation is that we now have a community center that is divided into a vocational training school and a sports and recreation center. More than two thousand people attend during the week, and 80 percent of them belong to other religious communities. The awareness of the need for such a place came when our faith community listened. People who had been marginalized and shamed for their lack of education now have the opportunity to acquire skills for various careers and to apply for employment. They receive better salaries and can now provide for their families. We would say they are enjoying life to the fullest because the church heard their cries and did not remain indifferent.

Just as people heard Jesus on the mountainside teaching the beati-tudes and affirming the arrival of the kingdom of God, people from our church heard about the kingdom's arrival in a very peaceful way, without imposition. It is similar to when Jesus responded to the question from John the Baptist, "Are you the Christ or should we wait for someone else?" Jesus could have boasted about his title, as we are accustomed to doing today, but instead he responded by saying, "The blind see, the lame walk, and the poor have the good news announced to them" (see Matt. 11:3–5). Some may ask if that is unquestionable proof of who he was. Our answer: of course it is.

Locally, we have tried to do the same by creating spaces where people can see the church and people of "authority" within it doing dirty work as if it were clean. We facilitate reflection times for the leadership of our church (which is 60 percent of the congregation) in order for them to discover for themselves what the church's role is as an agent of the kingdom of God. This has brought us out of the building and into the streets to serve with our actions. Quite a few years have gone by since that day we arrived in Fraijanes, and today we are still the ones who clean and adorn the streets and keep the waterways sparkling. That was our open door to connect a lot of people to the Good Shepherd. Today the purpose of all of the many facilities and community services we have is to connect people to Jesus.

After eight years of suffering the criticisms of our brothers and sisters from other churches concerning our missional strategies, we came to another realization: we needed to practice justice toward other congregations also. In an effort to extend our hands to them, we organized an extravagant dinner for all of the pastors and their wives, as well as a conference on ecclesiology, mission, and the kingdom of God. Everybody came, and forgiveness was the central theme at the event. We have since channeled many resources to these churches for various construction projects and other needs, which always makes them ask why we do it. To which we respond, "We are a church of and for the kingdom, and the table is the Lord's, not ours; everything that he puts on the table belongs to all of us."

Nine years have gone by since we first established connections. Today Fraijanes is not the same community. After many tears and a lot of persecution and opposition, we have finally become embedded in the everyday life of our community in proven ways that affect its health, education, culture, and many other areas of its life. There are townspeople trained in almost every technical area, people are enjoying better salaries and are taking care of their bodies in spinning and aerobic classes, and neighbors are receiving medical attention every day because it occurred to somebody that we should do more to inspire the government to act. Families who had old, corrugated tin roofs and cardboard walls for houses now have more decent housing with better roofing and sturdier walls.

But the most beautiful thing is that all of these changes have been made possible through grassroots community leaders. And we never flew our flag or imposed any norms. We have made changes as true cultural architects of the kingdom of God. We continue on our way, which we consider "The Way." We're always open to discovering new ways of connecting people to Jesus so we can say, as he did, "Come and see."

31 PARENTING FOR JUSTICE

How Can Parents Instill the Value of Justice in Their Children?

RUTH PADILLA DEBORST

We are a "small" family gathered for dinner tonight. Three of our girls are helping out at the Women's Meal, which serves homeless and underprivileged women who drop by our church every Thursday and pick up items from the Church Pantry. Our son Jonathan, frustration written all over his face, piles a second mound of stir-fry on his plate and asks, "We talk about the poor and we pray for people who don't have enough to eat. But what are we *doing* right now?" Aware that our family schedule is crammed full of school activities for the kids and graduate studies for the parents, I groan and ask inwardly, *Don't you see we are already stretched beyond measure! What with work, full-time graduate studies, and six kids, how can you expect anything else from us?* The faltering explanation I actually utter is: "Well, there is a time for everything and right now. . . . Besides, where are your sisters right now?" "Yes," he responds, unsatisfied, "but I mean as a *family*!"

RUTH PADILLA DEBORST grew up in Argentina and shares the parenting responsibilities of a blended and multicultural family of six kids with her husband, James. She is a missionary with Christian Reformed World Missions, President of the Latin American Theological Fellowship, a ThD candidate at Boston University, and director of Ediciones Certeza Unida publishing house.

231

Think for a moment about all you've discovered about our family through this snapshot. It's surely more than my husband would care to publicize! Yes, we are eight people: Dad, Mom, and six energetic teens and pre-teens. We are active in our local church, which in turn reaches out to the broader community. We have plenty to eat, and gather around the table for family meals. And you guessed it: our table talk includes soccer moves, drama schedule, complaints about teachers, and grandparents' health. But it also carries us into broader circles, touching on why people are poor, what the war is doing to children in Iraq, why we have chosen to bike around town instead of buying a car, what else we can do to quit contributing to global warming, and why we support a certain presidential candidate rather than another.

The question of this chapter is: How can parents instill the value of justice in their children? I'm not one to believe "one formula fits all" in any realm of life, so I intend to share how *these particular* parents have been learning to instill the *practice* of justice in their children. I am shifting the question slightly in hopes that others may glean some fruitful insights so that as God's people we may all— parents and children, young and old—more closely live out God's justice in God's world.

Having been freed from slavery in Egypt, God's people had a long desert road ahead until Egypt—its materialistic values, imperial ide- als, and violent relational patterns—was extirpated from their souls. It is in the middle of that steep learning curve that Moses reminds them of who should be at the very center of their lives:

> The LORD our God, the LORD is one. Love the LORD your God with all your heart and with all your soul and with all your strength. (Deut. 6:4 NIV)

And how are they to grow in this all-encompassing relationship with God?

> These commandments that I give you today are to be upon your hearts. Impress them on your children. Talk about them when you sit

at home and when you walk along the road, when you lie down and when you get up. Tie them as symbols on your hands and bind them on your foreheads. Write them on the doorframes of your houses and on your gates. (vv. 5–9 NIV)

God-talk, and discussion about God's good purposes for the entire creation, were not matters to be reserved for "religious" moments, circumscribed to formally assigned sacred spaces, nor limited to officially religious people, priests, or Levites. God's law of justice for all, which was particularly designed to protect the weak, the orphan, the widow, and the foreigner, was to be present in family conversations, at home and in the street, in the morning and at night. Markers, commonplace symbols, everyday rituals were to be developed that would make justice an ever-present ingredient of family and public life.

Our family is not in a Middle Eastern desert. Instead of the law, what is posted on our door is a sign reading "Jobs, not war," next to another one publicizing the name of our presidential candidate. But how do we build justice into the daily life of our family?

- *Through family prayer.* Yes, we pray for health and strength. But we also remember the victims of wars and cyclones, of injustice and greed, of famine and violence. We do so every day before our meals and in occasional family devotions. We want our kids to know that God welcomes these prayers, these conversations about the matters that concern God.
- *Through family dialogue about Word and World.* When we review the headlines during breakfast, mention is made about the Red Sox and the Celtics. But larger attention is given to news about social and ecological concerns, wondering how God, the creator and sustainer of all life, might look at and hurt over these matters. And when we read the Bible together after dinner, our conversation awakens wonder at God's love for all people and also awareness of God's heart for justice. For example, we read about Zacchaeus' conversion story, in which acceptance of Jesus into his life brought about repentance, a new social conscience, and very concrete economic consequences: he promised to give half of his possessions to the poor and five

233

times what he had extracted from anyone he had cheated. Jesus celebrated these steps toward justice as salvation.

- *Through music, art, movies, and literature.* The music that streams, or bangs and thumps, through our house could hardly be more varied: from Bach to Bob (Dylan, of course), from Vivaldi to Silvio (Rodriguez), from Handel to U2 and the Guaraguao . . . The common thread that weaves through most of the lyrics is justice. A favorite is Salomon Burke's "None of Us Are Free if One of Us Is Chained." On our wall hangs a poster of a family hero, Catholic Archishop Romero, murdered in El Salvador in 1980 for claiming, "Preaching that does not denounce injustice is not preaching of the gospel." Our family movie repertoire draws very little from Hollywood and plenty from foreign filmmakers who portray the lives and plight of real people, like *The Lost Boys of Sudan* (with Megan Mylan and Jon Shenk). And the books we recommend include plenty of fantasy to spark our kids' imagination, but also historical fiction. A favorite ever since their young years has been Jeanette Winter's *Follow the Drinking Gourd*, a book about the underground efforts to free slaves in the pre–Civil War U.S. All these creative expressions weave together to shape our intuitions and imagination, to draw us back to what is important: love of God and neighbor. They remind us we are not alone in the struggle for justice but are members of a choir that spans through the ages and across the miles. This weaving is so rich, none of us is even aware that there is no TV in our home dictating what we should wear, drive, eat, or look like!

- *Through sharing in a Christian community.* From family friends to Sunday services, from youth meetings to the Women's Meal, our family experiences of liturgy and song, dialogue and action all spring from deep wells of piety and spirituality. But we also look outward, engaging in the Christian communities around us. In that context, our children see that their parents aren't *that* crazy, even if our family does appear rather odd in comparison to those of most of their school friends. Or perhaps they realize we belong to a community composed of many people crazy enough to not fit in when things in our world are not the way

God intends them to be, when God's image is effaced in one of God's creatures or in nature, when human sin classes people by the color of their skin or the size of their bank accounts, or when human life is deemed secondary to personal or national gain. I am convinced that belonging to this crazy, global and local, boundary-crossing community is an essential source of encouragement and meaning-making for our children, just as it is for their crazy parents.

- *Through living it out.* I must confess that our lifestyle is not as simple, nor is our Christian stewardship as generous, as we would like. But my husband and I have made and continue to make very intentional choices about how we earn and spend money, what we do with our time, who we welcome into our home, how we treat people, whose needs we seek to be aware of, and what steps we take in pursuit of justice in our daily lives. One image from a couple years ago lingers in my mind and, most likely, in those of my children. Tears streamed down the rugged face of a tough security guard at the entrance of our Salvadoran neighborhood when we gave him a flashlight as a Christmas gift. "You treat us as people!" he choked through his amazement. "Why is he crying, Mommy?" our six-year-old asked. "Because he's a person!" explained her older brother. Small, daily interactions like this blend in with the special occasions, prayer vigils, peace marches, and signature campaigns in which we've chosen to involve our kids.

- *Through supporting the childrens' initiative.* I'll never forget our embarrassed pride when we discovered that our children had been selling colored paper with stickers—which they had glued together at home—to their fellow students. "We're raising money," they very naturally explained, "to put a roof on Rosa's house!" Another time, feeling burdened by the many children packed with their parents into public buildings after a hurricane had destroyed their homes, our kids spent three days baking cookies and making play-dough to brighten up the homeless kids' days. Obviously, this second initiative also demanded much collaboration from their parents, who had to be willing to purchase ingredients, surrender the kitchen for several days, and drive along muddy roads and precarious passes in order to reach the rural community.

Before concluding, I have no doubt some readers may react to our parenting choices on two counts. Some may deem these choices as placing unnecessary burdens on children, who should be left to enjoy the innocence of their age, free of the heavy concerns of adult life. My response? Yes, by all means! Children need free moments of imagination and play, enjoyment and excitement. (So, by the way, do adults!) But these need not be pinned together by painting a veneer of "okay-ness" when things are not okay, nor predicated on a lack of awareness of the darker side of reality, of death and its many expressions. Children will grow up far more able to face those inevitable dimensions of life if they have confronted similar challenges from within the security and loving assurance of their families.

Our parenting style could also be judged as far too "interventionist," or as "brainwashing." I am the first to recognize that our parenting most definitely shapes our children's vision of the world, their values and attitudes, priorities and preferences. But I would ask if this premeditated crafting is essentially any less marking than more hands-off, default-style parenting that, by invoking freedom of choice, actually leaves children adrift to the random influence of the media, peers, and whatever and whoever comes their way. Identity and vocation, sociologists and psychologists agree, are constructed in the interplay of the individual and her context. We all draw on the resources provided by our environment as we sort out who we are and what life is all about. So the issue is not *if* but *what* we plant.

Incriminating as our son's words might have felt when he denounced our family-wide over-absorption in our studies, I can only receive them as a wake-up call, and celebrate the fact that the seeds we've sought to plant are sprouting—seeds of love for God and for others and seeds of the hunger and thirst for justice. Our prayer is being answered before our very eyes, around our own kitchen table: "Your kingdom come, Lord, your just will be done, on earth as it is in heaven."

JUST TRADE

Commerce That Brings Justice to the Poor and Meaning to the Rich

NATHAN GEORGE AND LYNNE HYBELS

Anita, Bangalore, India:

Even in the stifling heat, even indoors, Anita wears a long scarf wrapped around her face and neck. Six months earlier her alcoholic husband had walked out, leaving her pregnant and indebted to a loan shark. When her baby was barely a month old, the men came to collect the money she did not have. After abusing Anita verbally and physically, they seized her infant son as collateral on the $70 loan. Alone, afraid, and certain she would never see her precious baby again, Anita covered her head with gasoline and set herself on fire. But women from a small local ministry heard about Anita and became advocates for her. Now, six months later, she is in a loving, Christ-centered community that had reunited her with her son and given her a job making cotton bags for a supermarket in the UK so

LYNNE HYBELS joined her husband, Bill, in starting Willow Creek Community Church in 1975. Lynne is the author of *Nice Girls Don't Change the World* and coauthor of *Rediscovering Church* and *Fit to Be Tied*. For years she has been involved in Willow Creek's ministry partnerships in Latin America and Africa. More of Lynne's writing can be found at her website, www.lynnehybels.com. After twenty years in software, **NATHAN GEORGE** moved with his family from the UK to California and founded a Fair Trade company, Trade as One. It sells products made by the poor, those with HIV/AIDS, and those making an alternative life for themselves after the abuse of slavery.

she can pay off the loan and build a future. Beneath the scarf, her horrific wounds are beginning to heal.

Annette, anywhere in America:

As Annette tossed the plastic bag onto the seat beside her and slipped the key into the ignition, her throbbing headache gave way to a dull sense of despair. She looked at the scattered contents of her shopping bag and wondered why she had bought any of it. She had come for a single item—a housewarming gift for her best friend, Beth. But as always the colorful displays stacked floor to ceiling and the clever marketing messages transformed every gadget, every bauble she saw, into a life-enhancing necessity. And now both her house and her life are full of them: trinkets for her to dust and re-arrange and sell in another stress-producing garage sale; cheap and unappreciated toys for her kids to break; plastic water bottles and disposable plates and Styrofoam packaging to fill her trash can. And for what? So a hot shot in a big city office could pay a poor peasant across an ocean a pittance for his backbreaking labor? So a corporate PR department could finance a cover-up of a production process that mortgages our planet's future? So Annette and her comfortable friends could spend more money, time, and energy decorating their empty lives? But why bother to think about it? Annette wondered as she maneuvered her car into traffic. What's the alternative?

Half the world faces the crisis of survival in extreme, dehumanizing poverty. The other half faces a crisis of meaning in an equally extreme, dehumanizing consumerism. The church, we would like to suggest, is the caretaker of the answer to both crises.

For those of us in the affluent developed world, the idolatry of our times is the notion that the more we consume, the better off we will be. The culture built around this idol of consumerism is powered by a self-centeredness that is not merely accepted, but honored as the foundation of healthy commerce and society. While preachers used to call it greed, economists now call it "rational self-interest." It places the individual's easily manipulated temporal desires at the center of his or her own little universe. As the dominant way of measuring status and deriving meaning, the drive to acquire produces countless human neuroses. These diseases of the soul are fed by corporations whose shareholders insist on ever-increasing profits. But it is not only our souls that suffer. An inevitable byproduct of our addiction to acquisition is the near runaway exploitation of this earth's natural resources. Through the liturgy of the media—TV, films, advertising—the gospel of consumerism promises to make us happy, keep us safe, and give us a place in the world. Or at least it offers to dull the pain of our confused and over-scheduled lives. Sadly, the gospel preached by the contemporary church seldom offers a thoughtful critique of our culture's pursuit of more.

On the other side of the divide, the ongoing lack of the bare necessities of life leads desperate men and women to mortgage their bodies, their labor, and their children just to survive. When the poor are also denied access to the rule of law, their desperation becomes fuel for an abuser's fire. Extreme poverty dehumanizes and denies the image of God placed in every human being. Men, women, and children become reduced to a cash value, to be exploited or excluded by an economic machine that has no conscience.

Surely it says something about the state of our collective imagination that we casually allow these two extremes—soul-dulling abundance and deadly lack—to co-exist. Surely we can do better than this. The writers of the Bible believed that the created world, though fallen, was still inherently good. The people of God were called to "have dominion over it"—to care for it and enjoy the fullness of its bounty. Nothing in the law suggested that creating wealth from the bounty of God's world was inherently inconsistent with the rule of God. In fact, a certain degree of acquisition is essential to thrive and to reflect the creative character of God that dwells in each of us.

However, the law and the prophets did adamantly condemn gaining possessions in ways that hurt or exploited others. In Isaiah 58 God refuses to accept the worship of people who perform acceptable public rituals, but behind the scenes they "do as [they] please and exploit all [their] workers . . . striking each other with wicked fists." The passage continues with God's definition of true worship: "to loose the chains of injustice . . . share your food with the hungry . . . provide the poor wanderer with shelter . . . clothe the naked." In the society God had in mind, the weak, the outcast, and the poor were to be afforded special protection. Justice and righteousness were paramount.

239

We believe that the unstoppable message of hope contained in Jesus' gospel can resolve the two contemporary crises presented in this chapter. We believe there is a way to stand against consumerism, subvert greed and, perhaps surprisingly, use the mechanisms of the market to bring Jesus' good news to the poor—both the materially poor and those trapped in the poverty of self-absorption.

What would it look like to live out this holy subversion?

- *Limit consumption.* We would prayerfully judge between healthy desires and ungoverned greed. We would move from mindless spending to conscious acquisition, making purchasing decisions slowly. While we wouldn't be paralyzed by guilt, neither would we hesitate to take practical steps to identify with those in need, such as fasting regularly in solidarity with those who are hungry.
- *Give more generously to people in need.* Perhaps we would give the full amount we save through consuming less. What better way to strip the consumerist mindset of its power than by giving? Giving to the point of personal sacrifice can break our addiction to consuming while it spreads the bounty of God's world.
- *Increasingly buy fair trade products.* Vendors committed to fair trade assure that products and services offer employment and hope to those generally excluded from the global economic market. Purchasing certified fair trade or "fairer than fair trade" goods allows us to "vote with our spending power" for a system which demands that living wages be paid to all workers; that children be freed from labor so they can play and go to school; that sound environmental principles be respected; and that the sick, the vulnerable, and the "least of these" be included and cared for.

In April 2008, Willow Creek Community Church in Illinois combined these principles in a month-long program called "Celebration of Hope: The Hunger Initiative." Church leaders and staff challenged the entire congregation to join them in a five-day subsistence diet based on the food and caloric intake common to the world's poor, and also to limit general consumption throughout the Hunger Initiative. The money saved through reduced consumption was then gathered and used for emergency food relief: volunteers purchased, packed, and shipped enough nutritional food mix to feed 15,000 children in Zimbabwe for one year. The church also addressed the issue of long-term food security through a partnership with Trade as One. Over the course of two weekends, Trade as One and Willow Creek staged a world market in the church lobby, with attendees purchasing nearly $250,000 worth of fair trade products—olive oil, rice, sugar, chocolate, coffee, shampoo, moisturizer, T-shirts, cards, stationery, purses, jewelry, scarves, and organic cotton shopping bags. These household items and gifts that would normally have been purchased in conventional stores guaranteed fair, living wages to men and women in the developing world who are often marginalized: people living with HIV/AIDS, women rescued from sexual exploitation, and families redeemed from forced labor.

Ongoing purchasing partnerships between fair trade companies and local churches could significantly contribute to a more just distribution of the world's abundance. Nearly 43 percent of Americans regularly attend church, creating an automatic constituency of almost 130 million people. What could happen if 130 million Christians embraced fair trade as a means of bringing good news to the poor and meaning to the rich? What if we began to see our spending, not just our giving, as a matter of discipleship?

In Britain the church has always led the fair trade movement. The largest fair trade companies were founded by Christians and in many communities the local church is still the primary place to purchase fair trade items. The fair trade logo is now recognized by over 70 percent of the population in the UK and fair trade products are in virtually every supermarket. The UK's largest fair trade company, Traidcraft, now listed on the London Stock Exchange, was formed as a for-profit company over thirty-five years ago by three Christian non-profit organizations who believed that business done well could be profitable, prophetic, and just.

An African proverb says, "The hand that gives is always uppermost. The hand that shakes is an equal." In contrast to the patronizing relationships so common in the history of international aid, fair trade allows those with abundant material resources to partner as equals with those in material need. Those of us who have enjoyed table fellowship with the global poor know their creativity, capacity for hard work, and their desire to take responsibility for their future. We are challenged by their authentic reliance on God and the vitality of their faith. The fair trade transaction is not simply about the flow of goods and cash. It is about the flow of life in God's kingdom—a flow of both material and spiritual abundance that blesses the poor with prosperity and redeems the sometimes shallow and disconnected lives of the rich.

The Church is uniquely positioned to bridge the ever-increasing gap between the poor and the rich—the gap that feeds global tragedies of disease, despair, and violence. With unequalled access to both, the Church can bring people like Anita and Annette into mutually redeeming partnerships. The question is: Will we? Will we humble ourselves enough to acknowledge how deeply we have distorted Jesus' gospel by dividing works from faith, action from proclamation, social justice from personal piety? Will we understand that the only antidote for our disease of materialism is a solidarity with the poor that moves us to action on their behalf?

The North American church seems to be awakening. It's possible this apparent awakening is simply an attempt to remain relevant in a more globally conscious world, but we believe otherwise. We see evidence that more and more Christians are grasping the full and compelling message of the kingdom of God: that through acts of faith and love we can call into being the new world of God's future kingdom. Tom Wright, Bishop of Durham in the Church of England, offered his assessment of the fair trade movement's importance in a personal communication to Paul Chandler, founder of Traidcraft: "The Fair Trade movement represents a leap forward into new possibilities. It brings the biblical vision of peace, justice, and fulfillment for all within touching distance. All those who are gripped by God's promises of a world set to rights in Jesus Christ should get on board and watch their faith turn into effective action."

U2 front man Bono calls on the church "to become the conscience of the free market. . . ." Will we rise to that challenge and harness commerce as a force for good? It's true that an isolated purchase here and there will not end global poverty. But we believe that a God who fed 5,000 with a child's lunch can use our small acts of faith, hope, and love to give rise to a movement that could foster economic transformation throughout the world.

For in the globally connected system in which we live today, Matthew 25 might read like this: "I was suffering from AIDS and despair in the Kware slum, but then you bought my rug and gave me hope for my future. I wanted to end my life until you taught me to make jewelry so that I could earn enough money to leave the brothel. My parents were murdered in the Rwandan genocide and I was living on the street, but you gave me a roof over my head and a job making greeting cards. Although you will never meet me, you helped me to feed my family by buying the silk purse I made for you."

CONCLUSIONS

JUST HOPE

What Good Can Come from Our Frustration and Anger at Injustice?

DOUG PAGITT

It has been a hard couple of years since my son was killed in the car accident and my stepdaughter was paralyzed. Living in our two-bedroom apartment with the five of us has been really difficult, especially with Toni in the wheelchair. But I really do appreciate your being here with us tonight. I have looked forward to this conversation on "making ends meet" for a few weeks now. I just got a job after being unemployed for three years and would really like to help other people who are struggling.

It was upon hearing those words that I sat in stunned silence behind the soundboard with Damien, this saint of a man. He was in his early thirties and was married to a woman ten years his senior, so he was parenting stepchildren a bit older than would be normally expected. He was certainly living a mature life. He had a sweet spirit and eager attitude to find where God was active in the world and join in. In fact, it was that desire that put him on Highway 45 heading north three years earlier. He was returning to Dallas from a conference at a church in Houston. It was that night, he told me, that his van was

DOUG PAGITT'S current professional endeavors include pastoring a holistic missional Christian community (www.solomonsporch.com), speaking and writing (www.dougpagitt.com) and owning businesses in Minneapolis, Minnesota, all in an effort to find creative, entrepreneurial, generative ways to join in the hopes, dreams, and desires God has for the world.

in a rollover collision. Everything was broken that night, he said—everything except, it seemed to me, his hope. Here was a man who had lived through the kind of pain that every father dreads, and yet he had something in him that called him to keep going.

I met Damien at a meeting where I was invited to be a guest presenter. The event, convened to discuss creative ways to live a simple and useful life, was hosted by a church in Dallas that had committed to practicing sustainable ways of life. This is of course the kind of thing that makes sense for a church of highly educated, upwardly mobile people living in the Dallas area. That is why Damien was so interesting to me when I first saw him and before I knew his story. He didn't fit the typical profile. He was biracial, slightly socially hesitant, and, judging by the logo on his T-shirt, not a member of the high-end fashion crowd. As I got to know him I learned that he was high school educated and was living an incredibly difficult story. He was the sound guy at the church. He told me he would probably not say anything out loud during the meeting: "I don't like talking in front of groups, but I do like making it possible for others to talk to one another." While the event itself was beneficial for the entire group, it was the time I spent with Damien that was most powerful for me.

During our conversation he talked constantly about hope, even the hope within him. I kept thinking that Damien should be given a "pass" to be as bitter as he wanted to be. I can't imagine anyone begrudging any anger he might have at God, the other driver, himself, or the entire world. Damien was cheated. His son and stepdaughter were cheated. They were victims. But he didn't see it this way.

This is why his conversation about hope and possibility was so shocking and so beautiful. What Damien showed me was not how to be hopeful in spite of heartache, but to hope because of heartache.

The partner of hope is frustration. When we are frustrated we are reminded that things are not as they should be—or could be. We know that children should not die from malaria, and we are right to be frustrated that not enough is being done to stop this epidemic. We would not be frustrated if malaria were unpreventable and untreatable; we would simply be resigned to the inevitable. But because another outcome is possible, we experience frustration, and wherever there is frustration, there can be hope. Similarly, in 1909 no one would be frustrated that they could not travel from Charlotte, North Carolina, to San Francisco within six hours. The expectation then was that it would take days and not hours. But this weekend there may be someone who is frustrated by a cross-country flight that takes more than five hours. This is not simply because we have become an impatient people. It is a result of knowing that five-hour, cross-country travel is an option. The gap between what is possible and what is actual frustrates someone at the departure gate in Charlotte, and it explains why frustration is the breeding ground for hope. In frustration, we choose to bond with the possible. We refuse to resign to the actual. That's why the antithesis of hope isn't the feelings of despair or frustration; it is the choice of resignation—the choice that relieves the feelings of despair and frustration by sacrificing the possible to the actual.

Hope disappears when we say that whatever will be, will be. When we are no longer looking for a better outcome, when we are no longer frustrated, we become hopeless people.

Situations of injustice can be a breeding ground for hope, for it is then, frustrated by injustice, that we see clearly what ought to be. In our frustration, in our refusal to resign ourselves to things as they are, our communities tell stories of struggle, tragedy, pain, and brokenness. By telling those stories, we keep resignation at bay and we dedicate ourselves, in hope, to participate with God in the dawning of a better day. We refuse to resign ourselves to the world as it is so it can become the world as it ought to be. That is when we are buoyed to keep living, to keep looking, to keep going. Some fear that to talk about injustice, struggle, and frustration will destroy the morale of a people or cause a gloomy spirit. But I find that this attempt to mute or hide difficulty and struggle actually cuts off hope.

We will never find hope if we only tell the satisfying stories of success. In stories of success we practice being nostalgic for the times gone by "when things were right." In that way, nostalgia may make us passive, but frustration and hope propel us forward in longing, yearning, reaching, praying, working, and waiting for the time to come when "all shall be well, and all manner of things shall be well." Only through the narratives of struggle are we liberated from nostalgia, plunged into the present moment of frustration, and propelled into the future with hope that will not disappoint.

Paul, writing to the first-century church in Rome, struck a similar note when he asked, "For who hopes for what he already has?"[1] Hope is about the future and what ought to be. This is why in the history of the nation of Israel we see constant struggle. This is why people of faith tell of Jesus being persecuted and crucified. This is why in confession we tell of our own failures and collective sin. We tell of these things because we are not people of resignation or nostalgia, but people of frustration and hope. We do not fear telling what is, for we are groaning for more than what is; we are committed to what ought to be.

That night in Texas, Damien dropped a lit match of hope into my bundle of frustrations. He helped me believe that today's injustices have been booby-trapped, that today's frustrations are pregnant, and that the seeds of a better day have already been planted.[2]

I am part of a faith community that uses the prophetic words of our people as the content for the music we sing. A year or so ago Cory wrote a song that has become an anthem for many of us who are seeking, and at times struggling, to keep our eyes open not only to what is but also to what ought to be and can be.

Believe

They tell you don't try
They tell you don't cry
They've pushed all your dreams aside
And they tell you don't cry.

But I Am.
I Am.
I Am.
I Am.

And some, they feel like giving up,
As the chains they feel are digging in,
And they keep asking, "What can you do?"
So don't try.

But I Am.
I Am.
I Am.
I Am.

And there is still hope,
Please believe.
Yes, there is still hope,
Please believe.
Believe that we can change,
Believe that God is just.
Believe that we can change,
Believe that God is just—
Just believe that we can change,
Believe that God is just—
Just believe that we can change,
Believe that God is just—
Just believe that we can change,
Believe that God is just.
Just believe that we can change.
Believe.

Cory Carlson

So may we be people of frustration in all times when we know that things are not as they are meant to be. And may we be those who participate in bringing about the very world whose absence and delay frustrates us. May we be children of a hope and a future. May the name of God, *I AM*, empower each of us to be people who echo with our own *I am* . . . "I am crying, I am trying, I am changing, I am hoping, I am believing."

May we, believing, be people of just hope.

JUST BEGINNING

What Are Some Good First Steps in Seeking Justice— for Both Individuals and Faith Communities?

TOMAS AND DEE YACCINO

"Forgive me if I sound angry. I am. You say you want to help? Okay, I hate my life and I don't know what to do. I don't want to give up, but it's better not to want anything, or dream, or think too much about anything. When I do, I just get frustrated that I can't do anything about it. I have enough trouble getting food on the table every day. I work so hard and nothing ever changes. People like you keep telling me you'll help me help myself. If you really want to help, listen, because whenever I try to say something, I am shut up or shut out. Nobody listens. I feel like nobody will ever listen."

TOM and **DEE YACCINO** have partnered in cross-cultural ministry for eighteen years. Trained in adult education and community development, they pioneered integrated grassroots development initiatives in Bolivia that catalyzed sustainable community-based responses to locally identified needs. Later they moved to the Dominican Republic and developed partnerships for Willow Creek Community Church. There they helped shape the Red del Camino (RdC), a church-based network focused on integral mission. Now they lead Del Camino Connection, facilitating global Kingdom connections with churches interested in supporting the RdC and passionate about participating in God's plan to make all things new. They live in the DR with their four children.

These are Madi's words. She's a single, middle-aged woman with four children from a small rural community in the Dominican Republic who cuts and styles hair for a living. Her motto: "Life sucks and then you die!" It's a catchy slogan for a T-shirt, a terrible philosophy of life. But in the context where we live and work, the fatalistic words fit, as they say here, "*como el anillo al dedo*" (like "a ring on your finger").

It's a cruel joke to tell them "life is good" or "life will someday become what you make of it." That is only true for those who, mostly for reasons beyond themselves, have been born and raised and still live in a context of incredible resource, endless opportunity, and free access to all they could ever dream or imagine. Those are the things that instill in some the audacious belief that they *can* make of life whatever they want.

Elsewhere, people learn differently. There is no glamour in watching your baby die from a preventable disease. There is no skill required for writhing in pain from a devastating illness for which you cannot afford medicine. There is no reward for wallowing in the hollowness of broken dreams you dared to have in spite of your circumstances. And if you are feeling a twinge of indignation because you identify with the experiences of these people "elsewhere" . . . keep reading. For you may be recognizing the single most important thing about the justice we seek for others—it is intimately connected to the tears we all shed when our world is not "as it should be."

The first thing we must do as we seek to change things that are not right with our world is to realize that the very way we see the world has been profoundly influenced, or programmed, by our background, history, and experience. These are all part of a historical, social, political, and economic system that most of us grow up accepting and believing is normal and right. And that system influences our thinking and actions in ways we are not aware of, which may result in us misusing our power in relation to others.

For instance, we say we want to help "others." What could be wrong with that? We are commanded by Jesus to "love our neighbor as ourselves."[1] But since we are predisposed to think from within the framework of a world superpower, or "empire,"[2] and operate naturally in terms of *using* people and resources, and of believing that having more is better, and that progress intrinsically means economic gain, we may miss what truly needs to happen to bring about justice. When we are part of the "20 percent of the population in the developed nations [that] consumes 86 percent of the world's goods,"[3] our help toward others may appear a bit as if we are throwing a lifesaver to a drowning person we inadvertently pushed into the water.

It is good to want to help, especially when that desire stems from a genuine broken heart that hates to see other human beings living in difficult situations. But we must do so understanding that we are prone to misguided actions based on some very real limitations in our perspective that unwittingly turn our good intentions into a tool for the oppression and injustice we seek to eradicate. And although most individuals could not put their finger on it, they sense that something is "not right" with the whole setup. How ludicrous it would seem to us, for example, if we were the younger, smaller brother sitting down at a family meal, and had to wait to eat the crumbs of our bigger, stronger brother because he happened to catch a chicken in the yard that we both share simply because his arms and legs are longer . . . and then we had to call him charitable, compassionate, or benevolent because he was giving us leftovers. But that is how our empire framework conditions us to think of the *stuff* of life and our place at the table.[4]

Jesus taught us another way. He called it the kingdom of God. The kingdom framework informs us that because we are all children of a loving, just, and good Father who happens to be the Creator and King of the universe, we can (and should) all freely share at the table without any unfair advantage of one over the other, or without having to compete to get our share, or protect our food from being taken by our brothers and sisters.

But only after we make this "kingdom" shift and put an end to our old "superpower" or "empire" way of thinking about everything will we be free to seek the just alternatives available as God intended. Only after we are willing and able to admit (and by admitting, repent) that because we are in some direct or indirect way a part of the problem, can we then go forward with our offers to be part of the solution. Notice we say "part" of the solution because it is only by walking together that we all find the way, which is the second valuable step toward seeking justice for others. Mutual, genuine,

254

trusting relationships allow us to participate together in reimagining the world as God intended it.

In Madi's case, for example, what she does not verbalize is as important as what she does. She is not saying, "Feed my hungry children" or "Give me a job." She does not even mention money. Not that she would ever decline those things were they offered her, but she is (without necessarily being aware of it) simply asking for a chance to have a say in the solution. When we take the time to listen, we honor people's stories. And what we hear them say is, "Even though it sucks to be me right now . . . deep down something tells me this is not how it should be. And I have something important to say and do about it."

The only way to really know what justice means in any given case is to walk together in the problem for a while . . . and walk humbly, acknowledging that no one person, society, or nation can fully grasp the complexity of the political, social, technological, ecological, economic, and spiritual systems that underlie poverty and injustice. Jesus captured it best by saying, "The poor you will always have with you."[5] Do we really fully grasp what he meant by that? Maybe he was simply offering us a way to humbly admit that none of us will ever fully know how to fix a problem that requires all of us to seek a solution together. By fleshing it out in community, we come up with innovative and creative "solutions" that truly make sense and offer real hope.

This leads to a third consideration when seeking justice for others. We need to begin with real, local efforts that are already working to make all things new—using things at hand, on a small scale that makes sense for the context, with everyone making whatever contribution they can. Be careful, though, to not misuse your power, knowledge, influence, and money to get *your own* plans accomplished. We all know that if you have enough of any of those things (especially money), you can make almost anything happen. Again, what could be wrong with that?

The problem is that within the framework of empire, power means, "We will tell you what to do," and knowledge means, "We know better than you," and influence means, "We are entitled to have our way," and money means, "We control what happens." Our superpower tendency is to make our own assessment of what is wrong, figure out the solution, get the resources we need to implement it, and bring it all in a neat little package to wherever we deem worthy of receiving it. And while our plans may be accurate in appraising the mess our world is in, and exceptional at raising a lot of awareness and money, they are usually ineffectual at translating efforts into sustainable transformational action where it counts. While our plans may attract donors because they come in convenient, measurable, super-sized combos that claim "we" can do something bigger, better, and faster than anyone else, they rarely deliver what they promise.

The point is that we can say anything. We can even write it down into a tight, strategic proposal. We can appeal morally and emotionally to powerful, affluent, and influential people so they unleash their compassion on others. But it's what really gets done with all that potential (and how) that matters. Large-scale programs planned and implemented from people in a position of power (as benevolent as they may be) often produce unintended large-scale consequences. Simple dreams from those at the top quickly become nightmares at the "bottom" because of insufficient knowledge of the complex realities. The results are practically impossible to evaluate because nobody can be held accountable for who does what, when, where, and how. "Over the past five decades some estimates show that over two trillion dollars (measured in today's economy) have gone into large scale big plan efforts to change the world—and that is not taking into account the private sector—and what is the result?"[6] We raise a bunch of money and awareness, give a bunch of money away, and twenty years later we have to invent another big scheme to make poverty history . . . again.

What would happen if the same amount were invested in tiny, healthy, kingdom "mustard seeds"[7] that are known for their ability to grow into trees so lush and beautiful that birds can nest in them? What would happen if the same superstar energy of hunger concerts were rallied for a few crazy Jesus-followers whose efforts were becoming signs of the kingdom of God in their communities?

Over the past thirteen years, we have had the privilege to bear witness to a network of churches from the global South whose actions breed justice and inspire hope.[8] We are anxious to capture their stories in order to describe what they do and how they do it from within a kingdom framework.[9] We would point, for example, to a faith community of seventy people in Curitiba, Brazil, who started composting and planted urban gardens, made soap from burnt oil, have sown recycled grocery bags to raise environmental awareness, and have gotten hundreds of at-risk kids off the streets using creative learning methods. We would tell you about a small rural Pentecostal church of one hundred members in the Dominican Republic whose mustard seed dream of communities living in good health resulted in a program with an impact on an estimated eighteen thousand people in their community, as well as six neighboring communities. Or a church in Costa Rica that wooed hostile neighbors into their faith community by their humble and patient service to them: cleaning up the streets and rivers, reforesting, and developing educational and recreational opportunities that otherwise would not have existed. Most recently, they worked with the local farmhands whom agricultural produce companies deemed unproductive (meaning over forty-five years old) and developed an organic farming project that creates employment, generates income for community service projects, and sells healthy organic vegetables for local and export markets. We would take you to see others who have become bridges to local markets for true fair trade,[10] who are refuges for people who are hungry and homeless, who have skilled businesspeople creating just forms of employment for "unemployable" people, who provide loans for small business enterprises who do not "qualify," or who rehabilitate "unworthy" people with addictions.

These things are not happening through big programs planned by powerful people, or impersonal systems costing millions of governmental or non-governmental funds or capital from multinational corporations. They are not the fruit of outside churches or independent donors from faith communities with their own sets of big plans to fight poverty and injustice. All of the initiatives are homegrown, grassroots efforts of a few local change agents (called the local church) that are sustainable, have a stake in the results, have built-in accountability and feedback for stop-gap solutions, and have the knowledge and capacity to make things work in their context. Some have begun with as little as nineteen dollars, others with absolutely nothing. Later, additional resources come from outside churches or independent donors who give in order to multiply what they've seen happen as they've walked side by side with these local Latin American faith communities.

The difference is that they all believe they are to be collaborators with God in *his plan* to restore everything in creation to its original design through Christ by contributing who they are, what they have, wherever they are, for however long it takes. They do it as citizens of the kingdom of God partnering with others who realize they can all do more together than any one of them can alone. Imagine what would happen if we all did our part in this divine plan—if we took our place at the Father's table and began seeking justice for others in kingdom ways, if we began walking humbly with others until we all could see clearly what would really make it right, and if we then began contributing fully to the things that are working. That kind of justice might actually inspire a person like Madi enough to say, "I don't hate my life so much anymore, and now I know what to do!"

A JUSTICE EMERGENCY

Will Justice Become Central to the Emergent Conversation?

ELISA PADILLA

I grew up in Buenos Aires (not Buenos Aires, Brazil, as President Reagan once said, but Buenos Aires, Argentina). I don't recall my parents ever trying to get into my head their way of understanding the gospel. Their impact was through their example. I have images of them running off to the rehab center to have Bible studies with drug addicts just coming off the street; loading up the beat-up VW with vegetables and fruit for buyers from a poor community; and taking pots of rice and beans to feed children of single working moms at the nursery. I remember the phone number of Amnesty International that sat by our phone during the years of military dictatorship in case, as I found out later, my father was ever abducted; the cover of the magazine *Mision*, edited by my father, with the picture of the warship *Belgrano* that was sunk by British forces—and the inside article denouncing the war as a military strategy to counteract growing civilian unrest and gain Argentine support; the simple but

ELISA PADILLA is executive director for the Kairos Foundation. Kairos works through publishing, theological education, community ministries, and the Kairos Retreat Center to encourage disciples of Jesus Christ to live out their faith in every area of life. Elisa and her family live in Buenos Aires, Argentina.

259

nourishing meals, the used clothes we inherited, the open home for all who needed a hand, whether it be for a day, a week, or months. Through the years it was this molding and kneading that shaped my thinking, my values, my relationships, my perspectives.

Church molded my ecclesiology. Leadership was shared and decisions were debated heatedly among all members, with "unity in diversity" being the motto. Active participation in service ministries (not just seat-warming attendance) was expected from all, putting into practice the priesthood of all believers. Plurality and variety of social classes (as opposed to having a church for the poor, another for the rich, this one for intellectuals, the other for charismatics) refuted the principle of homogenous units. Bible study and critical thinking about the issues of our times translated into practice the old saying, "with the Bible in one hand and the newspaper in the other." The inclusion of poor people, addicts, and outright misfits was not only allowed but encouraged, following the principle of a preferential option for the poor and marginalized. Ours was a church for sinners, which put us all at the same level of need.

Interpersonal relationships were worked on using confrontation in love and dialogue for reconciliation, for our community was considered "God's experimental vegetable garden" where we got a foretaste of what will be fully realized when the new kingdom comes in its fullness. Evangelism was not thought of from a position of superiority: we were simply "starving people who wanted to tell other starving people where we had found bread." The principles enclosed in these repeated phrases shaped my conception of church from early on.

When I was eighteen I decided, against the custom of my culture and family, to leave home and attend college in the United States. I will never forget the shock of arriving at the Miami airport, a city in itself, with horizontal elevators (which turned out to be trains) that took you from one terminal to the other. The intertwining highways; the zillions of cars; the huge homes with beautiful but empty gardens; the garages so full of things there was no room to put the car (but two or three would be parked outside each home!); the mailboxes saturated every day with advertisements that called out "Buy! Buy! Buy!"; the malls, gas stations, and church buildings, malls, gas stations, and church buildings, over and over again. . . .

260

It was the time of popular President Reagan, a time of nuclear build-up as a deterrent against the USSR; of support for military dictatorships throughout Latin America; of financing for the "contras" (the ex-military guard of the dictator Somoza) against the popular "Sandinista" government that had won the revolution in Nicaragua; of support for the evangelical President Ríos Mont under whose administration there were massive massacres of indigenous communities in Guatemala; of eternal embargo on Cuba ("Communism at our back door"), and no embargo on South Africa as it practiced Apartheid and kept Nelson Mandela imprisoned.

What was the position of my fellow students at Wheaton College, the "Mecca of Evangelicalism"? They were 90 percent Republican, and most of them attended church every Sunday (take your pick—there is a church on every block!). They were virtually all for nuclear build-up and militarism to defend freedom and democracy in the world, and nearly all had a strong sense that America was "the chosen and blessed people of God" entrusted with the responsibility of enhancing goodness in the world. Behind a desk in the student center sat a promoter of the Republican Party and a poster of an imitation Rambo figure, lined with a supply of bullets and holding a machine gun with the inscription: "Support a freedom fighter in Central America."

Freedom fighter? My group of friends (mostly Latin Americans) got ahold of a three-minute video that showed the "freedom fighters" in action: they surprised a wedding party in the countryside of the Nicaraguan border with Honduras. In a matter of seconds most of the "subversives" lay dead on the ground, including the bride and groom. The Belgian journalist who filmed it somehow got away (or at least his film did). The video made our fellow students really angry—not at the "freedom fighters," nor at their government that supported them as they systematically violated human rights, but at us for showing it and manipulating people's feelings. In spite of the opposition, we got ahold of more films of this type from El Salvador and Guatemala. We started a Central America group and organized meetings to bring awareness of what was going on, of that which the mass media never spoke.

But our supporters were few. "America—love it or leave it," we were told. Our shock was even greater when we found out our Christian college was giving then-Vice President Bush an honorary doctorate. We could not believe it. I will never forget our night walk in the nearby park. I felt indignant and frustrated, and let out all my tearful anger against God: How could Christians support so much injustice? How could they be so blind? Didn't the gospel have any effect on their political and social views? How could they accumulate so much wealth in the face of so much world hunger? If that was what it meant to be a Christian, I didn't want to have anything to do with Christians. I'd had it. The end.

In the dark silence of the night something clicked in my mind. The people, thoughts, and realities that had shaped and branded me so strongly during my eighteen years of life at home came back and began to flow again. They calmed my tears, soothed my thoughts, and massaged my heart: this was not the God I knew; this was not the Jesus I had chosen to follow. The God I knew was on the side of the weak and oppressed. I was not alone in my pain: the injustice committed was also God's pain; my tears were also God's tears. God also suffered the pain of the victims of violence and abuse. God also suffered the pains of creation.

Through the years I have read and reread these ideas and experiences in the light of new ones, and have reached a few conclusions. My first conclusion is that what I lived at home and church from an early age was what has been defined for about three decades as "integral mission." In the Latin America of the 1970s, plagued with military dictatorships, human rights abuses, and an increase of poverty, the traditional and preponderant gospel brought by North American missionaries presented no relevant response to the situation. Catholics saw the flourishing of Liberation Theology, which understood the Exodus as an applicable model for liberating the oppressed from the abuse of economic exploiters, dictators, and military regimes through armed revolution.

In evangelical circles, though most sectors held on to the traditional missionary message, a minority began to think, meet, write, and publish in another direction. "How does the gospel respond to a context of poverty, injustice, and abuse?" they asked. Preserving some valid contributions of Liberation Theology (like the contextual interpretation of Scripture, the effort to respond to social problems, and the use of kingdom language, among others) and of the social gospel (brought to Latin America in the eighteenth century), they proposed that the gospel was relevant to all of life (both personal devotion and piety on the one hand and social and economic justice on the other), all areas of life (family, church, work, society, politics, and economics), and all people (including different social classes, colors, and backgrounds). The gospel, they concluded, was integral and holistic. My church experience, as I see it now, was a sort of breeding ground for this theology of "integral mission."

My second conclusion is that the culture shock I suffered when I went to the U.S. to study wasn't only about going into a different culture; it was also the shock of discovering that some people in the world live with so many more resources than the rest. Lessons in global economics soon helped me understand what was going on. I learned about capitalism, the role of international banks and multinational corporations, unjust trade agreements, and embargos. The world economic order is such that it allows 4.6 percent of the world's population to consume 33 percent of the world's resources (according to World Bank 2004 statistics). That explains the cars, houses, lawns, garages, and overall wealth and consumerism that I found so baffling. This wealth is simply the consequence of the U.S. being the empire of the day, and it would be the condition of any other nation that reached that level of economic power and military control in the world.

My third conclusion is that the evangelical culture shock I experienced had everything to do with the good news of the kingdom getting so entangled with cultural values that it had taken on the culture's image. An individualistic message had shrunk the good news to the issue of salvation of one's own little self and getting one's own life right with God (thereby ignoring any concept of community or society). It became a spiritualized message that limited the good news to getting one's spirit in tune and healed, exclusive of material reality (of course, this was usually done in a warm, comfy home and on a full stomach!). A pragmatic gospel had prioritized strategies and results over and above content and quality. A verbal message had limited mission to speaking and preaching. An American gospel had prioritized being a citizen of the most powerful nation in the world over being a Christian with a radical lifestyle and a member of a worldwide community. The gospel of Jesus had been recast as

263

the individualistic, spiritualized, pragmatic, verbal infomercial of North American culture.

This means that if your gospel is only about yourself, your spirit, your converts, and your words, and in practice your highest loyalty is to your flag (which means you do not mistrust your authorities nor question the news you are fed), you can easily live in peace, accumulate wealth, and call it a blessing from God. In your naiveté and passivity you can support racism, land expropriation, inequality, abuses of power, wars for oil, nuclear build-up, economic exploitation, contamination, and all kinds of injustice, and still remain a good Christian, because your too-small gospel has nothing to say to the issues of your times.

The question I would like to leave with our readers is the following: what gospel will the Emergent movement embrace? In recent years we in the South have been hearing about this movement named "emergent" in the North. Most Christians in this hemisphere have no problem swallowing whole anything that comes from the "center of Christendom," whether it be the whirling of anointed jackets, "holy barking," falling over in church services, individualistic praise music translated from English, or American pop sound tracks in Latin American services. But others of us prefer to reflect and learn from our past, and submit every religious import to careful inspection.

In this analysis we wonder at times if the emerging movement is in danger of emerging into a new package of the same old content. You are in danger of repeating the old paradigms of "me and God," "the poor that need our help so desperately" (and we are so good that we give it), "excellence in praise" (which means paying professional musicians to give a good religious show), "homogenous units" (because mixing brings conflict), "we know how to do things best" (and since we contribute the money we decide how things are done), and "having a successful church" (measured in the size of the membership, of the annual budget, and of the church buildings). All this is done with doughnuts and coffee, a rock band instead of organ music, bare feet instead of shiny black shoes, jeans and T-shirts instead of suits and ties, candles and colored cloths instead of rigid pews, projectors and colorful images instead of red hymnals. It's the same content, just different wrapping.

264

My hope is that this book has forged and will continue to forge a path that leads in another direction. What would happen if we saw the gospel as all it was meant to be? What if it were allowed to explode out of its restraining capsule and become the Good News for all of life, for all areas of human activity, for all people? That would truly be excellent news! It would be wonderful news about reconciliation with God, other human beings, and all of creation. It would be amazing news for our families, homes, lifestyles, spending habits, and relationships. It would be tremendous news for our neighborhoods, cities, farms, and slums. It would be revolutionary news for our nations' policies on education, health care, immigration, security, and wealth distribution. It would include alternative news for our international political and economic structures, for our world order. It would be redeeming news for our ecosystems— forests, mountains, rivers, plants, animals, seas, lakes, and air. The gospel of a new and just order: this would be the most spectacular news of Jesus Christ for our world today.

NOTES

Introduction

1. Among the best introductions to the U.S. emergent conversation are Tony Jones, *The New Christians* (San Francisco: Jossey-Bass, 2008); Phyllis Tickle, *The Great Emergence* (Grand Rapids: Baker Books, 2008); and Doug Pagitt, *A Christianity Worth Believing* (San Francisco: Jossey-Bass, 2009). See www.emergentvillage.com and www.theooze.com for more information. For more on conversations in the U.K., see blogs by Andrew Jones, www.tallskinnykiwi.org; Jonny Baker, http://jonnybaker.blogs.com/; and Jason Clark, http://jasonclark.ws/. For Latin America, see http://www.lareddelcamino.net/es/. For Africa, see http://www.amahoro-africa.org/. For Australia, see http://www.spirited.net.au/blogs. There are many other online portals for other national, regional, and denominational networks too, discoverable through simple internet searches. Good places to find additional links include: http://emergingchurch.info/index.htm and http://godspace.wordpress.com/about-mustard-seed-associates/.

2. Since then, these trends have been detailed in three especially important books: Robert Wuthnow, *After the Baby Boomers* (Princeton: Princeton University Press, 2007); David Kinnaman and Gabe Lyons, *UnChristian* (Grand Rapids: Baker Books, 2007); and Dan Kimball, *They Like Jesus but Not the Church* (Grand Rapids: Zondervan, 2007).

3. For an appropriation of McLuhan's work in Christian ministry, see Shane Hipps, *The Hidden Power of Electronic Culture* (Grand Rapids: Zondervan, 2006).

4. My friend Ron Carucci says it well: "What we focus on determines what we miss."

5. My books *Church on the Other Side* (Grand Rapids: Zondervan, 1998) and *More Ready than You Realize* (Grand Rapids: Zondervan, 2002) grappled with these pragmatic ministry issues.

6. My *New Kind of Christian* trilogy (San Francisco: Jossey-Bass, 2005) along with *A Generous Orthodoxy* (Grand Rapids: Zondervan, 2004) recount my theological rethinking.

7. *The Secret Message of Jesus* (Nashville: Thomas Nelson, 2006) was key in this regard.

8. This process culminated in *Everything Must Change* (Nashville: Thomas Nelson, 2007).

9. So many other key writers have influenced us throughout this process. The missional church movement (see, for example, www.allelon.org and www.gocn.org), drawing from the seminal missiology of Lesslie Newbigin and David Bosch, has been indispensable. Dallas Willard helped us rediscover the message of the kingdom of God. N. T. Wright helped us see Jesus and Paul in a new light—in relation to the message of the kingdom of God. Brian Walsh and Sylvia Keesmaat's *Colossians Remixed* (Downers Grove: InterVarsity Press, 2004) gave us a way of reading the Bible through the lens of justice, thereby opening up new depths of meaning and challenge. There were also Jurgen Moltmann, John Howard Yoder, Richard Rohr, John Dominic Crossan, Leonardo Boff, Rita Brock, Diana Butler Bass, Phyllis Tickle, Ched Myers . . . the list goes on and on.

10. Some of our Catholic and mainline friends will no doubt say, "Of course. What's new about that? We've been saying these things for decades, or even centuries." Again, we can only respond by saying, "Yes, we're coming late to a conversation already in process. We hope we can join you and add whatever we can to what you've already been doing. Together, we still have a long way to go and a lot of work to do."

11. I regret that we weren't able to include Muslim voices too, because our conversation about justice must include our neighbors in Islam. But one book can only do so much, and there will be time and space for broader inter-religious justice conversations in the future.

12. See Matthew 6:33 and Amos 5:24.

What Is Justice?

1. Will and Lisa Sampson, *Justice in the Burbs* (Grand Rapids: Baker Books, 2007), 26.

2. Gary Haugen, *Good News about Injustice* (Downers Grove: InterVarsity Press, 1999), 72.

God's Call to Do Justice

1. Abraham J. Heschel, *Los profetas: Concepciones históricas y teológicas* (Buenos Aires: Ediciones Piados), 77, my translation.

2. Jimmy Carter, *Our Endangered Values: America's Moral Crisis* (New York: Simon & Schuster, 2006), 179. The growing gap between the rich and the poor is reflected in the following figures: "In 1969 the incomes of the wealthiest 20 percent of the world's population were 30 times higher than those of the poorest 20 percent of the earth's people. By 1990 that gap had doubled: the incomes of the wealthiest 20 percent were 60 times higher than those of the poorest 20 percent. The difference factor is now 83" (Bob Goudzwaard, Mark Vander Vennen, and David van Heemst, *Hope in Troubled Times: A New View for Confronting Global Crises* [Grand Rapids: Baker Academic, 2007], 20).

3. Michael S. Northcott, *A Moral Climate: The Ethics of Global Warming* (Maryknoll, NY: Orbis Books, 2007), 37.

4. E. F. Schumacher, *Small Is Beautiful: A Study of Economics as if People Mattered* (London: Abacus, 1974), 20.

Chapter 1 God's Justice

1. Abraham Heschel, *The Prophets: An Introduction* (New York: Harper & Row, 1962), 1:215.

2. Unless otherwise specified, all biblical citations are from the NRSV.

3. Grant LeMarquand, "From Creation to Creation: The Mission of God in the Biblical Story," in Ian T. Douglas, ed., *Waging Reconciliation: God's Mission in a Time of Globalization and Crisis* (New York: Church Publishing, Inc., 2002), 19.

Chapter 2 Just Son

1. Jim Wallis, *The Great Awakening: Reviving Faith and Politics in a Post-Religious Right America* (San Francisco: HarperOne, 2008), 58.

2. Rev. Dr. James Forbes quoted in Jim Wallis, *God's Politics: Why the Right Gets It Wrong and the Left Doesn't Get It* (San Francisco: HarperSanFrancisco, 2006), 16.

3. Obery Hendricks Jr., *The Politics of Jesus: Rediscovering the True Revolutionary Nature of Jesus' Teachings and How They Have Been Corrupted* (New York: Doubleday, 2006), 107.

4. Micah Challenge Call to Action statement, www.micahchallenge.org/english/knowit/Overview/.

5. Jim Wallis, "The Conscience of the State: Breakfast at the White House Can Be Dangerous to the Prophetic Vocation," *Sojourners*, March-April 2001.

6. United States Conference of Catholic Bishops, *Faithful Citizenship: A Catholic Call to Political Responsibility* (Washington, D.C.: USCCB Publishing, 2003).

Chapter 3 The Holy Spirit of Justice

1. For introductions to Pentecostalism in its global context, see Allan Anderson and Edmond Tang, eds., *Asian and Pentecostal: The Charismatic Face of Christianity in Asia* (Oxford: Regnum Books International, 2005); Harvey Cox, *Fire from Heaven: The Rise of Pentecostal Spirituality and the Reshaping of Religion in the Twenty-First Century* (Cambridge, MA: Da Capo Press, 1995); David Martin, *Pentecostalism: The World Their Parish* (Oxford: Blackwell, 2002); Lamin Sanneh and Joel A. Carpenter, eds., *The Changing Face of Christianity: Africa, the West, and the World* (Oxford: Oxford University Press, 2005). My pneumatological reflections in this chapter are indebted to conversations and correspondence with Bruce Ellis Benson, Cherith Fee-Nordling, Dale T. Irvin, Patrick Oden, Bowie Snodgrass, and Amos Yong.

2. For theological introductions to the biblical concept of *shalom*, see Walter Brueggemann, *Living Toward a Vision: Biblical Reflections on Shalom*, 2nd ed. (New York: United Church Press, 1982) and Perry Yoder, *Shalom: The Bible's Word for Salvation, Justice, and Peace* (Nappanee, IN: Evangel Publishing, 1987).

3. Nicholas Wolterstorff, *Justice: Rights and Wrongs* (Princeton: Princeton University Press, 2008), 65–95. Wolterstorff writes, "God desires that each and every human being shall flourish . . . and experience what the Old Testament writers call *shalom*. Injustice is perforce the impairment of *shalom*. That is why God loves justice. God desires the flourishing of each and every one of God's human creatures; justice is indispensable to that. Love and justice are not pitted against each other but are intertwined" (ibid., 82).

4. Jonathan Edwards writes, "There is God's justice, which is not really distinct from his holiness" ("Discourse on the Trinity," in *Trinity, Grace, and Faith*, ed. S. H. Lee [New Haven, CT: Yale University Press, 2003], 131).

5. Hans Urs von Balthasar writes, "By revealing his holiness God both manifests and communicates the distinctive fact that he is God, and by doing so he reveals his name" (*The Glory of the Lord: A Theological Asthetics*, vol. 6: *Theology: The Old Covenant*, ed. John Riches, trans. Brian McNeil and Erasmo Leiva-Merikakis [San Francisco: Ignatius Press, 1991], 64).

6. Emmanuel Levinas writes, "The Tetragrammaton—the 'explicit' Name, *Shem Hame-phorash*—is privileged. This privilege consists in this strange condition for a name of having never to be pronounced (except at the moment in which the high priest enters the Holy of Holies, on the so-called Day of Atonement—that is to say, for post-exilic Judaism, never)" ("The Name of God According to a Few Talmudic Texts," in *Beyond the Verse: Talmudic Readings and Lectures*, trans. Gray D. Mole [Bloomington and Indianapolis: Indiana University Press, 1982], 121).

7. Nicholas Wolterstorff writes, "Israel's religion was a religion of salvation, not of contemplation—that is what accounts for the mantra of the widows, orphans, the aliens, and the poor. Not a religion of salvation *from this earthly existence* but a religion of salvation *from injustice* in earthly existence" (*Justice*, 79).

8. I am following more recent attempts to interpret the Luke-Acts narrative as a whole as a theological document, e.g, Paul Borgman, *The Way According to Luke: Hearing the Whole Story of Luke-Acts* (Grand Rapids: Eerdmans, 2006); Joel B. Green, *The Theology of the Gospel of Luke* (Cambridge: Cambridge University Press, 1995); and Amos Yong, *The Spirit Poured Out on All Flesh: Pentecostalism and the Possibility of Global Theology* (Grand Rapids: Baker Academic, 2005).

9. Jürgen Moltmann has ushered in a pneumatological Christology that emphasizes the way the Son and the Holy Spirit work together throughout redemptive history. See Jürgen Moltmann, *The Way of Jesus Christ: Christology in Messianic Dimensions*, trans. Margaret Kohl (Minneapolis: Fortress Press, 1990); cf. D. Lyle Dabney, "The Advent of the Spirit: The Turn to Pneumatology in the Theology of Jürgen Moltmann," *Asbury Theological Journal* 48, no. 1 (1993): 81–108 and Peter Althouse, "Spirit of the Last Days: Pentecostal Theology in Conversation with Jürgen Moltmann," *Journal of Pentecostal Theology Supplement* (London and New York: Sheffield Academic Press, 2003).

10. Nicholas P. Constas, "Weaving the Body of God: Proclus of Constantinople, the Theotokos and the Loom of the Flesh," *Journal of Early Christian Studies* 3, no. 4 (1995): 169–94.

11. Dwight Friesen writes, "In the incarnation God became human as a continuation of God's hope for creation. God's hope for creation is peace or *shalom*—wholeness. This wholeness conjoins God, humanity, and the cosmos in a flourishing life, which simultaneously honors individuation and oneness" ("Orthoparadoxy," in *An Emergent Manifesto of Hope*, ed. Doug Pagitt and Tony Jones [Grand Rapids: Baker Books, 2007], 204).

12. In his Romans commentary Karl Barth writes, "What touches us—and yet does not touch us—in Jesus the Christ, is the Kingdom of God who is both Creator and Redeemer. The Kingdom of God has become actual, is nigh at hand (iii. 21, 22). And this Jesus Christ is—our *Lord*. Through His presence in the world and in our life we have been dissolved as men and established in God. By directing our eyes to Him our advance is stopped—and we are set in motion. We tarry—and hurry" (*The Epistle to the Romans*, 6th ed., trans. Edwyn C. Hoskyns [Oxford: Oxford University Press, 1968], 30).

13. Obery M. Hendricks Jr., *The Politics of Jesus* (New York: Doubleday, 2006), 101–12.

14. For a good overview of the Azusa Street revival and its origins in black Christianity, see Cecil M. Robeck Jr., *Azusa Street Mission and Revival: The Birth of the Global Pentecostal Movement* (Nashville: Nelson, 2006).

15. See Leslie D. Callahan, "Fleshly Manifestations: Charles Fox Parham's Quest for the Sanctified Body" (PhD diss., Princeton University, 2002); Iain MacRobert, *The Black Roots and White Racism of Early Pentecostalism in the USA* (New York: St. Martin's Press, 1988).

16. See J. Kameron Carter, "Race and the Experience of Death: Theologically Reappraising American Evangelicalism," in *The Cambridge Companion to Evangelical Theology*, ed. Timothy Larsen and Daniel Treier (Cambridge: Cambridge University Press, 2007), 177–98; and *Race: A Theological Account* (New York: Oxford University Press, 2008).

17. My reading of Romans 8 is shaped by Gordon D. Fee, *God's Empowering Presence: The Holy Spirit in the Letters of Paul* (Peabody, MA: Hendrickson Publishers, 1994) and Patrick Oden, *It's a Dance: Moving with the Holy Spirit* (Newberg, OR: Barclay Press, 2007), esp. ch. 5.

18. Jürgen Moltmann has helpful discussions of the Holy Spirit as the holistic presence and principle of the whole creation in *God in Creation: A New Theology of Creation and the Spirit of God*, trans. Margaret Kohl (Minneapolis: Fortress Press, 1993), 98–103, 185–214; *Trinity and the Kingdom: The Doctrine of God*, trans. Margaret Kohl (Minneapolis: Fortress Press, 1993), 57–60; and *The Spirit of Life: A Universal Affirmation*, trans. Margaret Kohl (Minneapolis: Fortress Press, 1992), 37ff.

19. I am indebted to Peter Rollins for the notion of our human subjectivity being an "iconic space" where God speaks to us, instead of us speaking to God; through God's Word, his reign of love and justice is made manifest in our Spirit-filled lives and communities (*How (Not) to Speak to God* [Brewster, MA: Paraclete Press, 2006], 20–43, 71).

Chapter 4 A Tradition of Justice

1. Diana Butler Bass, *A People's History of Christianity: The Other Side of the Story* (New York: HarperOne, 2009).

2. Bruce Winter, *Seek the Welfare of the City: Christians as Benefactors and Citizens* (Grand Rapids: Eerdmans, 1994).

3. *Letter to Diognetus*, Christian Classics Ethereal Library, http://www.ccel.org/ccel/richardson/fathers.x.i.ii.html, accessed April 15, 2008.

4. *New Advent Catholic Encyclopedia*, http://www.newadvent.org/cathen/06217a.htm, accessed April 15, 2008.

5. Raymond Mentzer, "The Piety of Townspeople and City Folk," in *A People's History of Christianity*, vol. 5, *Reformation Christianity*, ed. Peter Matheson (Minneapolis: Fortress Press, 2007), 23–47.

6. Lausanne Covenant, www.lausanne.org/lausanne-1974/lausanne-covenant.html, accessed July 10, 2008.

7. Mission Year, www.missionyear.org, accessed April 15, 2008.

8. Christian Community Development Association, www.ccda.org, accessed April 15, 2008.

9. Relational Tithe, www.relationaltithe.org, accessed April 15, 2008.

Chapter 5 (De)constructing Justice

1. To "deconstruct" is to show how a concept, belief, or practice is a human construction, often by telling the history of its development, showing its constituent parts, or showing inherent tensions among those parts.

2. Robert Reich, *Supercapitalism: The Transformation of Business, Democracy, and Everyday Life* (New York: Alfred A. Knopf, 2007), 444.

3. Stanley Fish, *Is There a Text in This Class? The Authority of Interpretive Communities* (Cambridge, MA: Harvard University Press, 1980).

4. Jean-François Lyotard, *The Postmodern Condition: A Report on Knowledge* (Minneapolis: University of Minnesota Press, 1984), p. xxiv.

5. Micro-narratives are local stories that people hold as true or relevant for themselves without claiming them as true or relevant for everyone, everywhere, at all times. The term contrasts with meta-narratives, stories that claim to be universal in a totalitarian way. Meta-narratives can colonize particular cultures by attempting to "cleanse" them of their micro-narratives and replacing them with the dominant meta-narrative. Some Christians claim that the gospel is a micro-narrative, others claim it is a meta-narrative, and still others believe it is a different kind of story entirely—a redeeming, reconciling, or healing narrative.

Chapter 6 Reading the Bible Unjustly

1. Anders Stephanson, *Manifest Destiny: American Expansion and the Empire of the Right* (New York: Hill and Wang, 1995), 5.

2. Ibid., xi.

3. Ibid., 8.

4. Kristina Bross, *Dry Bones and Indian Sermons: Praying Indians in Colonial America* (Ithaca, NY: Cornell University Press, 2004), 4.

5. Ibid., 29.

6. Ibid.

7. Ibid., 31.

8. Ibid., 149.

9. Ibid., 186.

10. Ibid., 187.

11. Stephanson, *Manifest Destiny*, 5.

12. John D. MacArthur, "Annuit Coeptis: Origin and Meaning of the Motto Above the Eye," http://www.greatseal.com/mottoes/coeptis.html.

13. Francis Paul Prucha, *Documents of United States Indian Policy* (Lincoln, NE: University of Nebraska Press, 1990), 141.

14. Ibid., 142.

15. Ibid.

16. Ibid., 157.

17. Steven T. Newcomb, *Pagans in the Promised Land: Decoding the Doctrine of Christian Discovery* (Golden, CO: Fulcrum Publishing, 2008), 13.

18. Ibid., 13–14.

19. Hilary E. Wyss, *Writing Indians: Literacy, Christianity, and Native Community in Early America* (Amherst, MA: University of Massachusetts Press, 2003), 92.

20. Ibid., 94.

Chapter 7 Just Torah

1. Mishnah *Avot* 1.15.

2. The Hebrew root *tzdk* yields a number of words, two of which are *tzedek* (usually translated as "justice" in the collective sense of broad social fairness) and *tz'dakah* (usually translated as "righteousness" in the individual sense of personal integrity and ethical conduct, the pursuit of social fairness, and dedication to keeping covenant with God). The second word often translated as "justice" is *mishpat*, which connotes civil order and regulation and so refers to justice more in the procedural, rather than absolute, sense. The commandments delineated in the Torah are sometimes categorized as *chukim* and *mishpatim*. A *chok* is a ritual commandment for which there is no earthly explanation; we are obliged to follow it because God said so. A *mishpat* is a law that has an explanation; *mishpatim* contribute to

272

a well-ordered society. Thus, justice is a quality of society as a whole, and righteousness is a quality of an individual.

3. A *tzadik* is a righteous person. We are commanded in Deuteronomy 16:20 to "pursue justice [*tzedek*], that [we] may live" (NET). For Jews, righteousness implies neither justification nor legal fastidiousness, but rather sensitivity and openness to others. Put another way, the righteous person is one who acts with *mishpat*, loves lovingkindness, and walks humbly with God (Micah 6:8).

My friend and teacher Daniel Sokatch likes to tell the story of two people who come across a never-ending stream of babies floating down a river. They begin to pull the screaming children one at a time from the river, but the stream never stops. Finally one of the two walks away, up the river. "Where are you going?" cries the other. "There are babies dying here!" "To stop whoever is throwing babies in the river," the first replies. In this story, of course, both rescuers are *tzadikim*, righteous ones; but only the one who goes to seek the source of the problem is a pursuer of justice in the broader sense (whether righteousness or civil order). In this essay, and in the Jewish liturgy more broadly, it is this more transcendent idea of justice to which I mean to refer.

4. There is at least one Sefardi (Spanish-Mediterranean) liturgy that asks for "peace, goodness and blessing, grace and lovingkindness, righteousness and compassion."

Chapter 9 Justice in the Gospels

1. Arundhati Roy, *An Ordinary Person's Guide to Empire* (New Delhi: Penguin, 2005), 3.

2. *Narmada Bachao Andolan* (NBA), or the Save the Narmada Movement. The government plans to build thirty large, thirty-five medium, and three thousand small dams on the Narmada River, displacing four hundred thousand people in the entire process. See http://www.narmada.org.

3. Brian D. McLaren, *Everything Must Change: Jesus, Global Crises, and a Revolution of Hope* (Nashville: Thomas Nelson, 2007), 220.

4. Jawaharlal Nehru, *The Discovery of India* (New Delhi: Penguin, 2004), 62.

5. UNHDR Report 2007.

6. Ibid., 21.

7. John Stott, *Essential Living* (Leicester, UK: InterVarsity Press, 1988), 65.

8. McLaren, *Everything Must Change*, 247.

9. Ibid., 178.

10. Amartya Sen, *Development as Freedom* (New Delhi: Oxford University Press, 2000), 18.

Chapter 10 Reading the Epistles for Justice

1. Psalms 9; 10; 35; 44; 71; 94; 98; 110; 118 (these psalms are all quoted by Paul in Romans); Isaiah 11; 61; 65:17–25; Ezekiel 34; 36.

2. Along with peace, Roman justice was part of the gospel of Roman salvation. The goddess Iustitia (justice) was closely identified with Roman rule, and Roman justice was one of the benefits of belonging to the empire.

Chapter 11 My Name Is Legion, for We Are Many

1. Ched Myers and Karen Lattea, eds., *"Say to This Mountain": Mark's Story of Discipleship* (Maryknoll, NY: Orbis Books, 1996), 50.

2. Richard Horsley, *Hearing the Whole Story: The Politics of Plot in Mark's Gospel* (Louisville: Westminster John Knox Press, 2001), 99.

3. Ibid., 100.

4. Melanie Bush, *Breaking the Code of Good Intentions: Everyday Forms of Whiteness* (Lanham, MD: Rowman & Littlefield, 2004), 219.

5. It's also worth noting that Jesus was quoting Deuteronomy 15:11. The previous verse in Deuteronomy says, "Give generously," and the following verse says, "Be open-handed to the poor and needy." Verse 4 reads, "There should be no poor and needy" because the land is bountiful. Clearly, using the verse to justify apathy toward poverty couldn't be less justified.

6. Bush, *Breaking the Code of Good Intentions*, 222.

7. Ibid.

8. Ibid., 223.

Chapter 12 Just Land

1. http://mcpwt.tripod.com/freecarson10.html and http://www.leonardpeltier.net/.

Chapter 14 Just Liberals

1. John Rawls, *A Theory of Justice* (Cambridge, MA: Belknap Press, 1971).

2. http://www.newsbatch.com/econ.htm.

Chapter 16 Just Family Values

1. U.S. General Accounting Office, *Defense of Marriage Act*, GAO/OGC-97-16 (Washington, D.C.: January 31, 1997), http//www.gao.gov/archive/1997/og97016.pdf, accessed September 2007. After passage of the Defense of Marriage Act of 1996, Congress requested that the Government Accountability Office (GAO) "identify federal laws in which benefits, rights, and privileges are contingent on marital status." The GAO identified thirteen categories and 1,049 federal laws involving marital status. In 2004, the list was updated by the GAO: "Consequently, as of December 31, 2003, our research identified a total of 1,138 federal statutory provisions classified to the United States Code in which marital status is a factor in determining or receiving benefits, rights and privileges" (http://www.gao.gov/new .items/d0435r.pdf, accessed September 2007).

2. Leo P. Ribuffo, "Family Policy Past as Prologue: Jimmy Carter, the White House Conference on Families, and the Mobilization of the New Christian Right," in *The Review of Policy Research*, March 1, 2006.

3. Organizations like Evangelicals Concerned or the unofficial groups in every major denomination (like the Association of Welcoming and Affirming Baptists) are good resources for those looking for an affirming view of Christian homosexual couples and their families. See also David G. Myers and Letha Dawson Scanzoni, *What God Has Joined Together: The Christian Case for Gay Marriage* (San Fransisco: HarperOne, 2005); and Roberta Showalter Kreider, *Together in Love: Faith Stories of Gay, Lesbian, Bisexual and Transgender Couples* (Kulpsville, PA: Strategic Press, 2002).

Chapter 17 A More Excellent Way

1. For distinct perspectives on globalization see Thomas L. Friedman, *The World is Flat: A Brief History of the Twenty-First Century* (New York: Farrar, Straus, and Giroux, 2005) and Richard Falk, *Predatory Globalization: A Critique* (Cambridge: Polity Press, 1999).

2. For serious attempts to present the complexity of the debate from multiple viewpoints, see William W. Chip and Michael A. Scaperlanda, "The Ethics of Immigration: An Exchange," *First Things* (May 2008): 40–46 and Carol M. Swain, ed., *Debating Immigration* (Cambridge: Cambridge University Press, 2007).

3. Martin Luther King Jr., *Where Do We Go from Here: Chaos or Community?* (Boston: Beacon Press, 1967). The fundamental query about any movement, its struggles, and its legacies should also deeply inform any national dialogue on immigration.

4. See Patricia Fernández-Kelly, "To Welcome the Stranger: The Myths and Realities of Illegal Immigration," *Perspectivas: Occasional Papers*, Issue Ten (2006): 9–22. See also Steven A. Camarota, "Immigrant Employment Gains and Native Losses, 2000–2004" in *Debating Immigration*, ed. Carol M. Swain (Cambridge: Cambridge University Press, 2007).

5. Although not a biblical scholar, conservative think-tank fellow James R. Edwards presents this view ("A Biblical Perspective on Immigration Policy," in *Debating Immigration*).

6. See Brian McLaren, *Everything Must Change: Jesus, Global Crisis and a Revolution of Hope* (Nashville: Thomas Nelson, 2007).

7. For a thorough outline of how trade agreements and immigrant and native employment are inextricably linked, see Douglas S. Massey, "Borderline Madness" and Steven A. Camarota, "Immigrant Employment Gains and Native Losses, 2000–2004," both in *Debating Immigration*.

8. I make this argument elsewhere. See Gabriel Salguero, "Multicultural Ministry: A Vision of Multitude," in *Perspectivas: Occasional Papers* 7 (2003): 86. See also Elizabeth Conde-Frazier, "A Spirituality for Multicultural Ministry," in ibid., 63.

9. Geraldo Rivera, *HisPanic: Why Americans Fear Hispanics in the U.S.* (New York: Celebra Books, 2008).

10. For a good summary of some of the most extreme positions and anti-immigrant hate speech, see the Anti-Defamation League's website, particularly the Civil Rights page, at http://www.adl.org/Civil_Rights/immigration.asp.

11. Craig Wong, "The Church's 'Third Rail' of Immigration," *Prism*, vol. 15, no. 3 (2008): 31.

12. I am using the neo-logism "Unitedstatesian" as a translation of *Estadounidense*. I do this as a linguistic acknowledgment that to use the word *American* to define only people living in the U.S. is to ignore that people living in other parts of North America, South America, and the Caribbean are also "American." Collapsing the word *American* solely into the U.S. context may be unhelpful to the dialogue on globalization and immigration.

13. For two great treatises from both a Catholic and Protestant perspective, see the United States Conference of Catholic Bishops, *Strangers No Longer: Together on the Journey of Hope* at http://www.usccb.org/mrs/stranger.shtml. See also M. Daniel Carroll R., *Christians at the Border: Immigration, the Church, and the Bible* (Grand Rapids: Baker Academic, 2008).

14. Reading postcolonially is a hermeneutic, or "optic," that recognizes the influence of empire, power, and imperial ideologies and their interplay with colonies and the colonized, as well as the irruption of the voices of the colonized, neo-colonized, or formerly colonized. There is a fertile list of postcolonial biblical readings and theologies. See, among others, R. S. Sugirtharajah, *Postcolonial Criticism and Biblical Criticism* (New York: Oxford University Press, 2002); Catherine Keller, Michael Nausner, and Mayra Rivera, *Postcolonial Theologies: Divinity and Empire* (St. Louis: Chalice Press, 2004); Musa W. Dube, *Postcolonial Feminist Interpretation of the Bible* (St. Louis, MO: Chalice Press, 2000); Richard Horsley, ed., *The Postcolonial Bible* (Sheffield: Sheffield Academic Press, 1998); and Fernando Segovia, ed.,

Interpreting Beyond Borders: The Bible and Postcolonialism 3 (Sheffield: Sheffield Academic Press, 2000).

15. I am borrowing from African theologian Engelbert Mveng's term "anthropological poverty." He speaks of a poverty that robs peoples of dignity, rights, economic access, etc. See Engelbert Mveng, "Third World Theology—What Theology? What Third World?: Evaluation by an African Delegate," in *Irruption of the Third World: Challenge to Theology*, ed. Virginia M. M. Fabella and Sergio Torres (Maryknoll, NY: Orbis Books, 1983), 217–21.

16. Edgardo Colon-Emeric, untitled presentation at the Sociedad Wesleyana's Durham Consultation on Hispanic Ministries, Duke University Divinity School, Durham, North Carolina, March 13, 2008.

17. Ibid. Colon-Emeric suggests a fresh interpretation of Stanley Hauerwas and William Willimon's seminal book in Christian ethics: Christians are not "resident aliens," but illegal aliens. See Stanley Hauerwas and William H. Willimon, *Resident Aliens: Life in the Christian Colony* (Nashville: Abingdon Press, 1989).

18. René Padilla, "Imperial Globalization and Integral Mission," *The Princeton Seminary Bulletin*, vol. 27, no. 1, new series (2006): 16.

19. See Michael Hardt and Antonio Negri, *Empire* (Cambridge, MA: Harvard University Press, 2000) and *Multitude: War and Democracy in the Age of Empire* (New York: Penguin Press, 2004).

20. In a conversation with Bishop Wenski of Orlando, Florida, at the National Faith Leader Roundtable on Immigration, March 10, 2008. Bishop Wenski cautions against the assumption that because something is legal it is necessarily moral. Good historical examples are the questioning of segregation, slavery laws, and South African apartheid.

Chapter 18 Just Perspectives

1. Tim Stafford, "Faith in God or in the Military?: Where Does a Weak Nation Turn for Help?" in *The Student Bible, New International Version* (Grand Rapids, MI: Zondervan, 1996), 726.

2. For more on cultures and economies of scale, read Bill McKibben's *Deep Economy: The Wealth of Communities and the Durable Future* (New York: Times Books, 2007).

3. Paul Hawken, "Indigene," in *Blessed Unrest: How the Largest Movement in the World Came into Being and Why No One Saw It Coming* (New York: Viking, 2007), 87–114.

4. "Who is our neighbor?" See Luke 10:25–37.

5. Office Cantonal de la Statistique, "Bilan et état de la population du canton de Genève en 2007: Résultats de la statistique cantonal de la population," Republique et Canton de Genève, http://www.geneve.ch/statistique/publications/pdf/2008/resultats/dg-rs-2008-05.pdf.

6. Geneva Economic Development Office, "International and Non-Governmental Organizations," http://www.geneva.ch/IGO.htm.

7. See Martin Meredith, *The Fate of Africa from the Heroes of Freedom to the Heart of Despair: A History of 50 Years of Independence* (New York: Public Affairs, 2005) for examples of injustices that the U.S. has supported.

8. See Will Hutton, *The World We're In* (London: Abacus, 2003). This book is part of the national dialogue in the UK about whether it should side more with the EU (and the European way of life) or with the U.S. (and the American way of life). The reader should note that the first two chapters can be received as quite anti-American, but the rest of the book is well worth the read.

9. Basler Mission and EMW, *Thuma mina: Internationales Ökumenisches Liederbuch/ International Ecumenical Hymnbook* (Munich: Strube Verlag, 1995). Maggie Hamilton and Päivi Jussila, eds., *Agape: Songs of Hope and Reconciliation/Lieder der Hoffnung und Versöhnung/Chants d'espérance et de réconciliation/Cantos de esperanza y reconciliación* (Oxford: Lutheran World Federation, 2003).

10. International Rescue Committee, http://www.theirc.org/what/resettlement_in_the_ united_states.html.

11. Type "Catholic Social Services" and your state into a search engine, and you'll find the website you need.

12. Thanks to Marius Brand in Cape Town, South Africa, for this recommendation.

13. The World Council of Churches, "In God's Hands: The Ecumenical Prayer Cycle," http://www.oikoumene.org/en/resources/prayer-cycle.html.

14. Matthew 5:43–45.

Chapter 19 Just Wealth

1. It was to Zacchaeus's advantage that in the first century there was no fixed tax for merchandise passing through customs. Tax collectors like Zacchaeus took advantage of this imprecision to commit fraud and extortion.

2. The law (Lev. 6:1–5; Num. 5:7) required that in certain cases of restitution, one-fifth of the money received unjustly was to be paid in addition to the restitution; in other cases, a double restitution was required (Exod. 22:4, 7, 9).

3. "Bendice Señor, nuestro pan" is a song and prayer by Federico Padura of Argentina, translation by Donald Wetherick. Sheet music published in Basler Mission and EMW, *Thuma mina: Internationales Ökumenisches Liederbuch/International Ecumenical Hymnbook* (Munich: Strube Verlag, 1995). The song is recorded by John Bell of the Iona Community with the Wild Goose Worship Group on the CD *Love and Anger: Songs of Lively Faith and Social Justice* (Chicago: GIA Publications).

Chapter 20 The Business of Justice

1. Rhett A. Butler, "Largest Corporations Agree to Cut Global Warming Emissions," http://news.mongabay.com/2007/0220-climate.html, accessed May 19, 2009.

2. Gaylord Nelson, Susan M. Campbell, and Paul A. Wozniak, *Beyond Earth Day: Fulfilling the Promise* (Madison, WI: University of Wisconsin Press, 2002), 18.

3. David Whyte, *Crossing the Unknown Sea* (New York: Riverhead Books, 2001), 24.

Chapter 22 Just Religion

1. 1 Corinthians 13:12.

2. Eboo Patel, a founder of Interfaith Youth Core, argues that whereas the fault line of exclusion in twentieth century America was race, the fault line in the twenty-first century will be religion.

3. See my chapter "The Sweet Problem of Inclusiveness: Finding Our God in the Other," in Doug Pagitt and Tony Jones, eds., *An Emergent Manifesto of Hope* (Grand Rapids: Baker Books, 2007), 189–99.

4. Paul F. Knitter's book *Introducing Theologies of Religion* is a good introduction to the discussion (Maryknoll, NY: Orbis Books, 2002).

5. http://religions.pewforum.org/reports.

6. Alexander Solzhenitsyn, *The Gulag Archipelago: 1918–1956* (New York: Harper, 2002), 75.

7. Luke 10:25-41.

Chapter 23 Just Cities

1. See Thich Nhat Hanh, *Being Peace* (Berkley: Parallax Press, 1996), 83–105.

2. See Marcus J. Borg and John Dominic Crossan, *The Last Week: What the Gospels Really Teach about Jesus' Final Days in Jerusalem* (San Francisco: HarperSanFrancisco, 2006), 1–31.

Chapter 24 Justice in the Slums

1. It is only after doing justice, reproaching the oppressor, and defending the weak and vulnerable that liturgy takes on its true meaning and worth. See, for example, the first chapter of Isaiah.

2. I use this term in reference to the innumerable Socializing Plans of the current government, most of which are inefficient, irrelevant, and designed only to catch votes.

Chapter 25 Just Suburbs

1. http://www.sierraclub.org/communities/2002report/north_carolina/.

2. http://www.theatlantic.com/doc/200803/subprime.

3. Brian McLaren, "Meditation," in *Justice in the Burbs: Being the Hands of Jesus Wherever You Live* (Grand Rapids: Baker Books, 2007).

4. Check out the site "I Love Mountains" (http://www.ilovemountains.org/) where you can enter your zip code and learn your connection to coal, even if that coal seems far removed from you.

5. World Health Organization, "Noncommunicable Diseases Now Biggest Killers," http://www.who.int/mediacentre/news/releases/2008/pr14/en/index.html, accessed March 11, 2008.

6. To learn more about where your food comes from, check out the Food Routes website: http://www.foodroutes.org/.

Chapter 26 Just Countryside

1. Michael Pollan, "You Are What You Grow," *New York Times Magazine*, April 22, 2007.

Chapter 28 More than "Just Us"

1. Note: Except for direct quotes from authors, I avoid writing out the name for YHWH (both privately and publicly) as a personal, if not meager, attempt to honor the holy name.

2. Founded by Charles Mason and born out of the historic and multicultural Azusa Street revivals of the late-nineteenth century, the COGIC represents the origins of Pentecostalism in the black church tradition.

3. The Black Church has been defined as (1) those eclusively black congregations that have arisen within mainline denominations; and (2) those communities of faith and denominations that have sprung up independently among people of African descent. In the end, the Black Church is any of the unique expressions of Christian faith as interpreted, expressed,

and lived by African Americans. See C. Eric Lincoln and E. Franklin Frazier's *The Negro Church and the Black Church Since Frazier* (New York: Schocken Books, 1974).

4. See James Cone, *For My People: Black Theology and the Black Church* (Maryknoll, NY: Orbis Books, 1989).

5. The term "womanist" was coined by Alice Walker's *In Search of Our Mother's Garden: Womanist Prose* (San Diego: Harcourt Brace Jovanovich, 1983). For a discussion of the tri-dimensional experience of racism, sexism, and classism and the worldview that arises as a result of these challenges among African American women, see Jacquelyn Grant, "White Women's Christ and Black Women's Jesus," *Journal of the American Academy of Religion* 64 (1989).

6. The terms "black" and "African American" are used almost synonymously, but the terms "colored," "negro," and "Afro-American" are used to mimic and mirror the language of the respective era.

Chapter 29 Suffering for Justice

1. H. R. Weber, quoted by David J. Bosch, "Processes of Reconciliation and Demands of Obedience—Twelve Theses," in *Hammering Swords into Ploughshares: Essays in Honour of Archbishop Mpilo Desmond Tutu* (Johannesburg: Skotaville Publishers, 1986), 164.

2. David J. Bosch, *Renewal of Christian Community in Africa Today*, message shared at PACLA I, Nairobi, Kenya, 1976. See also Desmond M. Tutu quoted by Simon Maimela in *Ploughshares*, 47–48.

3. Simon Maimela, *Ploughshares*, 49–50.

4. I take it as a given that there are many people of every and no faith who work for justice in their own context. Regrettably, Christians have often believed that they alone can do so. See also David J. Bosch, *A Spirituality of the Road* (Eugene: Wipf and Stock, 2001), 37.

5. Some of their leaders, including H. F. Verwoerd, studied in Germany at a time when the ideas that led to Nazism were starting to develop. Some think that this could have been a contributing factor to the development of Apartheid Policy.

6. For more about this idea, see David J. Bosch, *Transforming Mission: Paradigm Shifts in Theology of Mission* (Maryknoll, NY: Orbis Books, 1991), 299. The idea of the "super race" found a place in the church when Afrikaners identified themselves with the old Israel, chosen for a particular destiny. Each of the Western countries colonizing territories in the rest of the world did this as well, and, in a sense, it was also done by the liberation theologies, such as South African "Black Theology."

7. Bosch, *Transforming Mission*, 299.

8. During the two years prior to the *South African Christian Leadership Assembly* (SACLA) in 1979, we met every second month to prepare. Two things surfaced in every single meeting and again during the Assembly: black bitterness and white fear. The blacks were angry about discrimination and oppression, and the whites set up the Apartheid system out of their fear of being engulfed by the blacks and losing their identity, language, and land. It was at SACLA that, for the first time in the history of South Africa, such a great number (five thousand during the week and seven thousand over the weekend) from all races, churches, ages, languages, and cultures gathered for a week to try to understand each other and listen to what the Spirit was telling us about our lifestyle, politics, and work for justice and reconciliation.

9. More about this in my article "Memory and Forgiveness: Vehicles for Christian Reconciliation," in *Theologically Speaking*, October 1999.

10. Matthew 5:44–48; Luke 6:35.

11. We have a choice: an eye for an eye, or the Jesus way (Brian D. McLaren, *Everything Must Change: Jesus, Global Crises, and a Revolution of Hope* [Nashville: Thomas Nelson, 2007], 189). We can change both the way "we" live *and* the way "they" live, refuse to follow Donald Rumsfeld's thinking when defending "the war on terror": that we choose to change "their way of living" and not ours.

12. Maimela, *Ploughshares*, 42, 52. Tutu was "regarded as a 'political priest' for doing what the Bible teaches," i.e., working against evil. The Bible, then, he told the Apartheid Government, must be subversive.

13. McLaren, *Everything Must Change*, 183.

14. "Suffering for the sake of God (justice) and for that of the Gospel is an inescapable part of being a disciple" (Maimela, *Ploughshares*, 50).

15. The Special Branch was a much feared police unit often used to attack or intimidate individuals and movements resisting Apartheid. This branch of the police was also called the "Secret Police" or the "Security Police." It is rather ironic that, more often than not, it was the "Security Police" that made us feel *insecure*!

16. We learned anew how God sometimes moves in mysterious ways to protect his children when, in a roundabout way, we found out that the phones at the office and at home were tapped. We therefore were able to warn those who were underground to not call us on those lines.

17. It was obvious what was happening when the daily letter my husband used to write me during his frequent times away stopped being delivered regularly. Suddenly ten letters, written on consecutive dates, would arrive on the same day. We were delighted and amused— and somehow gratified by discovering that the "Secret Police" were also fallible. Once our friend Nico Smith, who had a post office box in a suburb far from our place, called us to say he had found in his mail a letter addressed to us at our *street address*! There was only *one* way it could have landed there!

18. If some in the group you belong to harbor any strong fears concerning the reason for the wrongs you are speaking against, they tend to spread rumors and stir up fear, which naturally leads to you being excluded, isolated, pushed to the periphery, or ignored.

19. An example of humiliation occurred when we held what was called a "Christian encounter." As a witness to the rest of the country, the more than two hundred whites attending the encounter were hosted by black families in what was then called a black township. A young black activist pastor was hosting a young white pastor. They were both ministers of the Reformed Church. The Special Branch, which knew about the whole arrangement, raided the house one night. Both young men were taken to the police cells. There the young white man was threatened that if he said anything in defense of the young black man, they would tell the press that they had found them together in bed. The threat of what was for him unspeakable humiliation was enough to intimidate the young white man into submission. Some days later, he was released. His friend was kept in custody without trial for seven months! This is an example of how someone wholeheartedly working for justice can be intimidated into committing injustice himself.

20. See how Jesus warns his disciples about "even small expressions of aggression like name-calling" (McLaren, *Everything Must Change*, 185). Some grassroots people use hate talk to dehumanize others simply because they cannot contain the threat they feel. But the political leaders and the Special Branch used it as a dangerous, finely honed tool.

21. During the early 1970s Beyers Naudé, the well-known Afrikaner minister of the Dutch Reformed Church, warned the Apartheid Government that if they did not change their policy, there would be blood flowing in the streets of Johannesburg. The report in the news media said that he had threatened to instigate violence, which would make blood flow

in the streets. It was just enough fact to make the fiction seem true and sow suspicion, even with those who knew Naudé as a nonviolent man.

22. For more information, go to the newspaper archives from the Apartheid era and look at pictures of political activists and people calling for justice. Then compare them to the pictures of the same people used in the press today, and it will be more than clear what is meant by this.

23. Later in this chapter I relate the story of how I lost my job.

24. Many people were banned, which meant they were not to be with more than one person at a time; were forbidden to attend meetings; could not preach, address groups, or give speeches; and had to report at the nearest police station once a day (in some cases once a week). Beyers Naudé was banned, and so was Winnie Mandela, who at that time was married to Nelson Mandela. Both, in their own spheres, did wonderful work for justice, despite living under the banning order.

25. A good friend, the Rev. Caesar Molebatse, like an untold number of others, was detained without trial. He was kept in solitary confinement in only his underpants. According to the law, even prisoners in solitary confinement were allowed to have a Bible, but the police at the Sunnyside Police Station in Pretoria denied him the privilege. The captain of this police station grew very aggressive when my husband, David, went every day to enquire about our friend.

During 1987 multitudes of children under the age of eighteen, who previously could not be arrested lawfully, were detained without trial. It was said that this was "for their protection" since the older teenagers, who could be charged when violating a law, instructed children between ages eleven and fifteen to act on their behalf during consumer boycotts. These boycotts were organized in defiance of the Apartheid Government, but because everything was more expensive in the black townships (because the local businesses were so small), many adults ignored the boycotts. They shopped instead at large chain stores in town where goods cost less. The older teenagers organized the children to check on all adults with grocery bags arriving on the buses into the townships. The children forced the adults to empty bags of maize meal, sugar, and bottles of cooking oil onto the dusty streets. In some cases, the adults were forced to eat the dry meal or to drink a whole bottle of cooking oil, with dire results. Once more, this is an example of working for justice and yet committing injustice in the process.

26. Steve Biko was banned in 1973, and four years later was tortured and murdered by the Apartheid Government for standing for the rights of blacks. He is one of the main icons of the struggle against Apartheid and for the humanity and dignity of blacks in their own right. He introduced "black consciousness" to South Africa, and used the phrase "black is beautiful," which he described as meaning: "Man, you are okay as you are, begin to look upon yourself as a human being." Ironically, though we agreed with these slogans, they led to what my husband, David, and I experienced as our worst suffering during the time of Apartheid: being rejected by our black friends because we, as whites, could never escape benefiting from the very same system that oppressed them.

27. Two sons of a pastor friend of ours died in such an "accident" when a police van struck them as they were returning home from a youth meeting at their church.

28. Despite the law at that time that stated that no person could be kept in solitary confinement for longer than ten days, our friend and co-worker Stanley Mogoba was kept there for three months and then served a sentence of nine years on Robben Island. After his release he was banned to a remote area in the northern part of South Africa, where his mother tongue was not spoken. Like many other people who also suffered extreme injustice during that time, Stanley harbored no bitterness and instead worked for justice, reconciliation, mutual acceptance, forgiveness, and peace.

281

29. White men with blackened faces traveled around a black township in white cars, petrol-bombing homes. Among the homes hit was that of yet another friend, Lukas Mabusela. One of his children slept beneath a window and was severely burned when a petrol bomb struck the burglar bars and splashed onto his bed. Similarly disguised white men later caused terror on the suburban trains when they randomly threw people, on their way to or from work, from the moving suburban trains.

30. Allan Boesak in *Ploughshares*, 279–88, especially 287–88. Dr. Boesak is a Reformed minister who, in 1984, formed the United Democratic Front (UDF) and challenged a government that was making merely cosmetic political changes. At the same time he continued calling for all the UDF members to never resort to violence. "Martin Luther King describes violence as begetting the thing it seeks to destroy. Instead of diminishing violence, it multiplies it" (McLaren, *Everything Must Change*, 191). "Through violence you may murder the murderer, but you can't murder murder" (ibid., 322).

31. More about this in the last part of this chapter.

32. Annemie Bosch, "Memory and Forgiveness."

33. Ibid.

34. Matthew 9:12; Mark 2:17; Luke 5:31. Annemie Bosch, "Memory and Forgiveness."

35. Luke 4:16–32. The reason why the people of Nazareth wanted to kill Jesus was the fact that he stopped reading from the passage in Isaiah 61 in the middle of a sentence, after the proclamation of "the year of the Lord's favor," and left out the announcement of "the day of vengeance of our God." The latter was what they craved—that is, for God to destroy the Romans.

36. "Despite the miraculous birth of the New South Africa . . . , the "child" has become *very* sick indeed!" (Annemie Bosch in a personal letter to G. Prové dated July 9, 2008).

37. Compare this, and the next paragraph, with what Tutu says about the treatment of blacks by the Apartheid system: "It . . . treats people as if they are a set of statistics to be juggled around, it uproots and dumps bearers of God's image, as if they were dirt . . ." (quoted by Simon Maimela in *Ploughshares*, 50).

38. "Remember, you yourselves were once foreigners in the land of Egypt" (Exod. 22:21 NLT; see also Matt. 25:35).

39. G. Prové is a Roman Catholic sister from the Netherlands who has been involved in mission and working for justice all her life. During the latter part of her ministry she has worked with people suffering with HIV and AIDS. In a personal letter, filled with gratitude and hope, dated May 20, 2008, she writes, "Lately, as I am aging . . . I become more and more aware how many hear the Word, and how very few *live* it. And yet, the number of those who honestly try to live it is growing: they are weaving a worldwide web/community of believers and slowly, slowly transformation is taking place.

"It takes a long period to experience this, but it is such a nice gift of growing old, to see that something has really changed for the better. I had such an experience last week in my local church community. We had a shared reflection on justice and peace with our Moslem brothers and sisters, mainly younger Moslems who already were organized in a group around the theme 'child and environment' since they needed support in the education of their children in this difficult and dangerous environment of the tumultuous city of Amsterdam. It was an excellent evening, after a brief introduction on what our respective books were saying about justice and peace (our priest for the Bible, a young imam for the Koran) there was an open exchange in which everybody participated, also shared how they try to live this commitment to justice.

"I recalled how some twenty years ago we had great difficulty to come to a real exchange on what it meant to be a multi-cultural community among Christians! This evening held a promise for the future, rekindled hope! Of course, all on a very small scale, and among only a few people, but at least real and tangible."

40. For many years Bob and Alice Evans of the Plowshares Institute in Hartford, Connecticut, came to South Africa and, through the University of Cape Town, offered courses in conflict resolution—i.e., mediating, arbitrating, healing, reconciliation, and in the run-up to the 1994 elections, education for democracy. We still urgently need this kind of training nationwide.

41. McLaren says, "The kingdom of heaven (or God) . . . comes to people who crave not victory or even freedom but justice, . . . and who are courageously eager to suffer pain for the cause of justice, not inflict it" (*Everything Must Change*, 183). Should someone with a certain mindset read these words, they could miss the last three words in the sentence and construe this pronouncement to be a motivation for suicide bombers who, incidentally, think they are giving their lives in the cause of justice—and possibly even of peace! Personally I find this too close for comfort. I would be more comfortable if the word "eager" could be replaced with "willing." See also Bosch, *Spirituality*, 27.

42. Lesslie Newbigin, *Proper Confidence: Faith, Doubt and Certainty in Christian Discipleship* (Grand Rapids: Eerdmans, 1995), especially the last paragraph in the book.

43. Judge the deed and not the person—see also Matthew 6:37 and Luke 6:37.

44. We were gathered in John Howard Yoder's home for a Koinonia-Group in Elkhart, Indiana, in 1978 and discussing non-violence. He said that we normally assume that, for instance, someone who breaks into our home and threatens our family can only be stopped by violence. "Is that true?" he asked. "Has anyone ever tried to reach someone like that through courageous words, instead of courageous violence?" (See John Howard Yoder, *The Politics of Jesus* [Grand Rapids: Eerdmans, 1994]. See also Bosch, *Spirituality*, 27; and McLaren, *Everything Must Change*, 189.)

45. Matthew 10:16 NIV.

46. In 2006 I asked Indian missionary and theologian Siga Arles (Bangalore) about persecution of Christians in India. He said, "Christian groups which are heavily dependent on foreign funds from fundamentalist groups tend to overtalk the persecution, anticonversion laws, and opposition to the Gospel. This is to arouse sympathy and to gain more money. But the larger reality about India is that we still have ample freedom for the Gospel. Where we have freedom, we need to wisely use it and share the love of God and serve people in such a way that they shall see the cross high and lifted up . . . and many shall get drawn to it without incentives. The church in India needs to speed up her work in the largely open parts of the nation. Instead, there is a slowness and a manipulation of the 'little opposition' that exists in parts of the country" (personal letter to A. E. Bosch, June 23, 2006). He added that Christians often brought suffering on themselves, not by the message they brought, but by the manner in which they brought it. In August 2008 about three thousand people were left homeless as a result of interfaith violence between Hindus and Christians. The Muslim community believed that Christians had murdered their leader, Laxmanananda Saraswati, and four of his followers.

47. See the Lord's Prayer and Matthew 6:14–15; 18:21.

48. See 2 Corinthians 12:9–10.

49. McLaren, *Everything Must Change*, 207–12.

50. "It is by this complete identification with the downtrodden . . . that Christ upset the powers that be" (Maimela, *Ploughshares*, 47); "this Christian attempt to opt for the poor . . . is one which is not often appreciated by the powers that be, because they construe [it] as being subversive" (ibid., 48).

51. See Acts 17:6b, *The Message*. For the inverse of "attacking everything we hold dear"—namely, leaving self behind, giving up what is dear to us, and becoming cross-bearers (sufferers) for the sake of others because we are followers of the crucified one—read David Bosch, *Ploughshares*, 164–68.

52. See the excellent article by Simon Maimela in *Ploughshares*, esp. 47, 50.

53. Bosch, *Ploughshares*, 165.

54. Matthew 5:9–12; 6:22–23, 35; 19:29; Mark 10:29–30; and Luke 5:35.

Chapter 33 Just Hope

1. See Romans 8:25.

2. Doug Pagitt and Kathryn Prill, *Body Prayer: The Posture of Intimacy with God* (Colorado Springs: WaterBrook Press, 2005), 31.

Chapter 34 Just Beginning

1. See Matthew 19:19; 22:39; Mark 12:31, 33; Luke 10:27.

2. For more on the "empire" concept see Brian McLaren, *Everything Must Change: Jesus, Global Crises and a Revolution of Hope* (Nashville: Thomas Nelson, 2007).

3. Statistic from *Consumption for Human Development*, Human Development Report 1998, United Nations Development Program.

4. Robert Guerrero, "Short Term Missions within Relational and Empowering Partnerships," paper presented at a missiology conference at Trinity Evangelical Divinity School, April 19, 2008.

5. Matthew 26:11; Mark 14:6–8 NIV.

6. *The White Man's Burden: Why the West's Efforts to Aid the Rest Have Done So Much Ill and So Little Good* (New York: Penguin, 2006), 11.

7. Tom Sine, *Mustard Seed Versus McWorld: Reinventing Life and Faith for the Future* (Grand Rapids: Baker Books, 1999).

8. Red del Camino (RdC) is a network of churches and pro-church organizations in Latin America who have inspired a movement whose main concern is to encourage churches in Latin America in their practice of integral mission. Visit our website at www.reddelcamino.org.

9. For more information see "The Work of the People" website at www.theworkofthe people.com for the "To be told series" and case studies on churches in the RdC Latin American Network.

10. For a unique discussion on fair trade see Claudio Oliver, "Feira Orgânica—ACV," http://blog.docaminho.com.br/videos/associacao-casa-da-videira-geral/feira-organica-acv/, accessed July 27, 2008.

Ashley Bunting Seeber and her husband Kilian live in Geneva, Switzerland, and are members of the Evangelical Lutheran Church of Geneva. Ashley is pursuing an MA in the Bible and Postcolonial Studies at the University of Sheffield in the UK. She enjoys running, traveling, cooking, and being a news junkie.

Brian D. McLaren is an author, speaker, networker, activist, and a former college instructor, church planter, and pastor. Author of about a dozen books, including *A New Kind of Christian*, *A Generous Orthodoxy*, *The Secret Message of Jesus*, and *Everything Must Change*, Brian is married to Grace, a high school teacher, and they have four young adult children. A resident of Maryland, Brian has traveled extensively in Europe, Latin America, and Africa, and his personal interests include ecology, fishing, hiking, music, art, and literature.

Elisa Padilla is executive director for the Kairos Foundation. Kairos works through publishing, theological education, community ministries, and the Kairos Retreat Center to encourage disciples of Jesus Christ to live out their faith in every area of life. Elisa and her family live in Buenos Aires, Argentina.

Proceeds from this book will help
three organizations in their work for justice:

In Latin America: La Red del Camino (www.lareddelcamino.net)
In Africa: Amahoro Africa (www.amahoro-africa.org)
In the U.S.: Emergent Village (www.emergentvillage.com)